Items should be returned on or before the last date shown below. Items not already requested by other borrowers may be renewed in person, in writing or by telephone. To renew, please quote the number on the barcode label. To renew online a PIN is required. This can be requested at your local library.
Renew online @ **www.dublincitypubliclibraries.ie**
Fines charged for overdue items will include postage incurred in recovery. Damage to or loss of items will be charged to the borrower.

**Leabharlanna Poiblí Chathair Bhaile Átha Cliath
Dublin City Public Libraries**

Baile Átha Cliath
Dublin City

Ballymun Branch Tel: 8421890

Date Due	Date Due	Date Due
29.9.17		

Manchester University Press

D1333681

The Anglo-Irish Agreement

Re-thinking its legacy

Edited by
Arthur Aughey and Cathy Gormley-Heenan

Manchester University Press

Published by Manchester University Press
Altrincham Street, Manchester M1 7JA, UK
www.manchesteruniversitypress.co.uk

British Library Cataloguing-in-Publication Data is available

Library of Congress Cataloging-in-Publication Data is available

ISBN 978 1 7849 9385 6 *paperback*

First published by Manchester University Press in hardback 2011

This edition first published 2016

Printed by Lightning Source

Contents

List of contributors

Arthur Aughey is a professor of politics in the School of Criminology, Politics and Social Policy, University of Ulster.

Paul Bew is a professor of politics in the School of Politics, International Studies and Philosophy, Queen's University of Belfast.

Cathy Gormley-Heenan is a senior lecturer in public policy in the School of Criminology, Politics and Social Policy, University of Ulster.

Thomas Hennessey is a reader in the Department of History and American Studies, Canterbury Christ Church University.

Gráinne Kelly is the policy and practice coordinator at INCORE (International Conflict Research), University of Ulster.

Cillian McGrattan an IRCHSS post-doctoral fellow in the School of Politics and International Relations, University College Dublin (UCD).

Elizabeth Meehan is a professor emeritus in the School of Law, Queen's University of Belfast.

Eamon O'Kane is a senior lecturer in politics in the School of Law, Social Sciences and Communications, University of Wolverhampton.

Henry Patterson is a professor of politics in the School of Criminology, Politics and Social Policy, University of Ulster.

Jennifer Todd is a professor of politics in the School of Politics and International Relations, University College Dublin (UCD).

Jonathan Tonge is a professor of politics and Head of the Department of Politics, University of Liverpool.

Preface

Arthur Aughey and Cathy Gormley-Heenan

It is a quarter of a century since the signing of the Anglo-Irish Agreement (AIA) at Hillsborough on 15 November 1985. The occasion was one of the dramatic moments in modern Irish history. At the time it was described by two constitutional lawyers (Hadden and Boyle, 1989: 1) as 'the most significant and carefully prepared development in the relationship between Britain and Ireland since the partition settlement of the 1920s'. It prompted an equally dramatic period in Northern Ireland's history, drawing onto the streets of Belfast a week later over 100,000 unionist protestors. It became the focus of political controversy on all sides, defining politics for the next decade and absorbing enormous public energy and effort, before the specific debate about 'a replacement of and an alternative to' the Agreement (the unionist position) and a 'transcendence' of the Agreement (the nationalist position) gave way in 1993 to the politics of the peace process. But even the peace process itself was bound up with the limits – but also the possibilities – of what had been done in 1985. Despite its central place in recent political experience, the twenty-fifth anniversary of the Agreement was marked in a very low-key manner. It did not go un-noticed, of course, and there was some reflective coverage in the press and on television, but it certainly lacked the attention devoted to other anniversaries such as Bloody Sunday, the Hunger Strikes or the collapse of the first power-sharing /Sunningdale Agreement. What coverage there was can be divided into two categories. The first involved reminiscence by senior figures in the making of the Agreement, such as former Taoiseach Garret FitzGerald and Sean Donlon, who was at the time general secretary at the Irish Department of Foreign Affair, and recollections by figures such as Ian Paisley (now Lord Bannside), then leader of the Democratic Unionist Party (DUP), and Seamus Mallon, then deputy leader of the Social Democratic and Labour Party (SDLP). The second involved taking a longer view, where commentators considered the impact of the Agreement on institutions, attitudes and practices. However, to use that fashionable contemporary expression, there was no sustained public *conversation* about the significance of the Agreement. Its anniversary evoked no sense of the drama of its time and evoked little popular engagement, not even in the blogosphere. Official commemoration was also low-key. There was a formal lunch at the Irish Embassy in London, attended by individuals involved in the negotiations but not by the current Prime Minister or Taoiseach. In the House of Commons, the Conservative MP Therese Coffey tabled an Early Day Motion acknowledging the occasion, noting that 'it led to significantly improved relations between the Governments of the UK and the Republic of Ireland'. There were only six signatories. The Agreement had been negotiated in secrecy by a tight group of politicians and civil servants and to be commemorated by that same, if diminished, tight group might be seen as a fitting tribute. Indeed, the Taoiseach's message sent to the anniversary lunch noted that it represented 'public service of the highest order', implicitly distinguishing it from the street protests and disruptive style of democratic politics which it provoked.

Why was there such a cool commemoration? Some reasons suggest themselves. In Great Britain, and especially in England, the lack of attention is perhaps understandable. The historian G.M. Young once proposed that it is often the case that what to a later generation is an arcane issue of little significance, to contemporaries was an issue of fierce controversy and intellectual turmoil. This applied to the matter of Home Rule for Ireland. Writing just after the end of the Second World War, Young thought that it was difficult for his generation, which rarely thought of Ireland at all, to imagine the political fervour of the previous generation which appeared to think of nothing else (Young, 1947: 104). Nations are as happy (or as miserable) in what they forget as in what they remember and Young's generation wanted to forget about the Irish Question. Similarly, the current generation of Westminster politicians does not want to think perpetually about the Northern Irish Question and its electorate wants to think about it even less. This is the politics of collective amnesia and it is welcomed by most people in Great Britain if only because what happened twenty-five years ago in Northern Ireland is for them almost pre-history. Surely this could not be the case with the supposedly history-minded publics of Ireland, north and south? However, if there is an Irish political curse it is precisely the curse of anniversaries and one could suggest that, in Northern Ireland, politics suffers from too many anniversaries. The decade 2010–20 has already been designated the 'decade of anniversaries' as preparations are made for the centenaries of the Ulster Covenant in 2012 and the Easter Rebellion in 2016. The competition for public attention can lead to anniversary-fatigue and this may have been the fate of the Agreement. Similarly, the anniversary of the Agreement coincided with a profound financial crisis in the Republic of Ireland where the term 'Anglo-Irish' was more likely to conjure up in the public's mind either the toxic debts of the Anglo-Irish Bank or the term 'agreement' to the willingness of the United Kingdom government to contribute to the so-called bailout package of 85 billion Euros. One could argue that the material crisis served to displace memory of the historical one. These reasons have some substance but they do not fully explain the way in which the marking of the Agreement lacked wider attention. A number of other reasons may be proposed.

The first is a reading of the recent past from present experience. Poetry, as Phillip Larkin once wrote, is like trying to remember a tune you have forgotten and, in some ways, coming to terms with the recent history of Northern Ireland is like trying to remember a tune that many who lived through it find convenient to forget or that, for the young, was never known. In that history the Agreement of 1985 is liable to be marginalised in the collective memory, if only because it has been overtaken by the more comprehensive Belfast/Good Friday Agreement (GFA) of 1998. If you like, 1998 has displaced 1985 as a major turning point in Northern Ireland's history. The second reason is a reading of politics from present practice. Politicians in Northern Ireland today dance, as Brian Walker once put it (1997), to a very different tune. There is a wish to consign to the category of heritage the violence, protest, disruption, instability and chaos of the 1980s and early 1990s. There is a temptation to apply a self-denying ordinance which runs: 'that was then and this is now'. This is not always the case, of course, but it has been true of the marking of the Agreement, if only because for unionists and republicans their protests against it, albeit for very different objectives, were both exercises in failure. This local version of the politics of amnesia may be very useful in a society often given to feelings of wild catastrophe and in a culture prone to feverish imagination. However, to adapt the famous expression of E.P. Thompson (1963), recovering the significance of the 'obsolete' Agreement from this 'enormous condescension of posterity' is now difficult for many people. But it is worthwhile trying to do so because the Agreement is of greater historic moment than momentary public recollection suggests.

In his hauntingly nostalgic duet with Hermione Gingold in *Gigi*, Maurice Chevalier remembers his time with her so well that he gets it wrong. Or so the song implies. Perhaps he only makes explicit what is implicit in all our remembering: the need to accommodate experience into a simplified narrative in order to make sense of complicated realities. The significance of historical moments, more so than personal ones, can become obscured by myths of recollection. Therefore, when it comes to remembering the Agreement, the title of Michael Portillo's radio series on historical understanding is appropriate: *Things we Forgot to Remember*, or how memory often conceals complex truths about the past. In short, we argue that important truths have been forgotten about the Agreement and frequently contemporary narratives conceal as much as they reveal. That is why it is important to re-assess its legacy one quarter of a century later.

This book has a number of objectives. First, it is intended to draw out the immediate impact that the Agreement had on the conduct of Irish politics. Second, it is concerned to identify its influence on how the Northern Ireland problem was subsequently conceived. Third, it considers the 'not only but also' influence on political discourse. The concern is not only with the Agreement's *momentary* impact but also with its claim to be an enduring *moment* of political modification. This idea is adapted from Bruce Ackerman (1998) who has identified what he calls 'constitutional moments', events distinctive in their political significance. The chapters interpret the Anglo-Irish Agreement as one reaction to what has been called (Smith, 1999: 77) the 'hardening of the categories' in Irish politics and in British-Irish relations. Each chapter explores the relationship between the historic 'moment' of the Agreement and the subsequent 'productive reassessment' (Bourke, 2003: xv) of political positions which occurred in the following decade. The contributors are cautious about claiming too much intention between the moment and the consequences of it. As Phillip Larkin believed, most things are never meant and much of what followed from the Agreement was not meant either. However, it is true to say that after the moment of 15 November 1985, nothing was ever quite the same again. How and why that was so is the subject of this book.

References

Ackerman, B. (1998) *We the People, Vol. 2: Transformations* (Cambridge: Harvard University Press).

Bourke, R. (2003) *Peace in Ireland: The War of Ideas* (London: Pimlico).

Hadden, T. and K. Boyle (1989) *The Anglo-Irish Agreement: Commentary, Text and Official Review* (London: Sweet and Maxwell).

Smith, M.L.R. (1999) 'The intellectual internment of a conflict: the forgotten war in Northern Ireland', *International Affairs*, 75: 77–97.

Taoiseach's message, www.dfa.ie/home/index.aspx?id=84745.

Thompson, E.P. (1963) *The Making of the English Working Class* (London: Gollancz)

Young, G.M. (1947) 'Government', in E. Barker (ed.) *The Character of England* (Oxford: Clarendon Press).

Walker, B. (1997) *Dancing to History's Tune: History, Myth and Politics in Ireland* (Belfast: Institute of Irish Studies).

Acknowledgements

The editors are grateful to all the contributors for their chapters. They appreciate their commitment to the project and for delivering on time to tight deadlines. Thanks are also due to Gillian McClelland for her assistance in preparing the final manuscript. The editors acknowledge the unfailing support at all stages of this book – from conception to completion – by all the editorial and management staff at MUP, in particular Tony Mason.

Arthur Aughey gratefully acknowledges the support of a Leverhulme Trust Major Research Fellowship which he held during the writing and editing of this book. He would particularly like to thank Sky Aughey for making him think afresh about moments in Irish history and how things change but also stay the same. He would also like to thank Sharon Glenn for her patience and good humour during the various stages of this book.

Cathy Gormley-Heenan gratefully acknowledges the financial support of the Institute for Research in Social Sciences (IRISS) at the University of Ulster and the moral support of colleagues, particularly those in the School of Criminology, Politics and Social Policy. Her greatest praise, as always, goes to Ronan and Hala Heenan, for their unfailing faith and optimism.

List of abbreviations

AIA	Anglo-Irish Agreement, also known as the Hillsborough Agreement
AIC	Anglo-Irish Conference
AIIC	Anglo-Irish Inter-Governmental Conference
DUP	Democratic Unionist Party
EC	European Community
EEC	European Economic Community
EU	European Union
GFA	Belfast/Good Friday Agreement
IFI	International Fund for Ireland
IRA	Irish Republican Army
IRCHSS	Irish Research Council for the Humanities and Social Sciences
LVF	Loyalist Volunteer Force
MEP	Members of the European Parliament
MRBI	Market Research Bureau of Ireland
NICS	Northern Ireland Civil Service
NIO	Northern Ireland Office
NSMC	North-South Ministerial Council
PIRA	Provisional Irish Republican Army
PUP	Progressive Unionist Party
RUC	Royal Ulster Constabulary
SDLP	Social Democratic and Labour Party
SOSNI	Secretary of State for Northern Ireland
SSPPR	Special Support Programme for Peace and Reconciliation
UDA	Ulster Defence Association
UDR	Ulster Defence Regiment
UFF	Ulster Freedom Fighters
UKUP	United Kingdom Unionist Party
UPRG	Ulster Political Research Group
UUP	Ulster Unionist Party
UVF	Ulster Volunteer Force
UWC	Ulster Workers Council

1 The Anglo-Irish Agreement: a constitutional moment?

Arthur Aughey and Cathy Gormley-Heenan

Introduction

2010 was the twenty-fifty anniversary of the Anglo-Irish Agreement (AIA), signed on 25 November 1985 by Margaret Thatcher for the United Kingdom and Garrett FitzGerald for the Republic of Ireland. The Agreement, a short document consisting of thirteen articles, established institutions by international treaty within which the two sovereign governments could consult on Northern Ireland policy and make determined efforts to resolve differences between them. The Preamble to the Agreement argued that any solution to the Northern Ireland problem meant acknowledging 'the rights of the two major traditions that exist in Ireland, represented on the one hand by those who wish for no change in the present status of Northern Ireland and on the other hand by those who aspire to a sovereign united Ireland achieved by peaceful means and through agreement'.

This was the basis for the three-part definition of the status of Northern Ireland in Article 1 of the treaty. Both governments affirmed 'that any change in the status of Northern Ireland would only come about with the consent of a majority of the people of Northern Ireland'; recognised 'that the present wish of a majority of the people of' Northern Ireland is for no change in the status of Northern Ireland'; and declared that, if in the future a majority wished for and consented to the establishment of a united Ireland, both governments would legislate to give effect to that wish. Under Article 2 the Anglo-Irish Inter-Governmental Conference (AIIC) was established to deal 'on a regular basis' with four areas of policy mainly, but not always exclusively, concerned with Northern Ireland: political matters; security and related matters; legal matters, including the administration of justice; and the promotion of cross-border cooperation. Though that Article specifically denied that there was any derogation from the sovereignty of either government it clearly gave to the Irish government an explicit role in the internal affairs of Northern

Ireland. Moreover, Article 3 made it clear that the Conference was to be no mean affair and, whether meeting at ministerial or official level, its business should receive attention at the highest level. At Maryfield, just outside Belfast, a joint Secretariat of Irish and British officials was created to service the Conference and that Secretariat was a symbol of a permanent Irish presence and influence in Northern Ireland politics. Article 4 underlined the requirement for the two governments to work closely together across the range of sensitive policy matters with the objective of securing peace, stability and prosperity. Furthermore, both governments committed themselves to promoting devolution in Northern Ireland that would have the support of representatives from 'both traditions'. Article 4 also conceded that the Conference should be the framework within which the Irish government might 'put forward views and proposals on the modalities of bringing about devolution in Northern Ireland, in so far as they relate to the interests of the minority community'.

It was also through the Conference that the Irish government would be able to influence appointments to public boards and to make suggestions on legislative proposals (Articles 5 and 6), on security policy (Article 7), on the administration of justice (Article 8), influence which cast the Irish government as an explicit defender of the interests of northern nationalists. Article 10 committed the two governments to promote 'co-operation between the two parts of Ireland concerning cross-border aspects of economic, social and cultural matters' in the absence of devolution. However, even if devolution were successfully engineered, the Agreement acknowledged that there would need to be machinery 'established by the responsible authorities in the North and South for practical co-operation' on cross-border issues. Devolution, in other words, might diminish the scope of the Anglo-Irish Conference but it would not eliminate institutions of intergovernmental and north-south cooperation. Provision was made under Article 11 to review every three years the operation of the Agreement and Article 12 permitted the two governments to establish an Anglo-Irish parliamentary body to monitor progress, the first meeting of which was held on 26 February 1990 in London.

The AIA was certainly a dramatic intervention in recent Irish political history, but was it of lasting significance? Assessing the significance of any historical event raises problems of interpretation, two of which are relevant here. There is, first, the experiential problem. Those who live through an event, especially if it helped to define or confirm their political dispositions, may give that event a different meaning to those who did not and the distinction here can be captured by the words 'historic' and 'historical'. The use of the word 'historic' presupposes the significance of an event, according it the status of a turning point or a dramatic quality 'out of the ordinary' while the use of 'historical' leaves that attribution open to debate as one of a sequence of similar (and 'ordinary') events. There is, second, the related problem of perspective where historians may come to review the historic claims of an event and suggest that its radical character has been much exaggerated. It was Michael Oakeshott (1962: 126) who argued that the further one got from even a supposedly revolutionary event the more it looked like a modification of particular circumstances, a philosophical expression of the more frequent reference to Chou En-Lai's famous response to a question about the significance of the French Revolution: that it is too soon to tell. One-quarter century after the signing of the AIA one can suggest that both the experiential and the referential have contributed to diminishing the significance of its historic character and the reason is obvious. The subsequent Belfast/Good Friday Agreement (GFA) of 1998 has encouraged a revision of the 1985 Agreement's place in contemporary Irish history. Again, one can propose two alternative political reasons why this should be.

The first of these reasons is an argument according to *immanence*. By this we mean the view that the broad institutional shape of the 1998 Agreement was always inherent in resolving the political conflict in Northern Ireland and integral to a just accommodation of interests and aspirations. This argument is most succinctly expressed in the saying, coined by the former SDLP deputy leader Seamus Mallon, that the 1998 Agreement was 'Sunningdale for slow learners' (Gillespie 1998). Power-sharing devolution in Northern Ireland with an all-Ireland dimension is rational and the Mallon formulation of the recent course of Irish politics has echoes of T.S. Eliot's poem *Little Gidding*. The meaning of all the many initiatives since the fall of the power-sharing executive in May 1974 was to return to where things had begun and to know it for the first time as the necessary solution. History is now and (a new) Northern Ireland and there is a particularly timeless quality to what is required. Such an understanding does not dismiss the contribution of the AIA but tends to confine it to the confirmation of one self-evident truth – the Irish dimension – in a larger, more comprehensive scheme. The second reason is an argument according to *transcendence*. By this we mean the view that the 1998 Belfast/GFA went beyond all previous attempts to resolve the Northern Ireland troubles. Rather than it being a return and a confirmation it represents an unfolding and a completion, albeit one which creates the conditions for a new beginning. If the first view is rather static, the second is more dynamic, but it is the sort of movement which – to adapt another of Oakeshott's terms (1962: 69) – resembles history 'as the crow flies'. In short, it is a local version of historical and political Whiggishness and one which enfolds facts convenient and inconvenient into a narrative of progress. In this narrative, the AIA is equally confined, either registered as an error replaced by an acceptable form of governance (albeit for very different reasons, the unionist and republican version) or one stage in the final achievement of an agreed Ireland (the nationalist version). Both the immanent and transcendent understandings have interpretative appeal, not only for those who have a partisan investment in the present but also for those seeking to make abridged sense of a complicated past. Indeed, one can argue that the period since 1998 has witnessed an uneasy, possibly temporary, reconciliation between the immanent and the transcendent views.

On the one hand, the dynamic of the second translates into the fact of the first. In this perspective, Northern Ireland is as it ought to be because it is already becoming what it should be. For nationalists and republicans, generally, the ultimate 'ought' of Irish unity takes on the shape of the 'is' – a devolutionary settlement in which they are involved in making things work. This has its attraction since they are not without hope that the 'is' – working the institutions of the Belfast Agreement – will deliver the eventual 'ought' – a united Ireland, a belief also shared in principle by the Irish government. The inherent truth is the sharing of power and the dynamic truth is the ability to move forward beyond it and both entail, especially on the republican side, movement from overthrowing the state to governing the state, *pro tem* (Bean, 2007: 135). On the other hand, for unionists – less generally and more tentatively – the reverse formula applies but has similar effect. Northern Ireland is becoming what it ought to be because it already has been accepted as it is. Even the leadership of the DUP, which had opposed the 1998 Agreement as well as the one of 1985, came to that position once it had negotiated modifications to the operation of the institutions in the St Andrew's Agreement (2006). In this version the inherent truth is the acceptance of Northern Ireland, the dynamic truth is the struggle to maintain it as an end in itself and both entail, especially on the DUP's side, movement from opposition to participation. And beginning and end in both cases are closely related and sometimes indistinguishable. However, both the immanent and the transcendent understandings of the 1998 Agreement perhaps no longer have the respective persuasive power they once had (see Wilson and Wilford 2008) and now that the Belfast Agreement itself is more than a decade old it provides an appropriate opportunity to re-assess the 1985 Agreement.

This introductory chapter proposes to do so by considering the event as a 'constitutional moment'. The concept we have adopted from the work of the American constitutional historian and theorist, Bruce Ackerman, and we adapt it for particular Irish circumstances. The second part of this chapter considers the appropriateness of Ackerman's model when judging the significance of the AIA. The third part revises the relevant insights of Ackerman in terms of an analogy of political change taken from Michael Oakeshott (1983), the 'dry wall' of history. The final part of this chapter uses the model which we have abstracted from the review of both Ackerman and Oakeshott to locate the matters addressed in the other chapters in the book.

A constitutional moment?

When he considered the history of the United States, Ackerman (1991; 1998a) argued that there were rare episodes of transformative deliberation (he identified only three) the outcome of which substantially altered the subsequent framework of politics. It was these episodes of transformative deliberation which Ackerman called constitutional moments and, to adapt a term popularised by Jim Bulpitt (1983), the distinction can be considered to be that between 'high' politics or the principles of association, and 'low' politics or the engagement of diverse groups and individuals to secure their respective interests. In short, such a moment involves not only a distinctive public attentiveness to the norms of politics but also re-constitutes in a decisive manner the way in which low politics are conducted. In this dualist conception, a constitutional moment is a short period of (high) drama, what one commentator (Rakove, 1999: 1931) called an occasion which 'speaks in a deeply sovereign pitch', but one with long-term (low) consequences, perhaps the most significant of which is that the (high) *exception* – the outcome of alterations to the decisional foundation of the existing order – subsequently becomes the *rule* of public expectation about (low) politics. Not everything changes, of course, but there is sufficient discontinuity for contemporaries to think that times have changed and for historians to write of a new political dispensation. If Ackerman's thesis represents an example of an historical turn in constitutional theory it also provides a normative account which tries to solve 'a problem associated with the passage of time' (Tushnet, 2004:3): how political legitimacy can be maintained across the generations. For Ackerman (1989: 474), traditional wisdom is challenged on behalf of principles which, 'though inevitably open-ended, do have rational content'. These 'transformative initiatives inspire mass involvement, passionate commitment, great sacrifice' but the result is a 'deepening dialogue between leaders and citizens that finally succeeds in generating broad popular consent for a sharp break with the received wisdom of the past'. Constitutional identity, then, is discovered in history but not as unchanging substance since that identity does not exclude change and is meaningless in its absence. Identity is not destroyed by change but maintained because of it and to believe otherwise is to deny the creative nature of political deliberation.

Reflecting on what he was to term revolutions 'on a human scale' which 'reorganize dominant beliefs and practices in a fundamental way within a relatively short period of time', Ackerman provides three criteria by which to assess a constitutional moment. The first is self-consciousness to which Ackerman gives pride of place. According to him, what makes a process radical is not violence but the intention of the agents to bring about a change which 'repudiates central elements of the status quo' (1999: 2284). The second is efficacy, for a constitutional moment must actually succeed 'in fundamentally reorganizing one or another area of social life' and the 'efficacy requirement' insists that such changes 'are and ought to be partial' (1999: 2285). The third is speed of implementation, what Ackerman calls the 'ten year test' (1999: 2287). He invites one to contrast the impact of a constitutional moment on political change over that period with one contained within the normal 'envelope of possibility'. The ten-year test strikes a balance between the extremes of everything changing and nothing changing. It rejects the alternative ideas that either 'wrenching change should occur suddenly, and all at once' or mere 'garden-variety evolution'. Big constitutional changes do not generally happen in such a short time 'without lots of people setting their sights on some big ideas, and working hard and long to make them into realities (though, of course, the actual results may well fall short of activists' dreams)' (1999: 2288). There are four ways in which this sort of change can be modelled (1999: 2279–80). The first assumes an invisible hand which leads different groups of actors to produce an outcome that none of them would have individually chosen; the second assumes the 'visible hand of self-conscious elites' who implement strategies to overcome those obstacles to the changes they think desirable or necessary; the third assumes evolutionary changes in the political mentality of communities; and the fourth assumes 'mass movements mobilizing on behalf of grand ideals, and elites struggling for authority to speak in the name of their mobilized citizens'. Though Ackerman accepts that these are ideal types, it is the fourth model which he believes appropriate to a *radical* constitutional moment.

Ackerman's analysis of change in American constitutional history is, of course, intentionally specific but it has been influential not only in the debate about the United States but also in other national and regional contexts where it has generated some interesting comparisons (see for example Eriksen, Fossum and Menéndez, 2003 and Wicks, 2006). Therefore it is not entirely inappropriate to review whether or how the AIA might qualify as a constitutional moment. To do so, it is important to point out very obvious differences, three of which are directly relevant. Ackerman's dualist project distinguishes between 'the will of We the People of the United States from the acts of We the Normally Elected Politicians of the United States' (Ackerman, 1989: 465). This assumes, first, that the people has an identity over and above its component interests, is conscious of itself as a collective 'we', is capable of deliberating on the basis of that commonality in exceptional times and can acknowledge itself as being a people by the very process of its constituted legitimacy. In the case of Northern Ireland one can argue that the question 'who is the people?' has been, and remains, a divisive matter of constitutional legitimacy. It lies at the heart of disputes about sovereignty and self-determination which continue to have ethnic and not just political connotations. The idea of the people has not intimated transcendence of everyday communal politics at the higher level of normative transformation. It has been associated, rather, with partiality of policy ('the institutionalization of sectarianism'). The second and related point is that, because of the unsettled question of who constitutes the people, Northern Ireland cannot sustain Ackerman's dualist conception of politics. Here the problem is that the normally elected politicians have found it difficult, if not impossible, to separate politics of constitutional moment from politics of the everyday and in this they have been in tune with the communal instincts of their respective electorates. To put that succinctly, the traditional rule of thumb has been a mutually frustrating formula of inertia: no first step because it may be a step towards Irish unity (the unionist position), no first step unless it is a step towards Irish unity (the nationalist position). Between 1921 and 1972 when unionists dominated the devolved parliament at Stormont and could think of themselves exclusively as the people of Ulster, high and low politics were justified absolutely according to the same end. In that period also, nationalists north and south could dedicate themselves absolutely to removing the border and constituting a unified Irish people. These were, in their opposite ways, fixed and final constitutional moments where the distinction between the phases, revolutionary and evolutionary, was erased. The third point is specific to the negotiation of the AIA. Ackerman's constitutional moments aimed to place the American people at the centre of constitutional thought, acknowledging how popular collective energies could be mobilised to transform the way in which politics is conducted, to alter how America understands itself and how Americans think of themselves. The model of change here is biased towards the fourth idea. Though there is an inescapably elitist dimension to the conditions in which a constitutional moment adapts elements of pre-existing constitutional vocabulary and practices in significantly new ways, Ackerman's historical citizens are directly engaged in this process of constitutional creativity from the bottom up (Ackerman, 1991: 44). The AIA, on the other hand, was a model of self-conscious elites, conducted confidentially, immune from popular mobilisation, top down and not bottom up. Of course, it was an enterprise to change the framework of politics but mainly the public reacted to an initiative which was directed at them rather than instigated by them and this judgement would apply as much to nationalists as it would to unionists.

As a number of critics have pointed out, there is a deeper problem of historical interpretation with the notion of 'constitutional moment' in the Ackerman model. In the introduction to a special symposium on his work in *The Yale Law Journal*, William Forbarth (1999: 1922–3) spoke of historians' 'shared misgivings about the triumphalist, Whiggish arc of Ackerman's moments', especially his neglect of the ambiguous, even contradictory, character of change and how older ways of constitutional practice persisted in the supposed new order. Indeed, it can even be argued that despite its democratic tone, the Whiggish note sustains an elitist view of enlightened decision-making *for* rather than *by* the people. Thus when the Whiggish progressive style is discounted, Forbarth continues, what remains is 'a somewhat different narrative of constitutional development – more constantly changing, more tenaciously remaining the same, involving force-and-fraud-ridden changes as well as more or less democratic ones, and arrayed into many overlapping periods of ordinary and constitutional politics and lawmaking'. That is a very important qualification and in the next section we try to adjust its insight to address the limits of a Whiggish interpretation of the AIA, precisely to understand what was of moment in what was signed at Hillsborough in 1985. If we accept that the model of change in the Irish case does not meet fully Ackerman's criteria, it is worthwhile reviewing Ackerman's three points. Certainly, the two governments were self-consciously changing established practices even if they were not necessarily challenging all of them. There was also a real sense, at least rhetorically, that the 'status quo was no longer an option' and that the Agreement was about ushering in a new dispensation, a 'quantum leap' as Bill Cash described it in the House of Commons (HC Deb., 17 Nov 1985). Efficacy is more doubtful and difficult to measure and there is a danger of attributing too much and too specifically to the Agreement but if we consider its stated objectives in terms of Ackerman's third point, the ten year test, then it is possible to make a case that momentous changes had taken place. By 1995, politics was being conducted in a very different register from the deadly predictability of the previous quarter century.

By 1995, there was a peace process in Northern Ireland. On 31 August 1994, the Provisional Irish Republican Army (IRA) had declared a complete cessation of military operations and the Combined Loyalist Military Command had reciprocated by declaring a ceasefire on 13 October. This cessation of political violence reflected a quickening of pace which had taken place already in political matters. Multi-party talks on the future of Northern Ireland – the 1991 Brooke and 1992 Mayhew rounds – had been conducted under the auspices of the two governments, revealing a greater openness in unionist attitudes to both the sharing of power within Northern Ireland and acceptance of an Irish dimension to any internal arrangements. However, it was the Downing Street Declaration of 15 December 1993 which set the principled template and helped create the political space for not only the ceasefires of 1994 but also for the institutions which were to be agreed four and a half years later. In a way, it has been persuasively argued, these developments were 'a footnote to the Anglo-Irish Agreement, which was now working in a way no one had intended' (Bew, 2008: 543). As Bew's formulation suggests, this unintended, though ultimately positive, consequence (which sits ill with Ackerman's Whiggish thesis) does not diminish but rather emphasises the historical significance of Hillsborough. If Ackerman's grand narrative, in its majestic sweep, is inappropriate in the Irish case what in particular can be retained to make sense of the AIA as a constitutional moment?

The dry wall

Ackerman (1989: 546–7) once used the analogy of the railroad to conjure the significance of constitutional moments in American history. Each time the train stops at a station there is a choice to be made because 'there is at least one other track, pointing obliquely toward a mountain range on the horizon'. Most of the time, these alternative directions are never considered since those in charge of the train usually continue to steam down the main line ahead. Sometimes, however, another track is taken and the (constitutional) moment of truth comes and goes as the train now begins to move more quickly into the unknown along a different track. 'As the smoke clears, the folks on the caboose look back and begin to see familiar mountains from a different angle; new mountains come into view for the first time.' People have to make sense of the new landscape in which they find themselves. Ackerman's mechanical understanding of historical change not only serves to stress radical choices of direction at such moments but also to emphasise the definitiveness of switching tracks. As a motivational metaphor designed to encourage laggards to board the train of history before it leaves the station, it is an analogy familiar to students of Northern Ireland politics (McKittrick, 1997). Whatever the utility for practical politicians to encourage movement, we suggest that this is not very appropriate for identifying the significance of the AIA. A more contextual and 'serial' understanding (Walker, 2003: 4–5) is required and for this we turn to Michael Oakeshott.

Oakeshott, of course, is celebrated for his scepticism not only of rationalism in politics but also of progress and purpose in history, all of which can be detected in Ackerman's thesis. Indeed, one could argue that he would think the historical insight which Ackerman supplies is compromised by his belief in history as a moral tale of progressive change periodically frustrated (see Ackerman, 1998b). For Oakeshott – and this could almost be taken as a direct reference to the Ackerman model – the ambition must be to escape from that abridgement of history which gives 'the new shape a too early or too late and too precise a definition, and to avoid the false emphasis which springs from being over-impressed by the moment of unmistakable emergence'. This is not to neglect the interest of such moments, merely a warning not to pitch the ambition of interpretation too high (1962: 13). Moreover, Oakeshott (1996: 26) thinks that if you posit a single (rail) road or main line, even one with branching tracks, 'no matter how slowly you are prepared to move along it or how great the harvest you expect to gather as you go, you are a perfectionist, not because you know in detail what is at the end, but because you have excluded every other road and are content with the certainty that perfection lies wherever it leads'. In its entirety, that criticism would be unfair to Ackerman but it does apply in part. It is not that one cannot tell a story about history but story transgresses into myth (or political utility) when history is given an 'over-all meaning' in order to make a case about the necessity of a direction or a destiny (Oakeshott, 1975: 105). And myth is 'a drama from which all that is casual, secondary and unresolved is excluded; it has a clear outline, a unity of feeling and in it everything is exact except place and time'. Moreover, 'every component is known and is intelligible in respect of its relation to a favoured present' (Oakeshott, 1962: 166). From an Oakeshottean perspective, then, we would need to treat with some scepticism Ackerman's threefold schema of self-consciousness, efficacy and speed with its intimation of intent, unfolding and fulfilment. Therefore, to understand the meaning of events after 1985 as the intended unfolding of the moment of the AIA and the Agreement of 1998 as somehow its fulfilment would be to put words into the mouth of history. Argument according to general design is an abstraction, to use a common Oakeshottean term, from a very complex set of 'goings on'. This scepticism about models returns us to 'the unavoidably contingent and circumstantial character of political life, and the recognition that this character is part of the very stuff of politics, not something that can sensibly be wished away to keep political theory morally pure' (Horton, 2005: 34). Since there is no general law of historical change, the unintended consequences of which Bew writes are what one would expect. Oakeshott (1983: 98) expresses this in his usual felicitous manner: 'The idea of change is a holding together of two apparently opposed but in fact complementary ideas: that of alteration and that of sameness; that of difference and that of identity.'

In *On History and Other Essays* (1983: 94), Oakeshott uses the image of a feature of the countryside, the dry wall, to suggest how historical events may be related one to the other. As he puts it, historical events 'are not themselves contingent, they are related to one another contingently'. The relationship is one of proximity and 'touch' and is 'composed conceptually of contiguous historical events' but with no place for 'the cement of general causes'. Rather the stones '(that is, the antecedent events) which compose the wall (that is, the subsequent event) are joined and held together not by mortar, but in terms of their shapes. And the wall, here, has no premeditated design: it is what its components, in touching, constitute'. If Oakeshott is correct, claims one of his sympathetic critics, 'the history of cataclysms, revolutions, epochs, and other supposed discontinuities fit as easily into this view of the continuum as does the recent history of Switzerland' (Auspitz, 1984). The image of the dry wall, then, conjures change in terms of continuity. But this continuity is not the continuity of permanent traits or fated behaviour (like the immanent view) but of contiguity, a contiguity that has space for events which can unsettle and disturb much of what went before. It is history of no grand design, unfolding or purpose (like the transcendent view), but one in which events are related one to another by their particular connecting shapes. One could argue that Oakeshott puts the constitutional moment in its place not as transformation but as adjustment. However, to understand the AIA as related to antecedent events and its placement as composing the connection of subsequent events still leaves open the key questions: how important an adjustment was that moment, to what extent did it modify the shape of events and how significantly did it rearrange the standing-in-relation of politics in Northern Ireland? Oakeshott's scepticism, in other words, can serve as a necessary corrective to Ackerman's grand historical model. The image of history as the dry wall of related events is a rather modest one because it is sceptical of two assertions: first, that there is in history some destiny to be fulfilled and second, that certain events or moments are of such revolutionary significance that all is changed utterly. To believe that the Agreement was a foundational event from which a radically new society emerged is misconceived but this does not deny its particular significance as an event which changed how things subsequently *did* stand-in-relation.

That historical adjustment opens up new possibilities but also closes down others. Some things come on to the agenda but some things also go off. Some things come up for debate but yet others appear settled, at least *pro tem*. Some things may improve but others may get worse. The dry stone wall of Northern Irish history changes shape, as does the perspective on the relations between its parts. The eccentricities, irregularities, inconsistencies and some might think, absurdities which result are not so much defects or irrationalities but characteristics of its political practice. Then again, these things are not 'set in stone'. They are not 'natural' but 'artificial' in the sense that they are the contingent outcomes of political artifice and so are always open to amendment. The questions then are: in what manner were circumstances modified by the AIA and what did the adjusted standing-in-relation mean for Northern Ireland?

Events, as Harold Macmillan well knew, can disorder the most care-fully laid relationships and they have often done so in Northern Ireland. For example, while the Agreement created a new potential for change it also created a new problem to be addressed. From one perspective, then, there exists a deep sense of contingency to all constitutional moments. But whereas the word contingency is usually taken to mean the fortuitous or the merely accidental, the term is used here to designate a connection between related circumstances. These recent related circumstances may be understood to compose (in another of Oakeshott's favourite terms) a political 'character'. This political character – one constituted by beliefs and sentiments which pull in different directions – may itself become modified and may at some future point reach out towards something new but 'what is already there' at one point provides us with some analytical purchase. The 'what is already there' is in this instance the AIA but, as the dry wall image suggests, this involves not the inevitable working out of a predetermined shape but shifting adjustments in the arrangement of parties, policy-makers and opinion, their manoeuvres and dispositions, in relation to one another. This was an observation made by Brendan O'Leary at the time (1987: 24), namely that the Agreement could be attributed to a purely pragmatic logic on the part of the British and Irish governments. We need to do something about Northern Ireland. Here is some thing, so let's do it. Far from being a dramatic departure it was 'the outcome of the policies and actions of state institutions'. To adapt another of Oakeshott's phrases, it would be certainly a very partial view that the grooves of politics are fixed and that no consequences followed the modi-fied standing in relation of communities in Northern Ireland which the Agreement delivered. The image of the dry wall is employed not only to indicate the sequence of events as choice placements and the rough inter-connection of political purposes over the last twenty-five years; it is also employed to emphasise the fragility of all arrangements and the potential for events or choices which disturb expectations. The dry wall image implies, of course, that there can be no administrative solution to politi-cal division, only a modification of relations in which those divisions can become possibly more constructive or stable and less destructive or unsta-ble. But in the long run it is impossible to say what effect adjustments to the standing-in-relation might have on Northern Ireland politics. The argument of this chapter is a modest one. It is that Oakeshottean scepti-cism does not deny the claim of the 1985 Agreement to be a significant constitutional moment but rather helps us to identify precisely what was significant about it. What changed in 1985 was not the fundamentals of politics and there was no beginning of a new normative order; but we would argue that what changed was that the parties to the Northern Ireland problem subsequently stood in a different relation to one another. In other words, the Hillsborough 'stone' was not just any stone but one of such form and weight that its presence had a significant effect on how later events arranged themselves. The next section suggests in more detail how the moment of the Agreement might have affected specific political dispositions as they adjusted to new constraints and possibilities. It also introduces the chapters in this volume which reflect on the historical significance of the Agreement by integrating empirical and theoretical perspectives. The intention is to draw out not only the impact the Agreement had on the conduct of politics but also to measure its influence on how the Northern Ireland problem was subsequently conceived. The concern is not simply, then, with its momentary impact but with its status as a constitutional moment.

Standing-in-relation

The first few chapters consider the strategic visions of the signatories to the Agreement and their popular reception. It appeared ironic that Mrs Thatcher's Conservative government, such a resolute defender of the principle of parliamentary sovereignty in its opposition to devolution for Scotland and Wales and internationally in its scepticism about European integration, accepted that the Irish government should have a say in the administration of one part of the United Kingdom. If it did seem out of character for Mrs Thatcher (indeed, she later thought better of it) it was not out of character with British constitutional thought for which Northern Ireland was always different. When power was devolved to Stormont between 1921 and 1972, home rule for Northern Ireland within the United Kingdom was exceptional. When the Northern Ireland parliament was prorogued and then abolished, the form of government known as 'direct rule' from Westminster was also thought to be exceptional. As Vernon Bogdanor (1999: 100) observed of the use of this term, no one at the time claimed that either Scotland or Yorkshire was under direct rule. The preparedness to accept intergovernmental arrangements for the governance of Northern Ireland can be put into a distinct British political context. On the one hand, a liberal exposition of British constitutional ideology can be found in Elizabeth Wicks's adaptation of Ackerman, *The Evolution of a Constitution: Eight Key Moments in British Constitutional History* (2006). For Wicks (2006: 198–200) the constitution has evolved through eight key constitutional moments from the Bill of Rights in 1688 to the devolutionary changes in 1998. Like Ackerman, the Whiggishness

of these key moments is evident because they elucidate 'the general movement towards democratisation of the constitution' and the entrenchment
'of a right to self-determination within the UK constitution'. Both 'developments' can be seen as 'a modern reconciliation of the need to pay
regard to the wishes of the people (as a group as well as individually)'.
Therefore British constitutional practice is 'flexible enough to evolve in
line with the changing priorities of society without endangering the core
principles' of the union state. The British ideology does not confuse logic
with politics or substitute a rational vision for the convenient. What is at
issue in the Northern Ireland case is the recognition of popular sovereignty in the constitution, expressed in terms of 'consent' but in a unique
international agreement which acknowledges its distinctive and exceptional circumstances. Though Wicks does not address the 1985 Agreement directly, it is clear from her argument that the new
standing-in-relation between the British and Irish governments and the
new standing-in-relation between Northern Ireland and the rest of the
United Kingdom that moment brought into being was in tune with that
tradition, if only because 'asymmetry has always been a feature of the
United Kingdom' and its constitution (2006: 167). Moreover, she accepts
that there is a distinction between the legal and the political conceptions
of sovereignty such that, while the principle of parliamentary sovereignty
is at the heart of British constitutional theory, government has been
flexible about it in practice when dealing with the realities of Northern
Ireland. 'The flexible view of sovereignty in Northern Ireland and the
entrenched right of self-determination' both complemented British
political priorities. On the other hand, a conservative exposition by Jim
Bulpitt (1983: 87) of the 'official mind' in Westminster agrees with Wicks
insofar as it claims that what the centre requires is 'relative autonomy'
from and 'quiet subordination' in the periphery. Because it never fully
developed a sense of the United Kingdom of Great Britain *and* Northern
Ireland as one and indivisible, the purpose of policy in Northern Ireland
was, as far as possible, to conjure it out of existence – that politics of
amnesia which we mentioned in the Introduction (1983: 230). This did
not mean a commitment to Irish unity but it did dispose the British
government to consider that exceptional measures for Northern Ireland
were actually the rule. If this meant standing in a new relationship with
the Irish government then so be it, so long as the calculated benefits
outweighed the calculated losses. And one of those calculated benefits,
apart from calculations of improved security cooperation, was securing
international support for Northern Ireland policy, in particular securing
the good will of the United States and Europe. Drawing on interviews
with many of the key British and Irish politicians and officials involved in
negotiating and implementing the Agreement, Eamonn O'Kane's chapter

examines British expectations of the AIA and the extent to which the AIA was altered during the negotiations. He demonstrates the inter-connection between the 'practical' and 'legal' aspects of the process, examining to what extent arguments that the agreement did not compromise British sovereignty are accurate and sustainable.

For the Irish government, the calculations were rather different. In his classic text *A Place Among the Nations* (1978), Patrick Keatinge arranged matters of Irish policy (albeit not exclusively concerned with the United Kingdom) according to the 'issue areas' of independence and identity; security; unity; and prosperity, and he showed how, especially on the question of Northern Ireland, that although these areas were ideologically linked they were often at odds in practice. Similarly, Garret FitzGerald once remarked that the challenge of foreign policy is 'to reconcile the ideals of a people with the protection of their interests *vis-à-vis* the rest of the world'. He thought that too often conflicts between the two had been largely ignored in Irish policy thinking (cited in Gillespie 1996: 144). This is not an exclusively Irish problem, of course, but the relationship between ideals and interests involves a distinctively Irish self-understand-ing, a self-understanding which may be said to constitute a large and venerable part of the Irish diplomatic mentality. It is idealism which is held to be definitive of Irish practice, not the crude calculation of interest, and FitzGerald's counsel was that it is often wise to modify idealism with a greater emphasis on protection of interests. One should not live by ideals alone but also by the stuff of getting (some of) what you want. The Irish self-image is of an exemplary small state, acting as a moralising influence amongst the big powers. On the other hand, the traditional Irish image of British policy in general, and on Northern Ireland in particular, has been the inverse. British policy has been thought of as self-interested or, if it ever rises to the tone of idealism, only speaks morally when its interests are at stake. In this view, the prevailing task of Irish *public* diplo-macy has been to encourage British governments to live up to those ideals in its relations with Ireland (which Wicks identifies as central to its consti-tutional tradition) – liberty, equality and justice. For most of the history of the Irish state, the *active* delivery of unity was left up to the British with all the contradictions that involved for notions of independence and self-determination. The Irish commitment was *passive*, an iteration of Irish unity (Articles 2 and 3) in its Constitution. As Clare O'Halloran (1986: 138) argues, there was at once naivety and hypocrisy in this position: 'a united Ireland would end divisions in Ireland and between Ireland and Britain when such divisions centred on the very question of unity.' The significance of the moment of the AIA is that it allowed for a more nuanced and satisfactory balancing of idealism and interest.

The 1985 Agreement allowed Dublin to re-orient boundaries and

connections in Anglo-Irish relations and to acknowledge openly that the
common interest which the two governments had in Northern Ireland,
what Brendan O'Duffy (2007) describes as a sovereign re-positioning
'from hierarchy to symmetry'. But it also permitted the Irish government
a new standing as a guarantor and advocate for the interests of nationalists within Northern Ireland. What is more, this new standing-in-relation
with London enabled the Irish government to provide a more plausible
and meaningful answer to the question posed in 1972 by Dennis Kennedy
of *The Irish Times*. The question of Irish unity, he asked 'might be not
how or when, but why' (cited in Keatinge, 1978: 82). The treaty signed at
Hillsborough provided an answer to the how and when – *consent* – and
displaced the why from an end to a means, from impotence to influence
on policy in Northern Ireland. That was indeed something of moment. As
Paul Bew argues in his chapter here, a new theme emerged, and this lay
in the insistence that the policy of the Irish state was directed towards
stability on the island of Ireland rather than the fast-track towards reunification – and it was this theme which was to triumph in the Downing
Street Declaration of 1993 and the Belfast Agreement of 1998.

That the AIA had a major influence on the thinking of the political
parties and the wider public is clear. That it had any institutional effects
is much more disputed: sceptics see it as simply adding a powerless layer
of thin inter-governmental institutions to existing institutions of (British)
governance. As Jennifer Todd reveals, drawing on recent research and
interviews with the policy-makers who negotiated and implemented the
Agreement, the public reaction, even if exaggerated, was more accurate
than the sceptical one. Her chapter shows how practices and norms
embedded in the AIA were displaced through other policy areas and
organisations, and how some key institutional arenas were partially
converted to new purposes by the influence of the Irish government. The
gradual, incremental process of institutional development, she believes,
opened new political opportunities, changed political expectations, and
thus helped to pave the way in part for the political and institutional
changes that followed in the 1990s.

Chapters 5–8 consider political calculations within Northern Ireland
as a result of the Agreement. If the Agreement meant that London and
Dublin stood in a new relation to one another over Northern Ireland then
the communities within Northern Ireland experienced a modification of
position as well in their relationships with one another and with the two
governments. Unionists felt that their relationship had been doubly disad-
vantaged. On the one hand, they were outraged by the actions of the
British government which had excluded them from consultation about the
Agreement's negotiation and appeared to marginalise them from its operation. That there was a palpable shift in how they experienced their new

position was captured by the then deputy leader of the DUP, Peter Robinson (1985), when he claimed that Northern Ireland (to mix our metaphors) had been placed on the 'window ledge of the Union'. This was a position which left unionists in 'a perpetual position of distrustfulness' (Cox, 1987: 84). On the other hand, unionists felt that as a result of the Agreement they stood in an unbalanced and asymmetrical relationship with nationalists who now had an advocate in the AIIC and in the Anglo-Irish Secretariat to promote their cause. In both cases they felt a profound sense of alienation, an alienation which translated into the grand refusal of 'Ulster says No'. As Tom Hennessey shows, though the Agreement of 1985 acknowledged that the status of Northern Ireland could not be changed without of the consent of the people of Northern Ireland, the actual status of Northern Ireland – whether it was part of the British or Irish States – was left undefined. The crux of the unionists' argument was that it did not recognise Northern Ireland as fully part of the UK and, in their view, bypassed their consent to a change in that status.

How best to deal with this precarious relationship promoted a fevered debate within unionism and helped to invigorate the loyalist para-militaries. The Agreement was understood to be designed to 'coerce' them (O'Leary, 1989) but to coerce them into what – power-sharing, joint authority, Irish unity – remained uncertain. Loyalists may have had their worst fears confirmed but they too had to engage in a re-examination of their options. John Tonge's chapter illustrates that beyond the immediate unity of opposition however, there lay sharp divisions among and between unionists and loyalists over the most appropriate means of resistance. These divisions reflected, first, broader ideological positions over the extent and nature of conditional loyalty to the British government and the responsibilities of allegiance accruing to UK citizenship and, second, moral issues surrounding the utility of the threat of violence to resist any shift towards Irish 'encroachment'. Internal rivalries within unionism and loyalism ensured that the unity of Protestant protest was soon to dissipate. Tonge's chapter analyses these internal tensions which eventually disposed loyalists to accept the north-south relationships in the GFA thirteen years later. If there was a substantial Anglo-Irish effect on unionist and loyalist dispositions, it was the determination that no leadership in the future should ever again be excluded in the way it had been in the years leading to Hillsborough. The anxiety was political – how to secure a sort of steady-state position by establishing Northern Ireland's position within the United Kingdom and determining that the national question remained firmly in the hands of the majority. The Agreement was a shock because, though there was an apparent endorsement of the principle of consent, unionist consent was not required for the signing of the Agreement itself. Unionists, of course, could not rule *out* the possibility of Irish unity but then they have always had to live with that prospect. The point was to make sure that it was not ruled *in* against their wishes and they feared the Agreement was an intimation of that possibility.

In what is, in retrospect, a rather insightful essay, Paul Bew and Henry Patterson (1987) wrote that two questions are linked in national-ist politics in Northern Ireland, the national question and the democratic question. The former has to do with the traditional pursuit of Irish unity and the latter with practices that discriminate against Catholics. The char-acter of its politics is defined by the balance and relationship between these two questions. To abridge severely, in the history of the Troubles the priority of constitutional nationalism was democratic and the priority of republicanism was unity. Moreover, the strategy of the IRA was to prevent a settlement acceptable to nationalists on (internally) democratic lines because that would compromise the objective of Irish unity – in the pursuit of which discriminatory practices, real and imagined, were func-tional to its strategy. In the course of the Troubles substantial reform of social and economic practices had been carried through by the British government, in fair employment legislation for example, such that the standing-in-relation of Protestants and Catholics was much more equi-table in 1985 than it had been in 1968. For the SDLP and its leader John Hume, the Agreement dealt effectively with what nationalists believed was the problem of a unionist veto on an Irish dimension. That block to nationalist aspiration had now been circumvented and Irish involvement in Northern Ireland affairs was no longer dependent on unionist consent. Indeed, it appeared that the direction of policy could only be towards deepening the all-Ireland dimension rather than diminishing or removing it, as unionists demanded. Compared with the situation in 1974 when the unionists and loyalists were able to bring down the power-sharing Exec-utive and the Council of Ireland, the standing-in-relation of nationalism and unionism was very different. Indeed, Hume could claim that the Agreement now demonstrated that the British government also stood in a different relation to the communities in Northern Ireland and was now *neutral* on the Union. The task for nationalist politics was to push forward in tandem the democratic and national agendas which the Agree-ment had made possible. Cillian McGrattan's chapter examines the devel-opment of equality discourse before and after the AIA and explores its influence on nationalist thinking. He suggests an alternative explanation for this discursive hegemony – namely, that for the SDLP and later for Sinn Féin, 'equality' principally meant equality for *nationalists*. The docu-mentary evidence suggests it was also a product of a traditionalist under-standing of the conflict on the part of Hume, and of a dedicated Sinn Féin policy of using equality issues to further their standing within the broader nationalist community. His chapter concludes with the suggestion that this understanding of equality qualifies a simplistic view of nationalist accommodation with unionism.

The republican project involved a strategy of process and transition. Process supposed that the end of Irish unity would be brought about by republican struggle and endorsed by a British government declaration of withdrawal from Northern Ireland. And the logic of process required that subsequent to that declaration, arrangements would be put in place which would provide for the swift transition to unity. The end presupposed the means for it was insufficient for republicans simply to 'aspire' to a united Ireland as constitutional nationalist rhetoric claimed. There needed to be a clear and irreversible dynamic which would ensure the fulfilment of that aspiration. In that transformative process, of course, unionist consent would not be necessary. The matter was to be resolved not by democratic persuasion but by coercion of the deed. The AIA, therefore, had an ambiguous impact on republican thinking. On the one hand, it was an initiative directed against the republican project and intended to frustrate its electoral ambition. From that perspective, republicans thought that constitutional nationalism was yet again betraying the national ideal. On the other hand, it was recognised as a blow to unionist morale, a political defeat for them of significant proportions and one which republicans believed would not have been possible without the sustained military campaign of the IRA. Republicans could not fail to be impressed by the mode of circumventing the unionist 'veto', the manner of the Agreement's negotiation (secretive) and its imposition (exercise of sovereign power). Both the manner and the mode of the initiative actually complemented the republican worldview of power and its exercise, suggesting that the British government might go further. In the right circumstances – and so long as republicans kept up the struggle – the British could become persuaders for Irish unity. Republicans could also recognise that there was a different shape and contour to politics in Northern Ireland following the Agreement and new possibilities were open for laying the stones in a different direction. Henry Patterson argues that the republican leadership's initial dismissal of the Agreement was to be followed by a realisation of what it demonstrated about the possibility of exploiting 'contradictions' between British statecraft and the Ulster Unionist community's rejection of the initiative. It is this shift in republican strategic calculations which represents one of the most profound and lasting impacts of the AIA. It flows from the intermingling of a Northern Irish consciousness and the movement's traditional all-Ireland ideology. His chapter proposes that at the same time as republicans were beginning to adumbrate their new peace strategy the IRA's campaign was focusing on keeping the pot boiling by a border campaign whose main victims were Protestants. It argues that there was no fundamental contradiction, from

the republican perspective, between these political and military engage-
ments. The Agreement, while denounced as an attempt to copper-fasten
partition, was also believed to illustrate the possibility of creating the
domestic and international conditions for encouraging the British state to
commit to Irish unity.

The final chapters consider international perspectives on the Agreement. For the British government certainly, one of its purposes was to
better manage the international perception of the Northern Ireland
problem. Elizabeth Meehan's chapter explores how cooperation in
Europe by the two governments and the overall dimension of European
integration helped provide a new language to redefine old problems. This,
of course, had been an aspect of John Hume's rhetoric for many years,
though the institutions of the Agreement were far from the pooling of
sovereignty which he believed defined the European enterprise. However,
even though the 'high politics' of Europe only periodically engaged with
the issue of Northern Ireland it encouraged more practical notions of
north-south cooperation and the formulation of policies affecting the
affairs of the islands of Ireland and Great Britain.

Following the Belfast Agreement of 1998, it has been suggested that
Northern Ireland has become a 'model' for other political conflicts to
adopt. This has affected how we now perceive the AIA. When viewed
from the conflict resolution paradigms of today, most theorists would
conceptualise it as one of several failed attempts to resolve a protracted
ethnic conflict through an intergovernmental approach, framing it as a
'ripe moment' misjudged and an exercise in exclusion, anathema in an era
which promotes 'inclusiveness' above all else. In a post-Cold War context,
conflict resolution theory has certainly developed, with models of success
and failure dissected to identify the combination of ingredients which can
be imported and exported to other regions in need. In the spirit of historical recovery, Grainne Kelly's chapter considers the changing dynamics of
conflict resolution theory prior to, and in the intervening period between,
the negotiation of the Anglo-Irish and Belfast Agreements and considers
how the AIA fits with – and has perhaps influenced – contemporary theories of conflict resolution.

As we have argued in this chapter, and as the subsequent chapters
examine in detail, some recent narratives puts words into the mouth of
history when, as we will see, the 1985 Agreement actually worked 'in a
way no one had intended' (Bew 2008: 543). To repeat, it is not our argument that it is impossible to tell a story about political history, only that
politics transgresses into myth when it is given an 'over-all meaning'
(Oakeshott 1975: 105). It becomes a myth when it is reduced to 'a drama
from which all that is casual, secondary and unresolved is excluded' and
in which every element 'is intelligible in respect of its relation to a

favoured present' (Oakeshott 1962: 166). We would suggest that the journalist Stephen Collins (2010) was closest to capturing the importance of the Agreement when he described it as 'a foundation stone in the process' by which relative though, for the moment, stable peace was brought to Northern Ireland. We think that the indefinite article before 'foundation stone' is appropriate and insightful for, of course, the 1985 Agreement was not the only event upon which everything was built. And we tried to give greater substance to that reflection by using Michael Oakeshott's metaphor of the 'dry wall' to capture how the Agreement stone modified, unintentionally or not, how parties to the Northern Ireland problem arranged their politics. Today politics is conducted in a different register from 1985. That register was neither provided for nor anticipated by the Agreement. What one can say is that even the failures of the AIA continue to have an effect.

References

Ackerman, B. (1989) 'Constitutional politics/constitutional law', *The Yale Law Journal*, 99: 3, 453–547.
—— (1991) *We the People, Vol. 1: Foundations* (Cambridge: Harvard University Press).
—— (1998a) *We the People, Vol. 2: Transformations* (Cambridge: Harvard University Press).
—— (1998b) 'The broken engine of progressive politics', *The American Prospect*, 38: May/Jun, 34–43.
—— (1999) 'Revolution on a human scale', *The Yale Law Journal*, 108: 8, 2279–349.
Anglo-Irish Agreement, www.dfa.ie/uploads/documents/angloirish%20agreement%201985.pdf (Irish version, accessed 19 January 2010) and cain.ulst.ac.uk/hmso/aia.htm (British version, accessed 20 January 2010).
Auspitz, J.L. (1984) 'On history and other essays – review', *National Review*, 36: 4, www.thefreelibrary.com/National+Review/1984/February/10-p5202 (accessed 19 January 2010).
Bean, K. (2007) *The New Politics of Sinn Fein* (Liverpool: University of Liverpool Press).
Bew, P. (2008) *Ireland: The Politics of Enmity 1789–2006* (Oxford: Oxford University Press).
Bew, P. and H. Patterson (1987) 'The new stalemate: Unionism and the Anglo-Irish Agreement', in P. Teague (ed.) *Beyond the Rhetoric* (London: Lawrence and Wishart), 41–54.
Bogdanor, V. (1999) *Devolution in the United Kingdom* (Oxford: Oxford University Press).
Bulpitt, J. (1983) *Territory and Power in the United Kingdom: An Interpretation* (Manchester: Manchester University Press).
Collins, S. (2010) 'Anglo-Irish Agreement had decisive impact on Republic's politics', *Irish Times*, 15 November.
Cox, W.H. (1987) 'Managing Northern Ireland intergovernmentally: an appraisal of the Anglo-Irish Agreement', *Parliamentary Affairs*, 40: 1, 80–97.
Eriksen, E.O., J.E. Fossum and A.J. Menéndez (eds) *The Chartering of Europe: The*

European Charter of Fundamental Rights and Its Constitutional Implications (Oslo: Arena, 2003).

Forbath, W.E. (1999) 'Constitutional change and the politics of history', *The Yale Law Journal*, 108: 8, 1917–30.

Gillespie, G. (1998) 'The Sunningdale Agreement: lost opportunity or an agreement too far?', *Irish Political Studies*, 13: 1, 100–14.

Gillespie, P. (1996) 'Ireland in the new world order: Interests and values in the Irish Government's White Paper on foreign policy', *Irish Studies in International Affairs*, 7, 143–56.

Horton, J. (2005) 'A qualified defence of Oakeshott's politics of scepticism', European *Journal of Political Theory*, 4: 1, 23–36.

House of Commons Debate (Hansard), 27 November 1985, vol. 87, col. 926.

Keatinge, P. (1978) *A Place Among the Nations: Issues of Irish Foreign Policy* (Dublin: Institute of Public Administration).

McKittrick, D. (1997) 'Blair offers a fresh start for Irish peace', *Independent*, 17 May.

News Letter (1985) 18 November.

Oakeshott, M. (1962) *Rationalism in Politics and Other Essays* (London: Methuen).

—— (1975) *On Human Conduct* (Oxford: Clarendon Press).

—— (1983) *On History and Other Essays* (Oxford: Blackwell).

—— (1996) *The Politics of Faith and the Politics of Scepticism* (New Haven: Yale University Press).

O'Clery, C. (1997) *The Greening of the White House* (Dublin: Gill and Macmillan).

O'Duffy, B. (2007) *British-Irish Relations and Northern Ireland: From Violent Politics to Conflict Regulation* (Dublin: Irish Academic Press).

O'Halloran, C. (1986) *Partition and the Limits of Irish Nationalism* (Dublin: Gill and Macmillan).

O'Leary B. (1987) 'The Anglo-Irish Agreement: meanings, explanations, results and a defence', in P. Teague (ed.) *Beyond the Rhetoric: Politics, the Economy, and Social Policy in Northern Ireland* (London: Lawrence and Wishart).

—— (1989) 'The limits to coercive consociationalism in Northern Ireland', *Political Studies*, 37: 4, 562–87.

Rakove, J.N. (1999) 'The super-legality of the Constitution, or, a federalist critique of Bruce Ackerman's neo-federalism', *The Yale Law Journal*, 108: 8, 1931–58.

St Andrews Agreement, cain.ulst.ac.uk/hmso/nistandrewsact221106.pdf (accessed 20 January 2010).

Tushnet, M. (2004) 'Potentially misleading metaphors in comparative constitutionalism: moments and enthusiasm', in J.H.H. Weiler and C.L. Eisgruber (eds) *Altneuland: The EU Constitution in a Contextual Perspective*, Jean Monnet Working Paper 5/04, www.jeanmonnetprogram.org/papers/04/040501-04.html (accessed 19 January 2010).

Walker, B. (1996) *Dancing to History's Tune: History, Myth and Politics in Ireland* (Belfast: The Institute of Irish Studies).

Walker, N. (2003) 'After the constitutional moment', The Federal Trust Online Paper 32/03, www.fedtrust.co.uk/uploads/constitution/32_03.pdf (accessed 19 January 2010).

Wicks, E. (2006) *The Evolution of a Constitution: Eight Key Moments in British Constitutional History* (Oxford: Hart).

Wilson, R. and R. Wilford (2008) 'Northern Ireland: polarization or normalization?', in R. Hazell (ed.) *Constitutional Futures Revisited: Britain's Constitution to 2020* (London: Palgrave).

2 British government and sovereignty: balancing legal restrictions and political ambitions

Eamonn O'Kane

The signing of the AIA was something of an unexpected departure for Mrs Thatcher's Conservative government from the perceived unionism of the Prime Minister. Why did Mrs Thatcher, whom the then head of civil service in Northern Ireland, Sir Kenneth Bloomfield, claimed was 'in sentiment the most deeply unionist of British prime ministers for a very, very long time' sign an agreement that was so unacceptable to Ulster Unionists? (Bloomfield, 2000) Ulster Unionism saw the agreement as a betrayal that undermined British sovereignty over Northern Ireland. The government, on the other hand, portrayed it as a practical exercise that had no implications for sovereignty and indeed strengthened the Union due to the Irish government's acceptance of the principle of consent (Article 1a; Hurd, 1999).

To explain the AIA from a British perspective it is important to examine the context in which the negotiations took place and the differing objectives that were in play amongst the government departments involved in the negotiations. This chapter highlights the differing dynamics that were evident within the British government and demonstrates that a guiding principle of the government was that whatever agreement was reached it must not infringe sovereignty and must be robust enough to withstand legal challenges in both the British and Irish courts. But the debate within British policy-making circles was over what the primary purpose of the agreement should be and what should be 'offered' to the Irish State in order to secure British objectives.

Background to the Agreement

The 1979 Conservative manifesto had proposed a broadly integrationist approach towards Northern Ireland, though this was dropped soon after the election. The approach of Mrs Thatcher's government in the early

1980s had been geared to creating the conditions that would allow for devolved government to return Northern Ireland. However, this was unsuccessful. During that period the Thatcher government was not inclined to acknowledge a role for the Irish government in discussions regarding how Northern Ireland was governed. Thatcher's first Secretary of State, Humphrey Atkins, noted that 'the South has as keen an interest [in Northern Ireland] as anybody else outside the United Kingdom' but underlined that 'it is our responsibility and nobody else's' (*Irish Times*, 19 August 1980). This echoed the point that Mrs Thatcher had made to the House of Commons in May 1980 when she asserted, 'The future of the constitutional affairs of Northern Ireland is a matter for the people of Northern Ireland, this government and this Parliament, and no one else.' (HC Deb., 20 May 1980).

The Thatcher government's clear assertions of sovereignty over Northern Ireland were in line with actions during the early 1980s that suggested Mrs Thatcher was determined to be a firm defender of British interests. Events such as her willingness to take a strong stance against other European states over Britain's contribution to the European Community (EC) budget, her actions in response to the Argentine invasion of the Falkland Islands in 1982 and her 'out, out, out' rejection of the New Ireland Forum Report's three proposals in 1984, seemed to underline this view. Mrs Thatcher's unequivocal defence of Britain's actions in the Falklands, for example, was welcomed by unionists. After the end of that conflict she told the House of Commons that, 'There can be no question of negotiations on sovereignty for the Falkland Islands. It would be a betrayal of those who fought and died' (HC Deb., 23 November 1982) In addition, the stance by Charles Haughey's Irish government of seeking to end the European economic sanctions against Argentina and the observation by the Irish Defence Minister after Britain's sinking the Argentine ship, the *Belgrano*, that, 'We felt that Argentina were the first aggressors. Obviously Britain themselves are very much the aggressors now', seemed to reduce further the likelihood of any increased right of consultation for the Irish government over Northern Ireland (*Irish Times*, 4 May 1982).

The change of direction that the AIA seemed to represent by the Thatcher government reflects the under-appreciated pragmatism that was evident in some aspects of Mrs Thatcher's policies (Armstrong, 1993: 204). There is a tendency to see sovereignty in zero-sum terms and Mrs Thatcher's defence of wider British interests was taken as an indication that absolute sovereignty would be upheld over Northern Ireland. As will be shown, in legal terms, this was indeed the Prime Minister's position. Beyond narrow legal considerations, Mrs Thatcher was persuaded that changes in how Northern Ireland was governed, and who was consulted over its governance, could be made as long as this did not impinge upon the issue of formal British sovereignty. Mrs Thatcher was willing to distinguish between formal sovereignty and practical governance on utilitarian grounds in a way that was to surprise many.

The reasons for this pragmatism lie in events within Northern Ireland rather than in abstract consideration of sovereignty or constitutional absolutes (though these considerations were key in limiting how far pragmatic/utilitarian considerations could be pursued). By 1983 the Thatcher government had made scant progress in Northern Ireland. Attempts at devolution showed little sign of succeeding. Although an Assembly had been created under Jim Prior's rolling devolution plan, the SDLP's rejection of the model meant it had little chance of success. The failure to achieve devolution on its own, however, would not necessarily have compelled the government to seek an agreement with Dublin: Direct Rule had been in place for a decade by that point. There had been some signs that Mrs Thatcher was amenable to attempts by Haughey to improve Anglo-Irish relations in the early days of her premiership. She met Haughey twice in 1980 which fuelled speculation that a breakthrough in inter-state relations was imminent. However, the relationship deteriorated sharply in 1981-82. Haughey's stance over the Falklands annoyed the British, as did the apparent over-selling by the Irish of the meeting between the two prime ministers in December 1980. The Irish were annoyed by the lack of consultation over Prior's plans and by what they believed was a mishandling by Britain of the 1981 hunger strikes. (The hunger strikes had a direct impact on Haughey, as the loss of two Fianna Fáil seats to H-Block candidates was instrumental in forcing him from office in 1981).

The situation in Northern Ireland had altered due to the increased tensions that emerged during the 1981 hunger strikes. The election of the IRA hunger striker, Bobby Sands, as a Westminster MP during the strike and the subsequent election of his former agent, Owen Carron, after his death were instrumental in Sinn Féin's 1982 decision to enter the political arena (the creation of the 'armalite and ballot box' strategy). Sinn Féin secured 10.1 per cent of the vote in the Assembly elections in October 1982 (the first Northern Ireland-wide elections they had contested) and in the 1983 Westminster election Sinn Féin's vote rose to 13.4 per cent and Gerry Adams was elected MP for West Belfast. Such results led to fears that Sinn Féin would displace the SDLP as the largest nationalist party and, as Jim Prior told Conservative backbenchers, Northern Ireland could become 'a Cuba off our western coast' (*Irish Times*, 11 November 1983). Britain now faced the challenge of dealing with the threat of republicanism on two fronts: the security and political arenas.

By 1983 the context of the relationship between Britain and Ireland had changed. The response of the British to this situation was to try a different approach: cooperating with Dublin rather than prioritising an accommodation between the main parties within Northern Ireland. One of the most influential interpretations of the AIA centred on the argument that it was an exercise in 'coercive consociationalism' (O'Leary, 1989; O'Leary and McGarry, 1993). Article 2b of the AIA stated that the 'Irish Government will put forward views and proposals on matters relating to Northern Ireland within the activity of the Conference in so far as these matters are not the responsibility of a devolved administration in Northern Ireland'. Article 5c states that 'if it should prove impossible to achieve and sustain devolution' the IGC will provide 'a framework within which the Irish Government may, where the interests of the minority community are significantly, or especially affected, put forward views on proposals for major legislation and on major policy issues ...' (see Appendix 1). This was interpreted by some as designed to induce the unionists to agree to power-sharing as a way to reduce the influence of Dublin in Northern Ireland affairs. If devolution was secured then the areas in which Dublin could be consulted by London would diminish as the IGC could only consider issues not devolved to a Northern Ireland administration. However, the argument that coercing unionists into accepting devolution was a *purpose* of the agreement is not persuasive. Whilst it is clear that the British government was in favour of devolution it is also clear that there was awareness amongst many of those who negotiated the agreement that it may have reduced rather than increased the likelihood of securing devolution (O'Kane, 2007: 59–64). As a result other explanations need to be sought to explain why the British government signed the AIA and these indicate that there were evident differences over both the objectives of the AIA and the type of agreement that should be entered into.

Divisions within the British government: from maximalism to minimalism

The realisation that progress towards devolution within Northern Ireland was unlikely, combined with the ongoing security concerns in Northern Ireland, account for the decision of the Thatcher government to negotiate the agreement. The impetus came from the Irish side but the approach was interesting to the British. For Mrs Thatcher the key was the security situation. David Goodall, the British civil servant who was one of the AIA's key negotiators, was discussing with Thatcher as early as December 1982, 'the sad fact that the only place in the world where British soldiers' lives were being lost in anger was in the United Kingdom' (Goodall, 1993: 126). This, it could be said, was the real *sovereign* issue insofar as it directly challenged the authority of the state. It was this concern with improving security in Northern Ireland that was a driving force for Mrs Thatcher. After a full term in office security had not improved, the unionists would not consider devolved government with an Irish dimension and the SDLP would not consider devolution without one. The result was that the British government were 'temporarily bereft of new ideas for tacking the Northern Ireland problem' (Goodall, 2010). As a result the approach made by the Irish civil servant Michael Lillis in September 1983 to David Goodall (at the behest of the Taoiseach, Garret FitzGerald, who took over from Haughey in 1982), which focused on the problems of security, 'alienation' of nationalists in Northern Ireland and suggested a willingness to review Ireland's constitutional claim on Northern Ireland as part of a wider agreement, was of interest to the government. Lillis notes that his approach was 'intended to engage the attention of a British prime minister whose entire focus on Northern Ireland was exclusively on security concerns and specifically on the defeat of terrorism' (Lillis, 2010). The problem was: what concessions should Britain offer to the Irish and would these infringe its sovereign authority?

According to Douglas Hurd, Thatcher's 'main aim in the negotiation was to shame and galvanise Dublin into effective anti-terrorist action, making as few concessions on points of interest to them as was compatible with that objective' (Hurd, 2003: 301). Thatcher realised that there would be a 'price' to pay for increased security cooperation with Dublin but it was on what this price should be that opinions differed. In her memoirs Thatcher recalls that 'I started from the need for greater security, which was imperative. If this meant making limited political concessions to the South, much as I disliked this kind of bargaining I had to contemplate it. But the results in terms of security must come through' (Thatcher, 1993: 385). The early negotiations discussed the possibility of a wider-ranging agreement than that which was eventually signed. The Irish position was clarified by FitzGerald at the Chequers summit in November 1983. According to Goodall, FitzGerald outlined what became known as the 'basic equation', 'outright Irish endorsement of the Union and closer security cooperation in return for an Irish role in the government and administration of justice in Northern Ireland' (Goodall, 2010). Garret FitzGerald was advocating what he termed 'joint authority' rather than 'joint sovereignty' and over the next year various plans were drawn up in line with what could be seen as the 'basic equation' (see FitzGerald, 1991: 501–10). The discussion on what can be seen as a maximalist agreement was scaled back to a more minimalist one around the time of the Chequers summit of November 1984, a result of the expansion of those involved in the negotiations on the British side, illustrating internal differences.

At the outset the talks had been conducted by the heads of the two

Cabinet Offices, Dermot Nally for the Irish and Sir Robert Armstrong for the British with their deputies Michael Lillis and David Goodall closely involved. The Foreign Office, under Sir Geoffrey Howe, also participated. But around the time Douglas Hurd succeeded Jim Prior as Secretary of State for Northern Ireland in September 1984, Mrs Thatcher 'widened the circle of those involved on our side of the talks to include senior officials in the Northern Ireland Office' (Thatcher, 1993: 399) though not the Northern Irish members of the Northern Ireland Office (NIO) (O'Kane, 2007: 49). This now meant that three government departments were involved in the negotiations, three departments that had differing priorities and responsibilities. The then head of the NIO, the Englishman Robert Andrew, later recalled,

> The Cabinet Office, having been asked by the Prime Minister to try and sort out an agreement, wanted to get an agreement and move onto other business as it were, as the Cabinet Office has many other things to do apart from Northern Ireland. The Foreign Office wanted an agreement for overseas political reasons: good relations with Dublin, good relations particularly with the United States. I certainly wouldn't say they wanted an agreement at all costs but they wanted an agreement and to reach an agreement was in itself an objective for them for these overseas political reasons. The Northern Ireland Office ... did want an agreement ... But we were conscious that whatever agreement was signed we had got to live with and work it whereas the other departments would be moving on to other business. (Andrew, 2000)

Goodall agreed that the NIO were 'more cautious' and 'acted as a sort of a brake on the thing, because they had responsibility for actually running the Province and they, I think rightly, thought that too many bright ideas by people who weren't responsible for running it would land them in a mess which they would have to deal with' (Goodall, 1999). The caution that the NIO injected into the negotiations frustrated the Irish government but also chimed with Mrs Thatcher's inherent unionism and instincts on sovereignty. Questions remain, however, whether a 'maximalist' agreement of the type under discussion in 1983–84 would have been possible. It is doubtful that the Irish government could have delivered the necessary constitutional referendum to remove Articles 2 and 3 from their constitution. Indeed Dermot Nally has stated that 'it would not have been possible to carry a referendum on 2 and 3, almost irrespective of what was in the agreement, because *Fianna Fáil* were opposing what was happening' (Nally, 2000). Although the Irish government felt frustrated by the NIO and were critical of Andrew's role in the process, the result was that from late 1984 the focus shifted away from trying to secure a wide-ranging agreement that would see Irish security forces deployed (at least temporarily) in Northern Ireland and have a sizable input into how Northern Ireland was governed in return for the removal of Articles 2 and 3 (something akin to joint authority) towards the more limited agreement that subsequently materialised, which Bew, Gibbon and Patterson usefully termed 'direct rule with a green tinge' (Bew, Gibbon and Patterson, 1995: 217).

In retrospect, given the fury that the more limited agreement caused amongst unionists, a maximalist agreement would have been far more problematic. It is also perhaps the case that the maximalist agreement may have proved too far a step for Mrs Thatcher. It is clear that the Prime Minister struggled with the increased role she was ceding to the Irish government over the affairs of Northern Ireland. Whilst Mrs Thatcher accepted the need to make some concessions to get an agreement she did not think these should be too great as she viewed the Irish constitutional claim on Northern Ireland as an unwarranted challenge to sovereignty and believed that the British had a right to greater security cooperation from the Irish government. As a result her attitude oscillated somewhat during the talks. David Goodall recalls,

> People have rightly said, I think, that for her, her head took her in one direction and her heart in another. So the thing tended to waiver a bit depending upon if she had been listening to Enoch [Powell] and Ian Gow. All her doubts would be sort of reinforced and then we'd work away at it again and then she'd come to see that even if she didn't like it, it would be a good thing, so it was a bit of a yo-yo really. (Goodall, 1999)

Indeed Garret FitzGerald portrays Mrs Thatcher as the main obstacle in the British government to getting an agreement. According to the former Taoiseach, the basic problem was 'how to persuade her'. 'Within weeks, the entire system of government was reorganised to how do you get round the prime minister? So the negotiation was not between Ireland and Britain, it was between Margaret Thatcher and the Irish and British ministers and Irish and British civil servants, effectively' (FitzGerald, 2000). Whilst this may overstate the case (not least given the resistance within the NIO) it was the case that Mrs Thatcher was troubled by the process (and ultimately became critical of the agreement). But for the Prime Minister security was the key consideration in negotiating the AIA.

Others within the British government, however, were not as apprehensive regarding the 'concessions' that needed to be made to the Irish government in order to secure an agreement. Geoffrey Howe was more enthusiastic about the process than Mrs Thatcher and more realistic about the 'price' that needed to be paid. As he recalled in his memoirs,

> If we wanted more effective cross-border security co-operation from the Irish government – as we all did, and Margaret most of all – then [Dublin] had to

be able to demonstrate an enhancement of their political role in the affairs of the Province. This less than heroic argument enabled us to keep both the Prime Minister and Cabinet sceptically in step and supportive of the continued search for a balanced package. (Howe, 1994: 417)

Goodall claims it fell to Howe and officials to convince Mrs Thatcher it would be 'suicide for an Irish Government to enter into a security arrangement with the British which had no political content, which would make the Irish Government in the eyes of their own electorate appear to be supporting British military and security activity in Northern Ireland without any political benefit from it. That was a point that Mrs Thatcher found extremely difficult to understand ...' (ICBH, 1997: 52). Howe, for his part seemed to view the AIA as a way of improving wider British-Irish relations. But Howe also highlighted another issue, one which overlapped with Mrs Thatcher's preoccupation with security and with Dublin's priority: the so called alienation thesis. According to this argument it was the alienation of nationalists from the institutions of the state in Northern Ireland, particularly those associated with policing and justice, which created the conditions that were conducive to the IRA campaign. The Irish saw this as a key issue that needed addressing and their prescription was for an increased role for the Irish state in Northern Ireland. This, they argued, would offer a route for nationalist grievances to be addressed via Dublin's input and so reduce the alienation that benefitted the IRA. In the early stages of the negotiation this argument had some appeal for Mrs Thatcher in so much as it seemed to suggest a way of getting Dublin to cooperate with the British government in dealing with the IRA. Howe notes that it was the emphasis that FitzGerald placed on the threat that the rise of Sinn Féin posed, when he met Thatcher in November 1983, which caused 'the first breakthrough' and persuaded her that 'the *status quo* was unacceptable' (Howe, 1994: 414–15).

The problem was that the British government did not really share either the Irish government's diagnosis or its prescription. Although the British were concerned with the rise of Sinn Féin, they did not concur with the view that this was symptomatic of the widespread alienation of nationalists from the institutions or structures of Northern Ireland. Douglas Hurd has argued that

I don't think we ever accepted the phrase alienation because there were a lot of Catholics, a lot of nationalists, who were actually co-operating perfectly well. But a lot of the things that direct rule tried to do in housing, education, labour laws and so on were really designed to bring the nationalist community more into the actual daily working of the Province. So there was a truth behind the phrase even though I think the phrase was rather over-used. (Hurd, 1999)

To accept that nationalist alienation was so widespread that only a role for the Irish government in Northern Ireland would address it would be a serious indictment of British policy (and sovereignty) in Northern Ireland since 1972. Hurd rejected Dublin's viewpoint, recording in his diary in March 1985: 'the truth is that we want a minimalist agreement, because we don't accept their [the Irish government's] basic analysis, which is that their involvement will rally the minority in a few months' (Stuart, 1998: 145).

So several reasons can be identified that help explain why the British pursued the initiative that led to the AIA. For Mrs Thatcher the desire to improve security cooperation with Dublin, along with an element of frustration at the lack of progress in attempts to restore devolved government in Northern Ireland, are key. For others in the policy-making circles wider international considerations were in play. For Howe there was a desire to improve relations with the Irish government more widely and undoubtedly there was a belief that an agreement with Dublin would be seen as helpful in the US. However, this was a secondary consideration for the British. Claims such as those made by Enoch Powell during the debate on the AIA in the House of Commons that 'The real reasons are that the Government were under external pressure which they could not resist ... This has been done because the United States insisted that it should be done' are unconvincing, with little evidence to support them (HC Deb., 27 November 1985). If that had been true, it would have identified a serious breach of sovereign purpose. Similarly, explanations that see the AIA as part of a wider plan to force Northern Ireland from the Union have little supporting evidence though they had wide currency within sections of unionism in the immediate aftermath of the agreement (Aughey, 1989; see also O'Kane, 2007: 59–66). It is interesting that in his account of the AIA, Lord Armstrong does not list international considerations amongst his nine 'ambitions' of the agreement. Security policy only appears at number eight and is part of the wider objective to, 'provide an institutional framework for improving cooperation between London (and Belfast) and Dublin on cross-border affairs (including security) and other matters of common interest, and for dealing with the sorts of disagreements bound to occur from time to time' (Armstrong, 1993: 205–6).

These intra-departmental differences and competing priorities within the British government help explain the decision to drop the idea of a maximalist agreement. But after the 'minimalist' agreement was signed the outrage that it provoked amongst unionists was caused in part by the belief that it did mark a fundamental shift in British sovereignty over Northern Ireland.

Sovereignty again

The British government were determined that the agreement should be 'fire-proof' against unionist attempts to topple it (as had happened with Sunningdale in 1974); legally defensible against challenge in the British or Irish courts; and should not infringe British sovereignty. The first of these was achieved by creating an agreement that was not dependent upon the participation of the Northern Ireland parties. The British government desired to see power devolved back to Northern Ireland but this was not the specific objective of the agreement. One of the aims was to 'create a structure that, while it admitted participation by the parties in Northern Ireland, did not depend upon it' (Armstrong, 1993: 205). The second objective was achieved by actually signing two different versions of the agreement. The British version recorded it was an 'Agreement between the Government of the United Kingdom and Northern Ireland and the Government of the Republic of Ireland'. The Irish version recorded it as an 'Agreement between the Government of Ireland and the Government of the United Kingdom'. This avoided the Irish signing an agreement that could 'use words which might be taken to signify a formal acceptance that Northern Ireland is part of the United Kingdom' (Hadden and Boyle, 1989: 15) and so be judged unconstitutional. In this regard the objective was achieved as a challenge to the AIA on these grounds, brought by the Ulster Unionists, Chris and Michael McGimpsey, was rejected by Dublin's Supreme Court in 1990.

The third issue, that the agreement would not be a derogation of British sovereignty, was addressed directly in the Agreement itself. Article 2b states 'There is no derogation from the sovereignty of either the United Kingdom Government or the Irish Government, and each retains responsibility for the decisions and administration of government within its own jurisdiction'. This clause was continually invoked by the government to counter suggestions that the AIA breached British sovereignty. Article 1(a) of the agreement also stated that 'any change in the status of Northern Ireland would only come about with the consent of the majority of the people in Northern Ireland' (see Appendix 1).

Mrs Thatcher sought to dispel suggestions that the agreement had implications for British sovereignty over Northern Ireland or was part of some plan to weaken the Union. In the opening speech of the debate on the agreement she asserted: 'I want to say something about what is not in the agreement. The agreement does not affect the status of Northern Ireland within the United Kingdom. It does not set us on some imagined slippery slope to Irish unity, and it is nonsense to claim that it might.' The Prime Minister noted that the British would 'listen to the views of the Irish Government' and 'make determined efforts to resolve differences' but 'at the end of the day decisions north of the border will continue to be made by the United Kingdom Government and south of the border by the Irish Government. This is a fundamental point. There can be no misunderstanding.' For Mrs Thatcher the agreement did not threaten the union but reinforced it (HC Deb., 26 November 1985). But not all on the British side presented the issue of sovereignty in such stark terms. Jim Prior, who had been Secretary of State when the original negotiations began but by 1985 had returned to the backbenches, agreed that legally the situation had not changed but there was a (necessary) perception in Northern Ireland that things had changed. 'We must ... accept that although it makes no difference to the status of Northern Ireland within the United Kingdom, in the eyes of the unionists it changes that status in Northern Ireland itself. Frankly, if it did not do so to some extent, there would be no chance of getting the minority community to accept it' (HC Deb., 26 November 1985). If it was accepted that the *status quo* was not working in Northern Ireland, then for things to change the *status quo* also had to change, an example of British pragmatism. The changes that the British government argued had taken place were not related to legal sovereignty but to a new practical mechanism whereby the Irish government could make representations on behalf of northern nationalists and in return would increase their cooperation with Britain in the security field.

As Hennessey demonstrates in this volume the Ulster Unionist interpretation of these changes was very different. Several Unionist MPs challenged the British on the point regarding sovereignty although one, Harold McCusker, rejected the debate telling the House, 'I shall not argue with the Secretary of State about sovereignty because the House can change what it means by that ... Sovereignty is what the Government decide it is' (HC Deb., 27/1 November 1985).

British insistence that sovereignty had not been breached was in legal terms upheld, given that the agreement withstood subsequent legal challenges. However, Prior's observations about perception, and the unionist reaction to the agreement, illustrated that the importance of sovereignty was not confined to the legal/constitutional sphere. For the agreement to work it was necessary that there was a perception amongst nationalists (and the Irish government) that things had changed in Northern Ireland. The British, though, wanted this perception to rest on issues such as a right of the Irish to have a mechanism to represent the view of nationalists, via the AIIC. They did not want it to rest on the perception of an executive role for Dublin over the internal affairs of Northern Ireland. The British were also hoping that there would be a perception amongst unionists that things had changed in a way that was advantageous to their position given the acknowledgement by the Irish government of the principle of consent in Article 1 and the commitment to greater security cooperation given in Article 9. However, unionists were not reassured on these issues to any great extent given that Dublin did not remove the constitutional claim over Northern Ireland and they either doubted Dublin's cooperation in the security field or saw it (like the Prime Minister) as something that they had a right to expect. For unionism it was the acknowledgement in the agreement that Dublin had a right to a say over Northern Ireland that was anathema and represented a clear *de facto* breach of British sovereignty even if the courts did not rule it a *de jure* one. Their suspicions were reinforced by the fact that they had been excluded from the negotiating process (whilst the leader of the SDLP, John Hume, had been consulted throughout by the Irish government).

So on the question of sovereignty a useful distinction can be made between the legal and practical spheres. Legally the agreement did not breach UK sovereignty over Northern Ireland. The Irish role via the IGC was, in the words of the Irish Taoiseach, one that went 'beyond a consultative role but necessarily, because of the sovereignty issue, falling short of an executive role ...'(*Dáil Éireann*, 19 November 1985). This quote is indicative of an underlying challenge for both governments when presenting the agreement. The Irish needed to portray it as a fundamental change to their role in Northern Ireland, the British needed to ensure that the Republic's role was not seen to be so great that it would alienate unionism entirely from the political process in Northern Ireland. Unionists were not at all reassured by the legal position and argued that Northern Ireland's position in the UK had been weakened and was far more conditional than before.

The outcome of the AIA: were British objectives achieved?

In the post-AIA, pre-GFA period, many commentators argued that the agreement had been a failure (Aughey, 1989; O'Leary and McGarry, 1994; Owen, 1994; Cox, 1996). Since the GFA there has been an attempt in some quarters to rehabilitate the agreement and portray it as a key contribution to the later peace process (Goodall, 1998; FitzGerald, 2003) though some accounts continue to argue that 'from a strategic point of view the AIA had ... been a failure' (Neumann, 2003: 146). The problem with evaluating the success or failure of the agreement is: by which yardstick does one measure it? A variety of aims can be identified for the agreement and a case can be made that they were not achieved. Mrs Thatcher was disappointed by the AIA and lamented that British 'concessions alienated the Unionists without gaining the level of security co-operation we had a right to expect' (Thatcher, 1993: 415) and by 1998 was claiming that 'I now believe that [Enoch Powell's] assessment was right ...' although she did not state which aspect of his assessment she agreed with (*Daily Telegraph*, 23 November 1998). Others within British policy-making circles have a different perspective. Goodall suggested 'Even the greatest enemy of the Agreement wouldn't have said that there wasn't greatly improved security co-operation as a result of the Agreement' (Goodall, 1999). Mrs Thatcher became disillusioned with the return for her utilitarian calculations, in a similar way to her disillusion with the Single European Act in 1986. In both cases she went against her natural (sovereign) instincts on pragmatic grounds, but by the time her memoirs were published in 1993 she clearly felt that the 'price' had not been worth paying.

In areas beyond security the agreement's record is also mixed. It certainly did not end megaphone diplomacy between London and Dublin; there were numerous high-profile public disagreements between the two states after 1985. Issues that the agreement highlighted, such as the accompaniment of army patrols by the Royal Ulster Constabulary (RUC), extradition of suspects from the Republic to Northern Ireland and the possibility of mixed courts or three-judge courts continued to cause frustration and disagreements. But some improvements can be identified: the growth of Sinn Féin was checked – at least until the peace process period when arguably the 'threat' posed by republicans was of a very different hue; changes were made to certain contentious policies that were seen as unacceptable to northern nationalists, such as the repeal of the Flags and Emblems Act; and some changes were made to the system of justice and on issues of employment and Catholic representation on public bodies (FitzGerald, 1991: 573–5). The issue is: at what point can we herald the agreement a success or damn it a failure? Given that there were competing objectives for the different departments and individuals involved in the negotiations it is hard to offer a definitive assessment on whether the agreement was a success or failure for the British government. It may be more useful to examine the outcomes of the agreement, both intended and unanticipated, than talk of its success or failure.

The AIA did play an important role in the politics of Northern Ireland and a strong case can be made that it was an essential contributory factor to the peace process that emerged several years later. As discussed elsewhere in this book, the Agreement did cause fundamental re-evaluations within unionism and republicanism, without which there may never have been a peace process or GFA. The impact of these re-evaluations, however, did not become apparent for several years. Whilst it is not too much of a stretch to make a link between the AIA and the peace process, it is too much of a stretch to suggest that the peace process was the intended and anticipated outcome of the AIA. The AIA was shaped by the differing priorities of the three British departments that were involved in the negotiations. This is perhaps not surprising. As the former head of the Northern Ireland civil service observed, 'People talk about "the British

Government" as if the British Government is a monolith. The British Government is never a monolith, there are different influences working there, particularly in relation to Northern Ireland' (Bloomfield, 2000). These influences were in play during its negotiation and the resulting problems of identifying what the objectives of the Agreement were, account for the differing opinions over whether it was a success or not. A quarter of a century later, it is more relevant to ask: was the Agreement beneficial to the politics of Northern Ireland? A compelling case can be made that because of the reaction that it provoked and the debates that it stimulated, the AIA was beneficial, though not perhaps in the way that was intended or anticipated in November 1985. Significantly, in the politics of Northern Ireland today, the issue of sovereignty is mainly noticeable by its absence.

Bibliography

Andrew, R. (2000) Interview with the author, 21 November.

Anglo-Irish Agreement, www.dfa.ie/uploads/documents/angloirish%20agreement%201985.pdf (Irish version, accessed 19 January 2010) and cain.ulst.ac.uk/hmso/aia.htm (British version, accessed 20 January 2010).

Armstrong, Lord, R. (1993) 'Ethnicity, the English, and Northern Ireland: comments and reflections', in D. Keogh and M.H. Haltzel, *Northern Ireland and the Politics of Reconciliation* (Cambridge: Cambridge University Press), pp. 203–7.

Aughey, A. (1989) *Under Siege* (Belfast: Blackstaff Press).

Bew, P., P. Gibbon and H. Patterson (1995) *Northern Ireland 1921–1994: Political Forces and Social Classes* (London: Serif).

Bloomfield, Sir K. (2000) (Head of Northern Ireland Civil Service 1984–1991) Interview with the author, 19 May.

Cox, W.H. (1996) 'From Hillsborough to Downing Street and after', in P. Catterall and S. McDougall (eds) *The Northern Ireland Question in British Politics* (London: Macmillan), pp. 182–206.

Cunningham, M. (1991) *British Government Policy in Northern Ireland 1969–1989* (Manchester: Manchester University Press).

Dáil Éireann Debate, 19 November 1985, vol. 361, col. 2562.

FitzGerald, G. (1991) *All in a Life* (Dublin: Macmillan).

—— (2000) Interview with the author, 6 June.

—— (2003) 'Parnell's people Home Rule by Alvin Jackson is a fascinating and original interpretation of 200 years of Irish history', *Guardian*, 26 July.

Goodall, Sir D. (1993) 'The Irish Question', *Ampleforth Journal*, XCVIII.

—— (1998) 'Actually it's all working out almost exactly to plan', *Parliamentary Brief*, p.54

—— (1999) Interview with the author, 24 June.

—— (2010) 'An Agreement worth remembering', *Dublin Review of Books*, 17 February. Available online at www.drb.ie/more_details/10-02-17/Edging_Towards _Peace.aspx# (accessed 22 March 2011).

Hadden, T. and K. Boyle (1989) *The Anglo-Irish Agreement 1985: Commentary, Text and Official Review* (Andover: Sweet and Maxwell).

House of Commons Debates (Hansard), 20 May 1980, vol. 985, col. 250.

——, 23 November 1985, vol. 32, cols 704–5.

——, 26 November 1985, vol. 87, col. 750.

——, 27 November 1985, vol. 87, col. 913.

Howe, G. (1994) *Conflict of Loyalty* (London: Macmillan).

Hurd, D. (1999) Interview with the author, 25 July.

—— (2003) *Memoirs*, London: Little Brown.

ICBH (Institute for Contemporary British History) (1997) *Anglo-Irish Agreement Witness Seminar*.

Index of Questions and Answers on Anglo-Irish Agreement (obtained by the author under the Freedom of information Act, 30 June 2006).

Lillis, M. (2010) 'Edging towards peace', *Dublin Review of Books*, 13: Spring, 1–20. Available online at www.drb.ie/more_details/10-02-17/Edging_Towards_Peace. aspx# (accessed 22 March 2011).

Millar, F. (2004) *David Trimble: The Price of Peace* (Dublin: Liffey Press).

Nally, D. (2000) Interview with author.

Neumann, P. (2003) *Britain's Long War: British Strategy in the Northern Ireland Conflict, 1969–98* (Basingstoke: Palgrave Macmillan).

O'Kane, E. (2007) *Britain, Ireland and Northern Ireland Since 1980: the Totality of Relationships* (Abingdon: Routledge)

—— (2007) 'Re-evaluating the Anglo-Irish Agreement: central or incidental to the Northern Ireland peace process?', *International Politics*, 44: 6, 711–31.

O'Leary, B. (1989) 'Limits to coercive consociationalism in Northern Ireland', *Political Studies*, 38: 4, 562–88.

O'Leary, B. and J. McGarry (1994) *The Politics of Antagonism* (London: Athlone Press).

Owen, E.A. (1994) *The Anglo-Irish Agreement: The First Three Years* (Cardiff: University of Wales Press).

Patterson, H. (1997) *The Politics of Illusion* (London: Serif).

Prior, J. (1986) *A Balance of Power* (London: Hamilton).

Stuart, M. (1998) *Douglas Hurd: Public Servant* (Edinburgh: Mainstream Publishing).

Thatcher, M. (1993) *The Downing Street Years* (London: Harper Collins).

3 Irish government and the Agreement: a dynamic vehicle for change?

Paul Bew

There is, of course, a powerful political temptation to develop a strong relationship with one side of the community in Northern Ireland at the expense of the possibility of a sympathetic relationship with the other. This could only have the effect of heartlessly raising false hopes among the long-suffering minority and at the same time increasing fear and intransigence among the majority. But our people are wise and they know that progress in Northern Ireland involves winning the confidence of both sides simultaneously, and they were right to question spurious claims about progress being made behind the backs of the people of Northern Ireland. (Garrett FitzGerald, 1982)

On 15 November 1985, the AIA was signed by Margaret Thatcher and Garret FitzGerald at Hillsborough Castle, Co. Down, ending months of negotiations and speculation. Article 1a stated that the two governments 'affirm that any change in the status of Northern Ireland would only come about with the consent of a majority of the people of Northern Ireland'. At the same time it failed to say exactly what the current status of Northern Ireland was, a point quickly latched on to by unionist critics of the agreement.

The Agreement established an Inter-Governmental Conference (AIIC) to deal regularly with political matters, security and related matters, legal matters (including the administration of justice), and the promotion of cross-border cooperation. The issue of 'political matters' was particularly sensitive. Article 5a said that the conference would look at measures to 'recognise and accommodate the rights and identities of the two traditions in Northern Ireland, to protect human rights and to prevent discrimination. Matters to be considered in this area include measures to foster the cultural heritage of both traditions, changes in electoral arrangements, the use of flags and emblems [and] the avoidance of economic and social discrimination'.

Article 5c stated that 'if it should prove impossible to achieve and sustain devolution on a basis which secures widespread acceptance in Northern Ireland, the conference shall be a framework within which the Irish government may, where the interests of the minority community are significantly or specifically affected, put forward views on proposals for major legislation and on major policy issues, which are within the purview of the Northern Ireland departments'. The Irish government interpreted this as covering an extremely wide range of issues in Northern Ireland. Under Article 2b the British government was also committed 'in the interests of promoting peace and stability' to make 'determined efforts to resolve any differences, which arise within the conference with the Irish Government' (see Appendix 1). The FitzGerald government and the Irish media interpreted this as giving them more than consultation but less than joint authority.

Dealing with Mrs Thatcher

After signing the agreement, Margaret Thatcher declared: 'I went into this agreement because I was not prepared to tolerate a situation of continuing violence' (Thatcher, 1985). The Treasury Minister, Ian Gow, a personal and political friend of Thatcher, resigned in protest, saying that 'the involvement of a foreign power in a consultative role in the administration of the province will prolong, and not diminish, Ulster's agony' (Gow, 1985). The Protestant Ulster Freedom Fighters (UFF) immediately declared members of the Anglo-Irish Conference (AIC) and Secretariat to be 'legitimate targets'. After the signing of the Agreement, FitzGerald approached Thatcher on the issue of seeking money from EEC countries for the International Fund for Ireland associated with the agreement. He was

> taken aback by her reaction. 'More money for these people?' she said, waving her hand in the general direction of Northern Ireland. 'Look at these schools; look at these roads. Why should they have more money? I need that money for my people in England, who don't have anything like this.' I was frankly quite nonplussed at this singular declaration of English nationalism on an occasion when I had expected rather to have to cope with what had so often been described to me as her 'unionism'. (FitzGerald, 1991: 568)

Something of the degree of secrecy in which the Agreement was drawn up was later revealed by the then Chancellor of the Exchequer, Nigel Lawson. He noted that the Agreement had largely been negotiated by the Cabinet, 'far too leaky to be taken into her confidence'. He believed that the only members fully aware of the details of the negotiations were Tom King, Douglas Hurd, and possibly the Defence Secretary, Michael

Heseltine. Lawson himself had considerable doubts about the Agreement but did not oppose it openly in the Cabinet; nor did any of his colleagues. Lawson believed that 'over the years there had been a succession of well-intentioned political initiatives launched to deal with the Irish problem, and each of them had ended in tears, if not in bloodshed. It had made me highly sceptical of the wisdom of any Northern Ireland initiative' (1992: 699).

Twenty-five years on, it requires an effort of will to recall the full impact of the emotional theatre of the signing of the AIA at Hillsborough in 1985. The sheer scale of the shock on the unionist side has ceased to reverberate. At the time, however, unionists certainly believed that this was the diplomatic breach which the Irish government had opened in Northern Ireland's defences and that a major obstacle had been removed from the road to Irish unity. So many other dramas have intervened subsequently: the Downing Street Declaration of 1993; the Framework Document of 1994; the Belfast/GFA of 1998 and the St Andrews Agreement of 2006. But, at the time, many educated unionists were convinced that the United Ireland was imminent; others, more sophisticated, felt sure that joint authority was the next step along the line. The incidentals of the Hillsborough signing: the Irish security detail lounging with its Uzis, while Harold McCusker MP protested bitterly and impotently at the gate, seemed to speak instructive volumes – the enemy had entered the gates and were here to stay. So too did the failure of the unionist counter-campaign; the huge Belfast City Hall demonstrations and the resignation of all parliamentary seats and the forcing of by-elections – which saw a slight rise in the unionist vote, but the loss of one parliamentary seat.

Above all, the AIA ushered in an era of direct rule with a green tinge, symbolised by the permanent presence of Irish government officials at Maryfield, Co. Down. The Secretariat took on a profound symbolic importance. The former unionist minister, Roy Bradford had popularised the phrase 'diktat' to describe the Agreement and this summed up the experience of marginalisation, a sense – felt by most unionists in Northern Ireland – that policy would now be determined by cliques in the Foreign Office; the NIO and, indeed, worst of all, the joint Anglo-Irish Maryfield Secretariat. And there was a deep popular assumption that what was being planned was the modalities of bringing about Irish unity. The agreement, of course, was novel in its explicit acceptance of a role for the Irish government in the affairs of the north as a defender of the interests of the nationalist community. This role was much less than the joint authority proposed by the New Ireland Forum, the major and recent official attempt to redefine and re-express the ideological purpose of Irish nationalism. The Agreement accorded to Dublin shared responsibility for all aspects of the administration of government – but it was more than purely consultative. Much of the confusion in unionist politics arose from the difficulties involved in coping with this fact. The Agreement also acknowledged that the British government would support a united Ireland if majority consent existed for it in the north. Here it was less novel: the same point was enunciated in 1973 at the time of the Sunningdale Agreement.

The AIA explicitly attempted to encourage devolution on a cross-community basis, but, despite a later inaccurate claim by Thatcher to this effect, it was not possible to 'knock out' its institutions by agreeing to power-sharing. In the absence of any agreement on devolution, the AIA gave a paradoxical shape to the governmental institutions of the north. In substance the system was, administratively and economically, increasingly integrated with the United Kingdom. This was intensified by the growing reliance of the entire community on the British subvention. Nevertheless, the new role of the Irish government in Northern Ireland affairs appeared to be irreversible, and for many this implied the eventual evolution of a formalised system of joint authority. However, if Irish nationalism could only be satisfied by the principle of movement then unionists certainly feared that joint authority, no matter how unacceptable to them, would even then not be the end of the matter. Joint authority would only be yet another temporary arrest on the journey towards Irish unity.

Consequently, Mrs Thatcher became a hated figure in certain unionist circles and it was thought that she, wittingly or unwittingly, had sold the pass to Irish expansionism. Ian Paisley told his congregation at the Martys Memorial Church: 'We pray this night thou wouldst deal with the Prime Minister of our country. We remember that the apostle Paul handed over the enemies of truth to the Devil that they might learn not to blaspheme. O God, in wrath take vengeance upon her, O Lord, and grant that we see a demonstration of thy power' (Bew and Gillespie, 1993: 188–9). In his most recent interview, Dr Paisley refers to Maggie in much more relaxed terms, criticising only a tendency to hit the wicked bottle 'hard'. No doubt, the fact that it looks increasingly clear that Margaret Thatcher's promise that she would one day look down from the heavens on a Northern Ireland firmly within the United Kingdom looks likely to be fulfilled, has helped this relative reconciliation. Nonetheless, the scale of this early anger requires explanation as much as does the later *glasnost*. It can be taken as a sign that unionists today no longer fear the imminence of unity, if only because the assumed institutional dynamic which they read into the Agreement of 1985 has been contained.

The recently released state papers for 1979 make Margaret Thatcher's eventual conversion to the strategy embodied in the AIA all the more surprising. It is sometimes said that Mrs Thatcher was an English nationalist not a United Kingdom unionist. There is some truth in this. But in her first year in office, her support for the Ulster Unionist case was well informed and tenacious. She revised some foreign documents in the Ulster crisis which, she felt, were too vague. She considered removing the voting rights of Irish citizens who moved to the United Kingdom, a retaliation for Dublin's feebleness on security policy cooperation. Mrs Thatcher never said that Northern Ireland was as 'British as Finchley' – a mountain of misquotations to the contrary – but she did say that the citizens of Northern Ireland should have the same rights as the British citizens of Finchley and in the end, she took a step which betrayed that position. In retirement, it was the one major British policy initiative taken in her name which she acknowledged to be a mistake (BBC News, 1998).

In 1980 the newly formed government of Charles J Haughey in Dublin viewed the Prime Minister in London with considerable suspicion and even fear. The recently released state papers show that John Hume had told the Irish government that Margaret Thatcher had no real knowledge of the history of Northern Ireland, and consequently no understanding of nationalist sentiment on matters such as discrimination and partition. The Prime Minister was believed to be fundamentally sympathetic to the case of the Ulster Unionists and unwilling to contemplate any new Dublin-friendly initiative. The Irish Department of Foreign Affairs responded to Hume's message by stating a hope that Mrs Thatcher's innate radicalism would win out and lead to a change in position. In the end, this judgement turned out to be correct, but it required a long labour involving a profound effort of persuasion by officials such as Sir Robert Armstrong and David Goodall on the British side, and a different Taoiseach, Garret FitzGerald, on the Irish side.

Enoch Powell might as well have been regarded as an intellectual forerunner to Thatcher. He continued to meet her regularly at events like the Tory Philosophy Group. Yet, Powell was not able to intervene on behalf of the unionist interest. Why? In part, this was a matter of personality. He never quite overcame his jealousy of Thatcher and thus never established a genuine intimacy. The Ulster Unionist Party (UUP) under Jim Molyneaux had expected that 'Enoch' would deal within the 'inside' world of government and would be able to compete with the Cabinet Office and Foreign Office for control of the Prime Minister's mind. It was not an unreasonable assumption, simply an incorrect one. When the dust settled, the anger over Molyneaux's old failure was a key element in the creation of a new UUP leadership under David Trimble in 1995. So, a mix of personal miscalculations and strategic error underlay the British approach – above all, however, the understandable impulse, *something* must be done.

The fact remains that there was a rational kernel at the heart of unionist dismay. As Bruce Anderson, the most pro-unionist of the senior metropolitan political commentators at the time, put it: 'Mrs Thatcher has insisted that there is no transfer of sovereignty, the fact remains that a foreign government has been given a say in the internal affairs of the United Kingdom – without even being required to renounce its own claim to Northern Ireland' (*Sunday Telegraph*, 18 November 1987). Why do this, unless British policy favoured a united Ireland? Why do this unless, under the influence of and with the persuasion of Irish diplomacy, the British had accepted the mutual advantage of a credible strategy of disengagement? In fact, there was a hidden absurdity to all this, but it was not visible at the time. The British proclaimed a victory – a new recognition of the north by the south – which was not a new victory but something they already possessed. In fact, a further enormous labour was required in the negotiations leading up to the GFA of 1998 to achieve the necessary transformation of the Irish Constitution. The logic of this negotiation lay in the perception, shared by everyone, that a new north–south relationship could not flourish in the presence of such a claim in the Irish Constitution, no matter how vacuous such a claim was in international law.

Irish issues

Only a paranoid reading of the Agreement's negotiation and implementation, however, would suggest that that something was without its own distinct boundaries of acceptability. Those boundaries were not exclusively set by the British government. The Irish government had its own limits of acceptability, though ones which it could rarely and openly articulate for reasons of nationalist ideology. The scholar Dr Enda Staunton's research in the files of the Irish government has thrown important light on this problem (1996: 45). Articles 2 and 3 of the Irish Constitution of 1937 did lay claim to Northern Ireland as a matter of territorial and legal right. But Irish officials at the start of the Troubles were well aware that this meant nothing in international law: that the international treaty of 1925, whereby Dublin recognised the Belfast regime, held sway. The British negotiating team seem to have been entirely unaware of this weakness in the Irish negotiating position; but they were, at least, conscious of the broad general position of Northern Ireland as part of the United Kingdom. It would have helped considerably in the propaganda battle of 1985 if the British government had pointed out publicly, as well understood by Dublin officials, that Ireland had already [in 1925] conceded Northern Ireland's legitimacy and that the 1937 Constitution could only have significance (real enough) at the level of internal Irish government thought and practice. Instead, the British chose to argue on the terrain of the Agreement of 1985 modifying the Irish Constitution; a losing argument, when, in fact, the Irish had given an irrefragable recognition in 1925. To suspicious minds, there could be only one reason for this and it was that the two governments had a common interest in concealing the constitutional transformation which was taking place.

But the dangers, after all, were far greater for Dublin. Why did the Irish elite take such a risk? The Department of Foreign Affairs always had its adventurers, but that hardly explains the broader operation of the state. On the Irish side, the most inscrutable figure is Dermot Nally, secretary to the cabinet since 1973. Bernard Donoughue's diaries signal Nally out as the most impressive of the Irish officials. In the mid-1970s he was obsessed, as was FitzGerald, with the idea that the British might do a scuttle and leave Northern Ireland as an unsustainable burden on Dublin. In retirement, he loved to re-tell the story of Jack Lynch's meeting with Jimmy Carter in 1980. The Irish foreign service advised Prime Minister Lynch that Mr Carter was not attuned to listening to complex stories; better to answer questions directly and simply. Taking this advice to heart, Lynch responded to Carter's question 'Do you want a united Ireland?' with a heartfelt 'Jaysus, no'. For Nally, the story happily summed up the real Irish policy and so the great advantage of the AIA was that it ruled out a unilateral British scuttle. Britain was now tied into Northern Ireland on the basis of a joint understanding with another sovereign power in a binding international treaty. In an Edinburgh document, *Northern Ireland – A Challenge to Theology*, Fitzgerald argued that under the terms of the Hillsborough Accord, the Irish government had responsibility without power in the north and in that sense 'nothing substantive had changed' (see McDonagh et al., 1987). This hardly worried Nally: he had once told the Irish cabinet that it was vital to Dublin that Britain stayed in the north, that all criticism should be toned down, lest Britain take it seriously and leave (see Bew, 2007: 521). Now he had Britain where he wanted it; chained to the grim rock of Ulster. Hardly surprisingly, but to the disappointment of London, megaphone Anglo-Irish diplomacy did not cease as a result of the AIA of 1985. In fact, it increased as incident after incident displayed. This was to be expected, as the one factor which might have controlled Dublin rhetoric (fear of unilateral British withdrawal) was now removed. In short, it was the boundary of influence which the Irish government was attempting to extend and not removing the border. Not surprisingly, when the *Sunday Independent* leaked copies of AIIC meetings it found that the British were using 'salty' language.

In September 1983 Garret FitzGerald instructed senior Department of Foreign Affairs official Michael Lillis to 'advance a particular line of argument to the British side, based on an analysis which he and I discussed' (Lillis and Goodall, 2010). Michael Lillis has recently outlined the elements of his analysis. The first issue was trust, specifically trust on the part of the nationalist community in the British security forces and the local judicial system. Lillis thought that the situation was beyond repair and feeding the alienation of young Catholics in favour of republican terrorism. The concern for the Irish government was that destabilisation in Northern Ireland would spill over into the South and that as things stood, it could do little to prevent this disaster happening. The second issue was one of policy logic. The transformation from alienation to trust could only be achieved by the direct involvement of the Irish government's security forces and courts on the ground, especially in nationalist areas where people would see them as 'their own'. This should be done not only for reasons of nationalist ideology but also for reasons of collective, mutual security. According to Lillis, the Irish understood 'a need to address the fundamental insecurities this project would inevitably create among unionists and that we should be ready in the interest of stability to do what was necessary to allay those insecurities, including reviewing the articles of our constitution which they read as constituting a territorial claim on Northern Ireland'.

Lillis noted an unmistakable subtext of this message. For such an initiative to succeed a new political and institutional structure would have to be created. In the mind of Lillis, in order to secure southern support this would have to be a system of 'joint authority' or 'joint sovereignty'. While this was not explicitly stated at this point, he believed that British officials fully understood the realities. That passage is a classic statement of the Irish government case. In his Oak Room speech of early 1982 Garret FitzGerald had said 'our people' are 'too wise' to seek to impose a framework on the unionists. FitzGerald here acknowledged that an imposed settlement would leave behind a legacy of sectarian distrust. However, Sinn Féin's strong performance in the general election encouraged the Irish Prime Minister to change his mind: he now pressed the British to impose a new deal. This is the meaning of the reference to 'alienation' in the Lillis document: it had to be addressed at all costs to protect the SDLP against Sinn Féin.

It has even been suggested that the election results of 1985 assisted the process of negotiation. In his *The Anglo-Irish Agreement* (1994: 17) E.A. Owen has written: 'The Northern Ireland elections of May 1995 provided the spur London and Dublin required to redouble their efforts to strike a bargain. Sinn Féin won fifty-nine seats on seventeen of the twenty-six district councils in the province, polling 11.88 per cent of the votes. This was double what the opinion polls had prophesised, and only 6 per cent less than the SDLP figure.' In fact, of course, the polls at this stage always underestimated Sinn Féin support, though one should not discount the employment of electoral fraud, on which subject the recent memoirs of Brendan Hughes are particularly helpful (Moloney 2010).

The trouble, however, lies with the issue which neither FitzGerald nor Lillis explicitly address even though it is, of course, the most important of all and goes to the heart of any serious historical judgement on the whole process. What if the new approach merely harvested the 'downside' already noted by FitzGerald but did not deliver on an upside in terms of sustained support for the SDLP against Sinn Féin? Was not Northern Ireland then placed in an even worse position? The electoral statistics are consistent with the view that Sinn Féin fell from a highpoint of 1983 (13.7 per cent of the vote) through to 1985 and that this fall was further stimulated by the immediate impact of the Agreement as shown by a relatively weak Sinn Féin performance in the four by-elections of January 1986. However, by May 1986, at two council by-elections in Magherafelt, in Sperrin and Erne East, the tide seemed to turn as Sinn Féin stabilised. In the general election of 1987, Sinn Féin polled 11.4 per cent of the vote, as against 11.8 per cent in the local government election of 1985. Some rural losses to SDLP were mainly, though by no means entirely, compensated for by a very solid urban performance. SDLP gains in Belfast seats appear to have been entirely at the expense of previous centre voters (the cross-community Alliance Party or from its former leader, Gerry Fitt) rather than from Sinn Féin. While SDLP generally did well in the 1987 elections, their leader John Hume actually polled fewer votes in 1983, whereas Sinn Féin president Gerry Adams actually polled more. In two West Belfast council by-elections on the eve of the Remembrance Sunday tragedy in Enniskillen, Sinn Féin outpolled SDLP by almost two to one in Belfast, even though the Alliance Party vote collapsed into the SDLP.

Yet, despite this, the implications of the AIA were, indeed, more radical than FitzGerald appears to imply. This was made clear in Sean Donlon's critical review of Mrs Thatcher's account of it in her memoirs (Donlon, 2010). Thatcher had claimed that the Irish government's role was no more than consultative in that it simply allowed the Irish ministers to put forward views and propositions on Northern Ireland matters. Donlon then quotes from the 'carefully negotiated' unpublished document which contained the agreed answers to the sixty questions most likely to be asked about the Agreement. The full 'catechism' answer is:

> The Conference will be more than just consultation in that the Irish side will put forward the views and proposals on its own initiative as well as being invited to do so: and there is an obligation on both sides in the Conference to make determined effort to resolve any differences: and one of the functions of the Conference will be to promote cross-border cooperation between North and South in Ireland.

Commenting on this analysis by one of its Irish architects, a leader in the *Irish Times* (30 December 1992) observed: 'The agreement was conceived as a dynamic vehicle for change, not as a bureaucratic instrument for the more convenient governance of Northern Ireland.' This encapsulated both the conceptual and strategic gulf between British and Irish approaches to what was signed at Hillsborough Castle. Fundamentally, the logic of the Agreement from London's vista was a shift away from the strategy of legitimising direct rule by the search for structures of devolved government based on power-sharing. As one senior NIO official has put it: 'Although the agreement paid lip service to devolution, it was really an admission that power-sharing in Northern Ireland had not worked and the nationalist interest could only be protected by Dublin' (Bew et al.,1997: 65).

In fact, there was an element of bravado on the Irish side insofar as the adventurers in the Department of Foreign Affairs were still prepared to push for joint authority-type initiatives until at least 1994. There is a wistfulness in the account of Michael Lillis when he talks about how Provisional Sinn Féin eventually negotiated a rather weak deal when compared with what seemed possible before 1985 and the opportunities which could have opened up thereafter. But the blame can not be laid at Sinn Féin's door alone. The Department of Foreign Affairs over-reached itself in British eyes in 1985 and, as a consequence, British policy became more sceptical towards official Dublin, an absolute measure of what was agreed in the Belfast/GFA.

The Prime Minister's foreign policy advisor, Percy Cradock, wrote of the AIA of 1985: 'This was based on an implicit bargain, on the one hand a say for the Dublin government in the affairs of Ulster, on the other hand, the greater security cooperation between the two governments.' Cradock added: 'It proved a disappointing bargain' (1997: 205). Cradock's remark, of course, did not stand alone. The memoirs of Margaret Thatcher and Nigel Lawson take the same line. The Conservative MP Ken Hind, then private secretary to the Northern Ireland Secretary of State, was in the same place when he addressed the British-Irish inter-parliamentary body. Famously, Gus O'Donnell, now the Cabinet Secretary, referred to the agreement as 'that f...ing awful agreement'. It is not difficult to see the logic of O'Donnell's remark. Deaths arising from political violence rose in 1986 from fifty-four to sixty-two while civilian injuries rose dramatically from 468 to 734. During 1987 there were almost 100 political deaths from political violence, double the figure for the last year of unalloyed direct rule. In the late 1980s and 1990s violence continued to rise steadily: loyalist paramilitary activity – 10 per cent of that of republicans in 1984 – was now almost on a par with republican violence. Moreover, republican militarism had been fuelled by the Libyan arms shipments, the great intelligence failure at the heart of the AIA on the British side. Playing with the casino's money – a phrase attributed to a senior Cabinet Minister – meant that the British government was paying for everything and thus it did not matter about the consequences of the AIA. This comment was a tacit admission that the initiative was something of a shot in the dark but one worth taking. This proved to be a dangerous assumption, and playing with the casino's money decisively lost its charm in a context of increasing violence and disorder.

Conclusion

Irish official comment – from Sean Donlon in the 1990s to Michael Lillis in 2010 – never addresses this British disillusionment. For Britain, the Agreement of 1985 was a disappointment, perhaps a mistake: this was the conventional wisdom of the NIO under Sir John Chilcot and Sir Quentin Thomas in the 1990s. A new approach, both to Sinn Féin and the unionists, was necessary – a new approach which, in the end, was successful – but a new approach which did not reflect that essential continuity of policy which even the wisest of Dublin commentators, such as former Taoiseach John Bruton, have insisted upon (see *Parliamentary Brief*, May/June, 1998). There is a relationship between the AIA and the Belfast/GFA but it is one of political 'contiguity' rather than of political 'unfolding'.

On the twenty-fifth anniversary of the Agreement of 1985 some of the surviving key figures on both sides met to celebrate their handiwork. Naturally enough, as is inevitable on these occasions, there was an understandable air of self-congratulation. The harmony of the event was only slightly affected by Dr Garret Fitzgerald's apparent failure to recognise Lord (Tom) King, the former Secretary of State for Northern Ireland. Dr Fitzgerald's vague reference to 'this gentleman' led Lord King to pointedly identify himself. It is perhaps unfair to read too much symbolism into this moment. Nonetheless, it should not be forgotten that when the framers of the Agreement moved on to pastures new, the fundamental responsibility for Northern Irish policy remained with the Northern Ireland Office and the Secretary of State. It was the strategic thinking in that office which laid the foundations for the settlement of 1998. This is why, despite the glow of contentment which surrounded the anniversary meeting, it seemed to refer to an event shrouded in the mists of time, even though the emotions generated by it were felt so profoundly by so many still living.

References

BBC News, 'Enoch was right on Ireland, says Thatcher', *BBC News*, 23 November 1998. Available online at http://news.bbc.co.uk/1/hi/uk_politics/220053.stm (accessed 22 March 2011).

Bew, P. (2007) *Ireland: The Politics of Enmity 1789–2006* (Oxford: Oxford University Press).

Bew, P. et al. (1997) *Between War and Peace* (London: Lawrence And Wishart).

Bew, P. and G. Gillespie (1993) *Northern Ireland: A Chronology of the Troubles 1968–1993* (Dublin: Gill & Macmillan), pp.188-9.

Cradock, P. (1997) *In Pursuit of British Interest: Reflections on Foreign Policy under Margaret Thatcher and John Major* (London: John Murray).

Donlon, S. (2010) 'Road to deal would have deterred lesser leaders', *Irish Times*, 15 November.

Fitzgerald, G. (1982) 'Oak Room Speech', *Irish Times*, 12 February.

—— (1991) *All in a Life: An Autobiography* (Dublin: Gill & Macmillan).

Gow, I. (1985) 'Public Statement: Letter from Ian Gow MP – Resignation'. Available online at: www.margaretthatcher.org/document/106174 (accessed 19 May 2011).

Lawson, N. (1992) *The View from No. 11* (London: Bantham Press).

Lillis, M and D. Goodall (2010) 'Edging towards peace', *Dublin Review of Books*, 13: Spring, 1–20. Available online at www.drb.ie/more_details/10-02-17/Edging_Towards_Peace.aspx# (accessed 22 March 2011).

McDonagh, E. et al. (1987) *Northern Ireland – A Challenge to Theology* (Edinburgh: Centre for Theology and Public Issues University of Edinburgh).

Moloney, E. (2010) *Voices from the Grave: Two Men's War in Ireland* (London: Faber & Faber).

Owen, E.A. (1994) *The Anglo-Irish Agreement: The First Three Years* (Cardiff: University of Wales Press).

Staunton, E. (1996) 'The Boundary Commission debacle 1925: aftermath and implications', *History Ireland*, 4: 2, 42–5.

Thatcher, T. (1985) 'Public Statement: Joint Press Conference with Irish Prime Minister', Hillsborough Castle. Available online at www.margaretthatcher.org/document/106173 (accessed 19 May 2011).

4 Elite intent, public reaction and institutional change

Jennifer Todd

The AIA of November 1985 produced intense public and political reactions in Northern Ireland. In successive polls in January and February 1986 (conducted respectively for the BBC, the *Belfast Telegraph* and the *Irish Times*), over 75 per cent of Protestants opposed the AIA and only 8 per cent approved of it, while only 10 per cent of Catholics opposed it and over half approved of it. Over half of Protestants believed it gave a decision-making role to the Irish state, while less than a third thought that role merely consultative, while the proportions were reversed for Catholics (Cox, 1987: 339; see also http://cain.ulst.ac.uk/issues/politics/polls.htm). The strongest and most intense response came from the unionists.

In this chapter, I make use of new data from a research project funded by the Irish Research Council for the Humanities and Social Sciences (Breaking Patterns of Conflict, 2007–10) to reveal the intent of the political elites who made the AIA and the nature of the institutional change that ensued. This shows that the AIA had a profound impact for the governance of Northern Ireland, although for different reasons than the Northern Ireland parties anticipated, or the governments intended.

The formal provisions of the AIA are well documented in this volume. It clearly stated that there would be no derogation of sovereignty, while reiterating the principle that Northern Ireland's consti-tutional status was dependent on the will of a majority in Northern Ireland, and granting the Irish government a role in policy-making in the AIIC and a permanent presence in Northern Ireland in the form of an Anglo-Irish secretariat. The Irish government would (in various formulations in the document) 'put forward views and proposals' within the remit of the conference (Article 2b) and 'put forward views on proposals for major legislation and on major policy issues' on matters 'where the interests of the minority community are significantly or especially affected' (Article 5c). The actual

Irish influence would depend on British decision and the remit of the IGC would decline as an agreed devolved administration was set in place in Northern Ireland (the declared aim of the governments) (Articles 2b, 4b; Hadden and Boyle, 1989: 22–5). Yet both governments committed themselves to 'determined efforts' to resolve any disagreements (Article 2b), a phrase which – according to British and Irish negotiators – signalled that this was to be much more than mere consultation (Witness seminar, 11 December 2006). The fifty-page 'catechism' written by officials which informed both heads of government in their subsequent dealings with the press described the conference as 'a unique mechanism' without executive functions and without derogation from sovereignty but 'more than consultative' with an 'obligation on both sides' to resolve any differences (Witness seminar, 11 December 2006; see also FitzGerald's speech in the Irish Dáil, 19 November 1985).

The AIA provoked an intense public response. The IRA, in their Christmas message, said it was 'a highly sophisticated counter-revolutionary plan' designed to 'isolate republicans' (*Irish Times*, 19 December 1985). Fianna Fáil, then the opposition party in the Irish state, initially rejected it as inadequate, a sell-out of Irish constitutional claims for the sake of a powerless conference, although on entry to government in 1987 they were happy to work the Agreement. The SDLP welcomed the Agreement, as did the Irish government parties. A clear majority (59 per cent) in the Irish state approved the signing of the Agreement, while only 29 per cent disapproved (*Irish Times*/MRBI poll published on 23 November 1985). Although there was slightly less support for the Agreement (47 per cent) amongst the British public (Cox, 1987: 349), there was much stronger support for it in the British Parliament with only a few dissenting voices.

Unionists and the wider Protestant community in Northern Ireland were outraged at the AIA. Protestant church leaders are usually significantly more moderate than the unionist political parties. In a public letter they reported the hurt and anger of their people who

> are deeply concerned that this form of secrecy will continue in the future with the exclusion of the Loyalist representation from the nerve-centre of decision making ... Presbyterians are apprehensive of the degree of vagueness that exists as to the role of the representatives of the Republic of Ireland. They are afraid that almost every aspect of domestic policy, e.g. security, education, social services etc, will be under the scrutiny of an outside power, not always sympathetic to the ethos of the majority of the Ulster people ... The greatest hurt felt by the loyalist majority is the role given to representatives of the Republic of Ireland in the administration of Northern Ireland. It is seen as an intrusion, a thorn in the flesh and something foreign and unacceptable above all grievances. This is the root cause of discontent. (*Irish Times*, 14 December 1985).

The political parties were stronger in their denunciation of the 'diktat' (see Aughey, 1989): the AIA was popularly described as a 'Trojan Horse', and unionists who associated with British officials who operated it were called 'Quislings' and 'collaborators'. Unionist MPs resigned their posts to provoke by-elections (held on 23 January 1986) to allow their constituents to express their dislike of the AIA. Their constituents responded with a very strong turnout and definitive rejection of the Agreement (Cox, 1987: 341–3). Mass public rallies were held, and loyalist paramilitary violence increased. A.T.Q. Stewart, the eminent historian, noted the breadth of unionist anger: 'It is not Unionist intransigence with which [Mrs Thatcher] now has to deal, but a kind of patriotism, the emotion of an entire religious community ... Even the we-mustn't-bite-the-hand-that-feeds-us Unionists are as deeply hurt as the we-will-eat-grass variety' (Stewart, 1986).

The unionist reaction, Mrs Thatcher reported, was 'much worse than I expected' and exaggerated Dublin's role: 'The decisions are made by us and will continue to be made by us' (interview with *Belfast Telegraph*, 17 December 1985). In the next sections I outline the intent of the makers of the AIA and the way it actually functioned to change modes of governance in Northern Ireland. In conclusion, I argue that while Mrs Thatcher was formally correct, substantively – both in its intent and its functioning – the AIA undermined core unionist assumptions about Northern Ireland. Also, if less dramatically, it challenged nationalist assumptions.

The Anglo Irish Agreement: the intent and interpretations of its makers

The AIA was negotiated by a small number of senior British and Irish civil servants and politicians, and implemented by a slightly larger group. We have talked to nearly all of these actors in a recent research project (Breaking the Patterns of Conflict) funded by the Irish Research Council for Humanities and Social Sciences and led from University College Dublin (see www.ucd.ie/ibis/bpc). Interviews and day-long witness seminars with key actors in the process where up to eight participants were questioned by academics, were taped and transcribed. Respondents included ex-Taoisigh and Secretaries of State for Northern Ireland, and very senior civil servants from both states. The transcripts will – after respondent approval – be opened to researchers. Pending this, the quotations used here are unattributed.

Both British and Irish negotiators shared the aim of restoring peace and stability to Northern Ireland. The Irish political elite had long argued that the problem lay in the *'insulation of Northern Ireland from Ireland'* (witness seminar, 7 September 2005; the first statement of this position was in Lynch, 1972). After the failure of the Sunningdale initiative in 1974, that insulation increased and the Irish government was effectively excluded from all input into Northern Ireland affairs. British-Irish relations in the late 1970s were described by an Irish official as *'poisonous'*. Meanwhile the surge of republican support in Northern Ireland after the hunger strikes of 1981 worried the government: should republicans become the main nationalist party in the north, it would delegitimate Irish government policies and destabilise the island as a whole. Peace and stability were thus an urgent policy priority on the Irish side. The British, in turn, were aware that the 'rolling devolution' initiative begun by Jim Prior in January 1982 was going nowhere, and for them *'the eggs were all in that basket at the time'* (witness seminar, 11 December 2006). As it became clear that this option was exhausted – and Mrs Thatcher saw it as a failure by summer 1983 – they were 'bereft of new ideas' (Goodall, 2010). None of their strategies had improved the security situation, the single most important concern for Mrs Thatcher and her closest advisors (interview 18 May 2010). Indeed Sir David Goodall (2010: 16) recalls Mrs Thatcher, as early as 1982, saying reflectively 'If we get back next time ... I think I would like to do something about Northern Ireland'.

From the Irish perspective, it was urgently necessary to show to nationalists in Northern Ireland that gradualist reform could be brought through peaceful lobbying and negotiation and could improve their situation. In the 1980s, it was common to speak of 'nationalist alienation': the term referred to restricted political opportunities, a daily sense of grievance in encounters with the security forces, continued economic inequality, and sensed cultural humiliation (see Ruane and Todd, 1996: 116-203). The New Ireland Forum (1983–84) brought together nationalists north and south, and the New Ireland Forum *Report* (1984: 4.2, 4.15, 4.16) argued that an Irish dimension of some form was necessary to give to nationalists 'effective political, symbolic and administrative expression of their identity' (4.15). This justified Irish input into policy-making in Northern Ireland in terms of a symbolic politics of recognition, and similar arguments were central to political rhetoric before and after the AIA (for example, Garret FitzGerald's Dáil speech, 19 November 1985).

In interviews and witness seminars, however, a much more practically and policy-oriented legitimation of the Irish dimension was given. The role of the Irish government in the IGC was presented as a means to institutional and policy change. Even the most mildly nationalist of the Irish respondents was critical of the counter-productive and (in their view) biased policies of the British government, particularly in respect to security. They believed that this lay at the root of nationalist public sympathy with republicans. Their response was to attempt to change not the fact but the impact of the British presence. They described the key idea as

'Irish in rather than Brits out' . Early suggestions of joint policing were eventually vetoed politically (by the Irish government) (see Lillis and Goodall, 2010), but the general idea of *'Irish in'* was followed in the AIA. Michael Lillis (ibid.: 5), one of the chief Irish negotiators, was explicitly interested in practical input and cooperation which would allow growth towards joint authority, even at the cost of renouncing constitutional claims. As I have argued elsewhere (Todd, forthcoming) the Irish presence agreed in 1985 can be conceived as a 'wedge' which could open up contest over the rules and logic of British institutional practices in Northern Ireland, and could be further developed as more opportunities opened. The Irish side inserted the wedge before being clear how precisely it would be used: they did so, however, with a very clear vision of what had to be changed.

The AIA promised to change the logic of British decision-making in three ways. First, it gave an institutional forum (the AIIC) in which to raise issues. The very existence of this as a legitimate channel allowed further lobbying (including in the US) when it did not satisfactorily resolve issues. Second, its very existence implicitly changed the meaning of sovereignty by taking the Irish government as a partner in conflict management, and moving Northern Ireland out of the domestic paradigm of British Governance. Third, it gave official (British and Irish) certification to liberal nationalist concepts of 'parity of esteem' and 'institutional recognition' of the different 'traditions' on the island of Ireland (Preamble, Article 4a). The Irish negotiators in the witness seminars and interviews placed primary emphasis on its potential practical impact. They needed to prove that the IGC could change the effects of the British presence and improve the situation of nationalists in Northern Ireland. From the first days of the Secretariat, they were busily involved in attempting to secure change in policing practices (in particular Ulster Defence Regiment (UDR) accompaniment by the RUC in relations with the public), constraints on marches, nominations of nationalists to state and semi-state bodies, palpable reform of security. Both Garret FitzGerald (19 November 1985) and Peter Barry (23 October 1986) emphasised these practical benefits in the Dáil, pointing out that a role for the IGC in improving conditions for nationalists would continue even in the event of devolution.

It is in this context that the Irish lack of concern for unionist worries must be understood. When asked by Christopher Farrington why they had not thought to balance Irish support for nationalists by explicit British support for unionists, one senior Irish civil servant replied *'The thinking of the Agreement was to redress an existing imbalance. Your question implies that you're approaching it on the basis of constructing a balance. But the thinking on the Irish side was that there's been a terrible imbalance which needs redressed ...'* (witness seminar, 11 December 2006) . From the Irish perspective this was the beginning of a process of change, although significantly less than the joint authority for which they had hoped (and which would indeed have been more egalitarian than the AIA). It was a chink in the perceived power imbalance within Northern Ireland, not a final settlement but a *'foothold'*, a *'building block'*, a wedge which they would use to further their aims to end nationalist alienation and ensure peace and stability. It was not a 'Trojan horse' which could surreptitiously lead to a united Ireland: by 1985, the Irish political establishment were clear that this could only come by consent, indeed by majority vote in Northern Ireland. It was however seen as a step that might possibly lead to *de facto* joint authority (Lillis and Goodall, 2010: 5; witness seminar, 11 December 2006). Most of all, it was an attempt to change the rules of the game of British governance in Northern Ireland. For the Irish, its virtue was precisely its capacity to change the form, not the fact, of British rule. While in the past, nationalists had been left with a choice of submission, subversion or insurrection, this was a wedge that would allow nationalists to work to change institutions gradually and opportunistically, within the existing political system, as far as joint authority (although there was no suggestion that it could ever 'trundle' unionists into a united Ireland).

The Irish did not expect unionists to welcome this, but it was significantly closer to unionists' own preferences than their own favoured joint authority option would have been. Indeed until close to the final date, some were unsure whether it would be more welcomed or more opposed by unionists or by nationalists. They had consulted with John Hume through the negotiations, but not with other SDLP leaders and until a few days before, they did not know if Seamus Mallon would support the agreement (see interview, witness seminar, 11 December 2006). Since it was a serious compromise for nationalists, they expected that unionists too should have to put up with it.

Why did the British accept this Irish wedge? Secretary of State for Northern Ireland, Tom King, suggested that in fact it was a British win, with the Irish accepting 'for all practical purposes and in perpetuity there will not be a united Ireland' although later he apologised to Parliament for this statement. Mrs Thatcher (1995: 402), without apology, wrote that the AIA left the British making the decisions while promising better security cooperation. The British makers of the AIA would not have disagreed with her but would have added important qualifications. Bew, Gibbon and Patterson (1995: 213-17) accurately describe these 'maximalists' (among whom they include the Cabinet Secretary, Lord Robert Armstrong, Sir David Goodall and then Foreign Secretary Sir Geoffrey Howe as seeing no essential conflict between Irish perspectives and British interests. In interview and a witness seminar, senior officials and politicians from the maximalist camp discussed their perceptions at the time. One senior official noted that one *'couldn't sit round the cabinet table in London and talk about Irish business without thinking of all the people who had done that before you over the last two hundred years. And here was our opportunity to add something to that story, something better than had gone before'* (witness seminar, 11 December 2006). The two hundred years at the British cabinet table between 1783-1983 of which the British actors were conscious went back before the Act of Union and spanned the expansion and contraction of empire. It encompassed a very wide range of possible and legitimate constitutional relations between the 'cousins' (Goodall, 2010: 15) of Britain and Ireland, and more generally of British-Irish, north-south, Protestant-Catholic, unionist-nationalist relations. This long historical view gave them significant *'flexibility'* and negotiating scope, and indeed some of those interviewed had still longer historical perspectives. Of course British state interests were paramount for them all, but the maximalist conception of the state and its interests was not of the territorial sovereign nation state of the twentieth century. A longer sense of history and a more global sense of geography, where the rise and fall of empire coexisted with continuity of the state, let them define Ireland as close to British interests and identities, but the specific form of partition and Union which was put in place in 1921 much less so (witness seminar, 11 December 2006; interviews, 18 June 2009, 7 May 2010, 18 May 2010). For this wider group of British officials and politicians it was simply a matter of *'flexibility'* in relations while respecting the interests and perspectives of each side. This flexibility, however, put them at odds with unionists' territorially bounded concept of the United Kingdom.

Significant numbers of the Conservative party were willing to test out the AIA in 1985 because of their concerns about security and their belief that the Irish state could help in this respect. The new willingness to rely on the Irish state was furthered by its diplomatic initiatives when, in the course of countless dinners and meetings, the Irish interest in peace and stability was explained (FitzGerald, 1991: 468, 569; interview, 15 December 2009). After 1985, some of the British political establishment wished to limit the impact of the AIA, in part because of their own sense of the impropriety of Irish intervention, in part because they believed that the fact of the Agreement was defeat enough for unionists, without adding more substance to the symbolism, in part, perhaps, because they felt enough attention had been given to Northern Ireland (interviews, 27 November 2008, 18 June 2009) But if the Irish influence was not advanced as quickly as the Irish desired, neither was it pulled back: rather British-Irish strategic cooperation on Northern Ireland increased. A senior

Irish official who had worked with taoisigh on Northern Ireland issues from the early 1970s to the mid-1990s described the difference between the early period when the Taoiseach's input was disregarded and his attempted communications refused and the later period with frequent informal phone calls and consultations between Prime Minister and Taoiseach.

If unionist definitions of the union, and Northern Ireland's place within it, were not shared by senior British politicians and officials, nor were Irish nationalist objectives and assumptions. British and Irish senior politicians and officials were acutely aware of the differences of views, perspectives, backgrounds, aims and assumptions on each side, and the different interests embodied in the very different forms of each state. As one senior politician pointed out, this was not the first international agreement where the parties who signed it expected it to fulfil differing aims (interview, 18 May 2010). The AIA was designed not to mask these differences but to accommodate them. What changed in the 1980s was that key members of the British political elite came to see that they could not restore political stability in Northern Ireland while continuing to accommodate unionist perspectives. When instead they emphasised the long historical view with its potential convergence with Irish perspectives, new political options opened out. The shift was subtle but important, opening the British government to a level of Irish input into the gover- nance of Northern Ireland, and moving them away from a territorial notion of sovereignty. From a British (maximalist) perspective, this kept the key aspects of sovereignty – freedom of decision-making on issues of high politics – while acknowledging the unusual and difficult situation of Northern Ireland. The interviews and witness seminars confirm the insight of Jim Bulpitt's (1983) analysis of the logic of Conservative state- craft, not least the dual vision which prioritises the high politics of the state-centre and is tolerant of a very wide range of administration in the regions. Unionists were right that the AIA made Northern Ireland anom- alous within the Union, but from a long historical perspective such anom- alies were not unprecedented. But if from a British perspective, the AIA met both British and Irish interests and perspectives, what exactly it would imply in institutional and policy terms was left open.

The effects of the Agreement

Different groups had radically different views of the effects of the Agree- ment. From the British maximalist perspective, the AIA would have no radical constitutional consequences. It would open other policy matters to discussion and debate on their merits, taking into account conflicting views in a divided society. For the Irish government, it would begin to move towards a balance in the politics of Northern Ireland. For Fianna Fáil, Sinn Féin and sections of the British elite, it would simply be of symbolic significance. For the unionists it would let nationalists have more of an influence on policy than themselves, it would remove the unionist voice, it would lead to a gradual, creeping increase in Irish and nationalist influence. Nationalists in Northern Ireland were rather more sceptical of its potential impact.

What then were the effects of the AIA? Streeck and Thelen's (2005) typology of mechanisms of incremental institutional change provide a way of thinking about informal processes of institutional change. As I have argued elsewhere (Todd, forthcoming), the effects of the AIA can be defined as (i) layering, which helped change specific policies although significantly less than the Irish had hoped and unionists had feared; (ii) displacement, which generalised Irish influence through the field of strategic thinking about Northern Ireland and (iii) conversion, which changed political opportunities for nationalists, and thereby changed their aims and strategies.

First, the AIA created a new layer of institutions. The IGC was not itself a decision-making body but it could help set the political agenda, influencing those with decision-making powers, either directly (when they attended IGC meetings) or indirectly, by helping define policy orientations which would then be insisted upon by the Prime Minister or responsible members of the cabinet. For the first years, the members of the Secretariat and British and Irish governments were very slow to claim any effect of the IGC, because it might further inflame the unionists with whom negotiations were sought. However later reports show that significant changes were achieved:

- Curbs were put on Orange marches through nationalist areas, and the police stood firm against Orange pressure. The process began in summer 1985 and continued for more than a decade.
- There was a swift repeal of the Flags and Emblems Act, in response to Irish demands (FitzGerald, 1991: 573).
- The Irish government added its weight to pressure for a stronger Fair Employment Act (eventually enacted in 1989).
- The Secretariat nominated 'massive' numbers of nationalists onto public and semi-state bodies (Lillis and Goodall, 2010)

While significant, the changes were outweighed for the Irish actors by the failure to achieve change in areas to which they gave even greater priority:

- Joint British-Irish courts were proposed in the IGC and were immediately vetoed by British judges at the highest level.

- Policing reform had been promised in the AIA. Article 7c defines the objective of 'making the security forces more readily accepted by the nationalist community'. The reforms suggested did not take place. For example, the proposed accompaniment of UDR personnel by police in their relations with the public was never consistently implemented. These issues were raised repeatedly in the IGC. The Irish members of the Secretariat made a log of each proposal made by them, the date and recorded everything that happened in respect to it. They had long discussions with British army and police chiefs, who are reported to have blamed each other for the deadlock. Senior Irish politicians and officials are evidently and visibly still angry about this lack of response (witness seminar,11 December 2006).
- Change in a whole set of security-related issues was painfully slow. Irish civil servants described *'stand-offs'*, *'no meeting of minds'*, *'polar opposites'* in discussions on security in the latter half of the 1980s (interview, 8 January 2009). Below the apex of the NIO and Northern Ireland Civil Service (NICS), there was reported resentment and bureaucratic inertia which was (so some Irish officials believed) designed to block change (interviews, 19 September 2008, 15 January 2009). This changed only after 1998, in part through the detail of the 1998 Agreement, in part through the Prime Minister's willingness directly to order cooperation and break the veto power of other institutions.

In short, the IGC did not come to bypass other loci of decision-making. Veto-power remained with the judiciary, the NIO and in full SOSNI, the military and police. The new layer of institutions changed the issues that came onto the political agenda (policing, equality, marching, symbols, courts) and the frequency with which they appeared on this agenda, but it did not typically change the outcomes or the loci where decisions were made.

The AIA however had unanticipated effects in the form of 'displacement' (the 'diffusion' of new models 'which call into question existing, previously taken for granted organizational forms and practices' (Streeck and Thelen, 2005: 19) The very presence of the Irish government in the IGC and Secretariat meant that 'you got a sovereign government, the government of the United Kingdom, agreeing to have within its institutions a group of people from another jurisdiction to advise it on how to rule part of its own territory, and ... under Treaty obligations, to make determined efforts to resolve differences' (interview, Irish official, 16 January 2009). This was a new set of rules of conflict management, and, at the level of strategic thinking and planning, *'Irish in'* became the norm in all areas to do with conflict regulation in Northern Ireland. The Irish state played a key role in the Brooke and Mayhew talks in the early 1990s, and was a crucial actor in the talks which led eventually to the 1998 Agreement.

Displacement also took another form, with senior British policy-makers becoming significantly more willing to open Northern Ireland to international influence. The process was painful, with President Bill Clinton going against British advice in granting visas to republicans Gerry Adams and Joe Cahill. John Major and his Cabinet eventually accepted that there would be a US role – guided by the two governments – in the Northern Ireland peace process, while with Tony Blair's premiership, that role was – at least temporarily – welcomed. Lord David Owen (2002: 22) notes that this marked a major change in British policy. The process was promoted by the prior opening of Northern Ireland to Irish influence so that the Irish could legitimately lobby in the US when their advice was ignored. It was also eased by that prior opening: the threshold whereby Northern Ireland was seen as sufficiently 'different' to warrant a level of external advice had been passed in 1985.

Equally older institutional arenae were 'converted' to new purposes. The media and the public sphere more generally became populated with political elites from the Irish state, and northern nationalists and Catholics newly nominated onto state bodies, together with nationalist and unionist politicians. This was the period of the Cultural Traditions Group, when the many varieties of nationalism and unionism were publi-cised and officially recognised (Crozier, 1989, 1990) and of the Commu-nity Relations Council. Republicans were marginalised, but constitutional nationalists in the SDLP were on every public body and the legitimacy of nationalist aims was no longer questioned. Indeed these aims were calmly asserted by the conservative nationalist figures now populating the public sphere. Even satire (the temporarily popular late-night television programme, *The Show*) kept a firm balance between nationalism and unionism (Ruane and Todd, 1990). Common sense, as it was broadcast and discussed, had changed: now nationalist alienation, nationalist rights, nationalist equality, paths to a united Ireland, parity of esteem were concepts that became part of public debate in Northern Ireland while before they were voiced only by 'extremists' from the margins. Now liberal nationalism – equal institutionalisation of nationalist and unionist identities – could be used as an argument, not a winning one, but a plau-sible one which sometimes won. The evident prominence of nationalists and nationalism in the public sphere and the opportunities for further political advance prompted more nationalists to participate in Northern Ireland politics in order to change it incrementally: voting for nationalist parties increased after 1985 and within this bloc, the SDLP increased its share of the vote (O'Leary and McGarry, 1996: 321). Most important of all, republicans too saw the prospects of gradual change in the institutional matrix of Northern Ireland, and saw opportunities there for further advance.

That advance had to wait until after the peace process and settlement of 1998. By 2010 most of the positions long advocated by the Irish government in policing and criminal justice, in respect to marches, public culture and equality had been enacted in a British-initiated reform process. The AIA began the process of change, but it accelerated only when other factors – the prospect of a stable multi-party agreement – gave enough sense of urgency to motivate change in established intra-state regimes.

Explaining the unionist response

The narrative presented above shows that unionist responses to the AIA were highly rational – all varieties of unionists had reason to be deeply disturbed. The AIA did not change the fact of British sovereignty but it did change its meaning in a way that did not suit either unionists' interests or unionists' assumptions about the place of Northern Ireland in the United Kingdom. The long historical sense of British policy makers – sometimes themselves from old Irish land-owning families – was not shared by twentieth-century Ulster unionism, although perhaps an earlier generation of Irish unionists would have understood it (Jackson, 1995). Ulster Unionists instead looked to sovereigntists – Enoch Powell, Ian Gow and Margaret Thatcher herself – to express and protect their interests. But Thatcher and her closest associates – because of their over-riding emphasis on security – saw the need for new moves. Once the AIA was in place, a threshold had been crossed and it was hard for the British to row back without signalling state weakness. In the 1990s, as it became clear that Anglo Irish cooperation was necessary to get peace and settlement negotiations started and to keep them moving, the ideas – if not the letter – of the AIA were generalised.

If the British view was disturbing to unionists, the Irish view was even more so. The wedging strategy met the worst fears of many unionists, that they would be 'trundled' into a situation – joint authority – that they had always explicitly opposed. The Union would, the Irish agreed, be maintained short of an explicit vote for change, but for unionists it might be a form of union not worth fighting for. Subsequent events showed truth in their fears. Notwithstanding the slow progress of reform – by 1995 policing, criminal justice, security and marches were still deeply disputed – the potential for increasing Irish and nationalist influence remained. Moreover in some spheres change had come quickly: the newfound legitimacy of nationalist discourse meant that unionists had lost a key cultural resource – the defining of political common sense. The involvement of the Irish government with the British in all strategy was, eventually, accepted by unionists, although they became more relaxed about it only in the context of the loosening of the Union in 1997 and the explicit asymmetry between its different parts and with the amendment of the Irish Constitution in 1998 to express an aspiration to unity not a claim to sovereignty.

The AIA also challenged the constitutional assumptions of many nationalists and republicans. The division among northern Catholics as to whether or not Irish input would be substantial and would substantially better their position reflected in part different views of the British state itself, and its capacity for incremental change. By the 1990s, the republican leadership also came to accept the view that significant change could come gradually, and that the impact of British sovereignty could be decreased short of a united Ireland.

All parties in Northern Ireland found new motivations to negotiate after the AIA: O'Leary and McGarry (1996: 250–60) emphasise the slowness of reaching a settlement, but also detail the movement towards negotiations from the late 1980s. Republicans wished to accelerate the pace of change, perhaps precisely in order to create a form of union that unionists would not want. They became convinced that a gradualist and peaceful strategy could change the impact of British rule and could be worthwhile, at least as an interim goal. Nationalists in the SDLP wanted to increase their say in daily politics, and to decrease the British role. Devolution, on their understanding, would not replace the Irish dimension but rather decrease the British. Unionists too decided to negotiate in order to close the door opened by the AIA. They accepted that there would be an Irish dimension but if they could make it voluntary and symbolic, they would remove the 'wedge'.

Was the AIA a major constitutional moment? Yes, in that it changed the character of Northern Ireland and the meaning but not the fact of British sovereignty in Northern Ireland. It did not have immediate effects on policies and institutions. Its impact was over a longer term, and is still not fully played out. Public and in particular unionist reaction anticipated the institutional effects of the AIA long before they happened, and that reaction diverted state attention from reform to negotiations. When, after 1998, reform came back onto the agenda, Irish influence remained (though still far from decisive) through a renewed British-Irish Inter-Governmental Council, and through now habitual informal contacts. The AIA was significant because it held out long-term possibilities of radical change and legitimated new policy directions. These have only partially been realised. The prospect of creeping joint authority, with or without devolution, remains as one – although far from the only – possible future for Northern Ireland.

References

Aughey, A. (1989) *Under Siege: Ulster Unionism and the Anglo-Irish Agreement* (Belfast: Blackstaff).

Bew, P., P. Gibbon and H. Patterson (1995) *Northern Ireland 1921–1994: Political Forces and Social Classes* (London: Serif).

Bulpitt, J. (1983) *Territory and Power in the United Kingdom: An Interpretation* (Manchester: Manchester University Press).

Cox, W. Harvey, (1987) 'Public opinion and the Anglo-Irish Agreement', *Government and Opposition*, 22: 3, 336–51.

Crozier, M. (1989) *Cultural Traditions in Northern Ireland: Varieties of Irishness* (Belfast: Institute of Irish Studies).

—— (1990) *Cultural Traditions in Northern Ireland: Varieties of Britishness* (Belfast: Institute of Irish Studies).

FitzGerald, G. (1991) *All in a Life: An Autobiography* (Dublin: Gill and Macmillan).

—— (1985) *Dáil Eireann*, Debate, 19 November.

Hadden, T. and K. Boyle (1989) *The Anglo-Irish Agreement: Commentary, Text and Official Review* (London: Sweet and Maxwell).

Irish Times/MRBI poll published on 23 November 1985.

Jackson, A. (1995) *Colonel Edward Saunderson: Land and Loyalty in Victorian Ireland* (Oxford: Clarendon Press).

Lillis, M and D. Goodall (2010) 'Edging towards peace', *Dublin Review of Books*, 13: Spring, 1–20. Available online at www.drb.ie/more_details/10-02-17/Edging_Towards_Peace.aspx# (accessed 22 March 2011).

Lynch, J.M. (1972) 'The Anglo-Irish problem', *Foreign Affairs*, 50: 4, 601–17.

Mallon, S. interview, witness seminar, 11 December 2006.

New Ireland Forum (1984) *Report* (Dublin: Stationery Office).

O'Leary, B. and J. McGarry (1996) *Politics of Antagonism*. 2nd expanded edition (London: Athlone).

Owen, D. (2002) 'The resolution of armed conflict: internationalization and its lessons, particularly in Northern Ireland', in M. Elliott (ed.) *The Long Road to Peace in Northern Ireland* (Liverpool: Liverpool University Press), pp. 22–40.

Protestant church leaders, *Irish Times*, 14 December 1985

Ruane, J. and J. Todd (1996) *Dynamics of Conflict in Northern Ireland : Power, Conflict, Emancipation* (Cambridge: Cambridge University Press).

—— (1990) 'Cross channels: The Show', *Graph*, 8, Summer.

Stewart, A.T.Q. (1986) 'Why loyalist feeling of betrayal runs so deep', *Irish Times*, 14 January 1986.

Streeck, W. and K. Thelen (2005) *Beyond Continuity: Institutional Change in Advanced Political Economies* (Oxford: Oxford University Press).

Thatcher, M. (1995) *The Downing Street Years* (London: Harper Collins).

—— (1985) interview, *Belfast Telegraph*, 17 December.

Thelen, K. (2003) 'How institutions evolve. Insights from comparative historical analysis', in J. Mahoney and D.Rueschemeyer (eds) *Comparative Historical Analysis in the Social Sciences* (Cambridge: Cambridge University Press), pp. 208–40.

Todd, J. (forthcoming, 2011) 'Institutional change and conflict regulation: the Anglo-Irish Agreement (1985) and the mechanisms of change in Northern Ireland', *West European Politics*.

5 Unionism and consent: problems with a principle?

Thomas Hennessey

The 'principle of consent' – today defined by the unionist community in Northern Ireland as their 'right' not be subsumed within an all-Ireland polity either inside or outside the United Kingdom against their will – has its own history and, having a history, shows evidence of its changing character. In 1912, Ulster Unionists pledged themselves in solemn Covenant 'throughout this time of threatened calamity to stand by one another in defending ourselves and our children our cherished position of equal citizenship in the United Kingdom, and in using all means which may be found necessary to defeat the present conspiracy to set up a Home Rule Parliament Ireland' (Stewart 1967: 62). They did not consent to being ruled by an all-Ireland Parliament as envisaged in the Home Rule Bill of 1912. Here they stood on the principle of A.V. Dicey (1973: 16) who believed that Home Rule was 'a plan for revolutionising the constitution of the whole of the United Kingdom'. As such, it required the consent of not only those living in Ireland but also the consent of all citizens.

In 1920, when the Government of Ireland Act partitioned the island of Ireland and created Northern Ireland, Section 75 of the Act provided that 'the supreme authority of the Parliament of the United Kingdom shall remain unaffected and undiminished over all persons, matters and things in Ireland and every part thereof'. The Act established a Northern Ireland Parliament and a Southern Ireland Parliament. It also looked forward to the ultimate 'reunion' of Ireland, by the consent of both Irish Parliaments, and made provision for a Council of Ireland to help facilitate this and empowered the two Parliaments 'by mutual agreement and joint action to terminate partition and set up one Parliament and one Government for the whole of Ireland' (Preamble: Government of Ireland Act 1920). Thus the constitutional principle that the Parliament of Northern Ireland should decide whether or not to consent to a united Ireland was first enshrined in 1920. By now the notion of consent was no longer conceived in universal or British terms but in particular or Northern Ireland terms.

The government of the Irish Free State, which had recognised its border with the United Kingdom of Great Britain and Northern Ireland in 1922, did so again in 1925 by a tripartite agreement with the governments of Northern Ireland and of the United Kingdom. It was Eamon de Valera's administration in 1937 which formally laid claim to Northern Ireland. Eire's new constitution, *Bunreacht na hÉireann*, declared in Article 2 that: 'The national territory consists of the whole island of Ireland, its islands and the territorial seas.' Article 3 stated that pending the 're-integration of the national territory', the Irish parliament and government had the right to exercise jurisdiction over the whole of the island although it chose, voluntarily, not to apply this to Northern Ireland. This became known as 'the territorial claim'. According to the Constitution, Northern Ireland was a part of both the Irish nation and the independent Irish state – it was not part of the United Kingdom. Thus the Irish state formally challenged British sovereignty in Northern Ireland and ignored the consent, not only of the Parliament of Northern Ireland, but also of the majority of its population to being part of the Irish state.

In 1948, Eire – as the former Irish Free State was known from 1937 – formally declared itself to be a republic. As a response the Labour government passed the Ireland Act a year later; the key clause of which stated that Northern Ireland would remain part of His Majesty's Dominions unless the Northern Ireland Parliament voted to leave the United Kingdom (Ireland Act 1949, Clause 1 (1) B). For the first time since the abolition of the Council of Ireland in 1925, Northern Ireland's constitutional destiny was explicitly transferred from Westminster to Belfast – although the UK Parliament retained overall sovereignty. Following the proroguing of the Northern Ireland Parliament in 1972, Westminster passed the Northern Ireland Constitution Act 1973. The Act transferred the principle of consent to a united Ireland from the Northern Ireland Parliament to the Northern Ireland electorate (Northern Ireland Constitution Act 1973, Section 1). This was an attempt to reassure the unionists that there could be no change in the constitutional status of Northern Ireland without the consent of a majority of the people there. For unionists this became the 'constitutional guarantee'. For nationalists it remained the 'Unionist Veto', a mechanism to block any political progress.

The provisions to settle north-south relations set out in the Sunningdale Agreement of 1973 were published in the form of a joint British and Irish government communiqué. Article 5 dodged the question of the Republic's territorial claim to Northern Ireland in the form of parallel declarations by the Irish and British governments:

The Irish Government fully and solemnly declared that there could be no change in the status of Northern Ireland until a majority of the people of Northern Ireland desired a change in that status.	The British Government solemnly declared that it was, and would remain, their policy to support the wishes of the majority of the people of Northern Ireland. The present status of Northern Ireland is that it is part of the United Kingdom. If in future the majority of the people of Northern Ireland should indicate a wish to become part of united Ireland, the British Government would support that wish. (Sunningdale Communiqué, 1973)

While both declarations stated Northern Ireland's status could not be changed without the consent of a majority its people, only the British declaration defined Northern Ireland as *part of the United Kingdom*. The Irish declaration could not. In Irish law Northern Ireland was de jure *part of the Republic of Ireland* and only *de facto* part of the United Kingdom. The Irish part of the parallel declaration did not depart from this position. From a unionist perspective the Irish declaration was worthless.

In 1973, the British government acquiesced to pressure from the Irish government and the SDLP and accepted a Council of Ireland with *executive* functions. It was the ability for the Council to evolve, and extend, its executive power, which was to give the institution the appearance of an embryonic all-Ireland government. A *de facto* all-Ireland state could evolve incrementally without any formal transfer of sovereignty and without unionists having to consent formally. Ultimately, Sunningdale collapsed in the wake of that most dramatic withdrawal of unionist consent – the Ulster Workers Council strike of 1974.

The Anglo-Irish Agreement: unionist responses

Until the signing of the AIA in 1985, unionists had felt increasingly secure about the constitutional guarantee and the principle of consent. However, this changed once Margaret Thatcher had put her name to the AIA, declaring the AIA to be 'the most formal commitment to the principle of consent made by an Irish Government' (HC Deb., 18 November 1985). In Article 1,of the AIA, it was stated that the British and Irish governments:

   (a) affirm that any change in the status of Northern Ireland would only come about with the consent of a majority of the people of Northern Ireland;

   (b) recognise that the present wish of a majority of the people of Northern Ireland is for no change in the status of Northern Ireland;

   (c) declare that, if in the future a majority of the people of Northern Ireland clearly wish for and formally consent to the establishment of a united Ireland, they will introduce and support in the respective Parliaments legislation to give effect to that wish
(Hadfield, 1989: 192–8).

The psychological trauma of the event for unionists should never be under-estimated. Though the Agreement makes much of the principle of consent as a 'subsequent', i.e. to give effect to Irish unity, the Agreement had ignored the principle of consent as an 'antecedent'. Not only had it been done without unionist consent. It had been done without consultation.

James Molyneaux, leader of the Ulster Unionist Party, opposed the AIA on the grounds that it would 'destroy any possibility of achieving peace, stability and reconciliation – three words that have found themselves by accident in the Agreement's preamble'. In 1984, the UUP leader had endorsed the policy paper *The Way Forward*. The main thrust of that paper was 'equal British rights for all British citizens'. The key paragraph, for Molyneaux, was this:

> The time is now ripe for both communities in Northern Ireland to realise that, essentially, their problems will have to be solved in Northern Ireland by their political representatives and that any future prospect for them and their children is best provided for within the Northern Ireland context. This will require a mutual recognition of each other's hopes and fears. Only rights can be guaranteed, not aspirations.

The next phrase used by Molyneaux was 'probably the most telling for an Ulster Unionist leader to use': it was the responsibility of the majority to persuade the minority that the Province was also theirs and to build a consensual Northern Ireland. Now, to Molyneaux's great regret, those proposals for achieving peace, stability and reconciliation within the bounds of Northern Ireland 'have been snuffed out by the Anglo-Irish agreement, and that document must be regarded as so much waste paper'. The second casualty of the agreement was stability, because stability depended on a known way: consent. 'But how can there be a known way when there is no consent?' He added: 'I have to say honestly and truthfully that in forty years in public life I have never known what I can only describe as a universal cold fury, which some of us have thus far managed to contain' (HC Deb., 26 November 1985).

For the Democratic Unionist Party's deputy leader, Peter Robinson, the debate on the AIA, in the House of Commons, provided 'a unique occasion for Ulster Unionist representatives, because it is not often that a man gets the opportunity to deliver the oration at his own funeral'. When Mrs Thatcher signed the Agreement, 'she was in reality drafting the obituary of Ulster as we know it in the United Kingdom'. The Hillsborough Agreement (as the AIA is also known) was 'but the tip of the iceberg'. Robinson believed the AIA was clearly a framework for further agreements. What other reason could there be for a front cover entitled, 'The Republic of Ireland No. 1 Agreement'? Robinson noted that John Hume, of the SDLP, had 'at least been honest with the people of Northern Ireland in saying that the Agreement was a process, that it was "a first step"'; later adding that there were to be 'progressive stages' (HC Deb., 26 November 1985). This, according to Robinson, was the familiar nationalist tactic of trying to circumvent the principle of consent by re-defining it as a veto on progress. It was clear that this process was 'intended to take us out of the United Kingdom. Yet the people of Northern Ireland have democratically expressed their wish to stay within it. The agreement is intended to trundle Northern Ireland into an all-Ireland Republic.' If the AIA had been 'intended to do us good', Mrs Thatcher 'would have been only too willing to allow the unionist community to be consulted. She would have been only too pleased to take it along with her and to ensure that the representatives of the unionist people in Northern Ireland could have some input to the discussions.' But she did not; whereas the government of the Irish Republic was 'only too happy' to give John Hume that facility – as were the Secretary of State to the Vatican, the President of the United States; as were the United Nations and the European Community. 'But those who were to be affected by the deal were kept in the dark.'

Robinson noted how the British government had established the 1982 Northern Ireland Assembly (it would be suspended in the wake of the AIA) on the basis of widespread acceptance throughout the community; this meant there had to be 'cross-community support'. He pointed out that throughout the years all party leaders had spoken about the necessity for consent in Northern Ireland and that Northern Ireland could not be governed without the consent of the minority:

> If that is true, I have to tell the government that they can never govern North-
> ern Ireland without the consent of the majority. Do they have that consent?
> Have they tried to access whether there is such consent? Will they test
> whether there is consent? The people of Northern Ireland have the right and
> entitlement to be consulted about their constitutional future (HC Deb., 26
> November 1985).

Enoch Powell put the traditional Diceyean argument for the consent of the part (Northern Ireland) being bound up with the consent of the whole (UK Parliament). In a disquisition on the constitutional fabric of consent, he described the AIA as 'unacceptable and deeply offensive' to Northern Ireland as it represented a dilution in the responsibility of Parliament for the governance, the law and the administration of the United Kingdom: 'We are now proposing to see made a unique and unprecedented breach in that position, an unprecedented arrangement whereby a formal position is allocated to another country in respect of the conduct of affairs in the United Kingdom'. The affront was not lessened but rather sharpened because that agreement related to only one part of the United Kingdom: 'It is indeed a specially unique, an unprecedented, proposition that we should endow another country with an institutional right within the United Kingdom, a right of proposal and statement of views, a right formalised in a conference, to influence the administration and the law of a particular part of the United Kingdom' (HC Deb., 27 November 1985). As a Member of Parliament from Northern Ireland he was sent by his constituents to the House of Commons to sit as an integral participant in that assembly. By so doing he and his constituents expressed 'not only their consciousness and their purpose of themselves being a part of the United Kingdom, but their will that they, like the rest of the United Kingdom, should live under law which is made, and exclusively made, by the Parliament of the United Kingdom'. To send Members to sit in Parliament was to consent to the right, and the exclusive right, of Parliament to make the law under which one lived (which is why Sinn Féin did not send elected Members to sit in the House of Commons). What was incompatible with that claim, and with the legislative power of the House of Commons, was that it should be exercised differently in respect of different parts of the United Kingdom: 'We cannot all come here accepting law made by a majority in this House, because we are all part of the United Kingdom, and then see that law imposed differently – different law made for the different parts of the Kingdom.'

He argued that the fact that Parliament passed separate Scottish legislation was because, under the Treaty of Union, the Scots retained the right to their own legal system and 'behind it lies the assent of that particular part of the kingdom to be legislated for in that way – and more than assent, for not many Scots would accept that this House had a right, by virtue of being the Parliament of the United Kingdom, to pass English law which was to be applied in the courts of Scotland'. Therefore, there was a counterpart to the undoubted right of Parliament to make the law for the United Kingdom. It was that,

> wherever it makes law differently for certain parts of the United Kingdom, it can do so only in accordance with the wishes, and normally at the petition,

of the people of those parts of the United Kingdom ... We recognise it wherever we legislate privately by bylaw or otherwise and differently for different
places in the realm, but we do that only on the petition and with the assent
of those for whom we legislate.

This was recognised when a previous Parliament passed two Acts confer-
ring devolved administration and legislation upon Scotland and Wales,
but refused to bring that into effect until the people of Scotland, in respect
of Scottish devolution, and Wales, in respect of Welsh devolution, 'had
uttered their agreement – agreement which in the event they withheld in
the terms in which it was required by that legislation'. To claim the right
to impose, upon a part of the Kingdom, law – differential law – which
that part had not asked for or assented to was to undermine the moral
authority of the House of Commons and: 'to strike at the very essence of
that compact between the electorate and Parliament upon which parliamentary sovereignty depends.' Law, pointed out Powell, was made in the
UK only in a particular way – by both Houses through a certain legislative procedure that eventually received the assent of the Crown; so:

> no one will be able to say ... that the people of Northern Ireland are under
> an obligation to accept—whatever might be the meaning of the term
> "accept" in that context—the Anglo-Irish agreement that has been made
> between the two Prime Ministers [of the UK and Ireland]. We are again
> straining beyond its moral limit the authority of this House when we demand
> that by a resolution of the House we shall have the power to impose the will
> of government upon a portion of this country differentially from the rest (HC
> Deb., 27 November 1985).

In addition, what worried unionists such as Harold McCusker, was talk
in the AIA about 'the majority of the people of Northern Ireland' opting
for Irish unity. It did not say a large majority; it could mean a bare majority. There was no safeguard here at all for unionists:

> If the population is 49.9 per cent Protestant and the remainder is Roman
> Catholic or nationalist, the government will seek to establish a united Ireland.
> Legislation would be introduced and supported in the respective Parliaments
> to give effect to the wish of an 'undefined majority. Why do they not talk
> about 'widespread support in the future?' We are constantly told that there
> cannot be government without widespread support ... (HC Deb., 27 Novem-
> ber 1985)

It was noticeable that no other option was given in the AIA, apart from a
united Ireland. Once more reverting to a Diceyean notion of universal
consent, McCusker called for a referendum in the United Kingdom:

If the people of the United Kingdom say to me that they no longer want me, it will simply be echoing what the government are saying anyway and they will have to live with the consequences of that decision. That referendum cannot deliver me against my will into an Irish Republic. I will not go to the Irish Republic and what might flow from whatever the developments might be would be something with which everybody in the United Kingdom would have to live. I am not scared of a referendum. I am prepared to live with its consequences. (HC Deb., 27 November 1985).

How was the constitutional case for the unionist position on consent re-expressed after 1985? A coherent expression of it can be found in a report of the 1982–86 Assembly that had been boycotted by the SDLP and now dominated by unionists outraged by the AIA. That report pointed out that Northern Ireland was an integral part of the United Kingdom and a *distinct entity* within the United Kingdom as made clear by its correct name – the United Kingdom of Great Britain *and* Northern Ireland. This status derived from the creation of the United Kingdom and could be seen in the preamble and the first Article of the Act of Ireland (Ireland) 1800. These made it clear that the Kingdom rested on a treaty entered into by two Kingdoms – Great Britain and Ireland – and on the legislation of the two Parliaments that gave effect to that treaty and created a new Parliament. It was noted that the Acts (one in each Parliament) of Union declared that the two Kingdoms were to be united 'for ever'. The Acts did not provide any mechanism for amending or terminating the Treaty they embodied. The major change that had occurred to the United Kingdom since the Treaty, namely the secession of the twenty-six counties of southern Ireland, was given effect to by another Treaty made between His Majesty's Government and an Irish provisional government formed by an elected parliamentary body representative of those twenty-six counties. This latter Treaty was then embodied in legislation as the Irish Free State (Agreement) Act 1922. The Acts of Union were, therefore, amended in a procedure similar to that by which they were enacted. It was also noteworthy, deemed unionists, that in other major changes to the Acts of Union relating to Ireland as well as to Scotland, the UK Parliament had taken care to ensure that the changes were acceptable to the people of both parts respectively. In the light of the above, the provision in Section 1 of the Northern Ireland Constitution Act 1973, commonly 'although erroneously' called the 'guarantee', while reiterating the position of Northern Ireland, did not establish its status, but provided a procedure whereby that status, created by the Acts of Union, could be altered. In that sense, the 1973 Act created uncertainty about the Union.

The unionist position was that, although Northern Ireland's status as part of the United Kingdom derived from the creation of the United Kingdom in 1801, Northern Ireland as a unit distinct from the rest of

Ireland derived from the government of Ireland Act 1920. And the 'democratic basis of that unit' – consent – was displayed in the elections of 1920
in both southern and Northern Ireland. The existence and status of
Northern Ireland were 'explicitly' recognised in the 1921 Anglo-Irish
Treaty entered into by the negotiators appointed by the Dáil. That body
itself ratified the Treaty. Therefore, 'to refer to Northern Ireland as an
artificial unit when it corresponded to the social reality in the island of
Ireland, and was accepted and endorsed by a majority of the people of
both parts of Ireland, was inaccurate and insulting'. And the 1925 tripar-
tite treaty between the United Kingdom, Northern Ireland and Irish Free
State governments constituted a *de jure* recognition of Northern Ireland
and was registered by the Free State government at the League of Nations.
However, the *de jure* recognition of Northern Ireland contained in the
Treaties of 1921 and 1925 was abrogated by the Irish adoption of the
1937 Constitution. Articles 2 and 3 prevented any *de jure* recognition of
Northern Ireland (Northern Ireland Assembly Report, 1986: 33–5). And
since those Articles had not been removed or amended by the AIA, then
unionists could not possibly consent to any of its provisions.

The Belfast Agreement: when is consent not consent?

In 1986, the unionist-dominated Northern Ireland Assembly had considered, formally, the declarations in Article 1 of the Agreement in order to
test the claims that the AIA recognised the principle of consent. Article 1a
of the AIA, claimed unionists, went no further than earlier statements by
the Republic of Ireland's governments since 1937. Article 1a was virtually
identical to the Irish declaration in the Sunningdale Agreement. The
Boland case of 1974, when a former Irish minister had unsuccessfully
claimed in the Supreme Court that the Irish government had recognised
Northern Ireland as part of the United Kingdom by consent, showed 'that
it was beyond the competence of any Irish government to recognise
Northern Ireland in any meaningful way'. The references to the AIA's
declaration as a treaty were also insignificant in the light of Sunningdale,
the Boland case and the 1925 Treaty. Article 1 did not go as far as the
1925 Treaty, and if it had done, the Boland case showed that it would be
unconstitutional. Article 1b was merely a statement of existing fact and
added nothing to the significance of Article 1a. Unionists, therefore,
concluded that Articles 1a and b were merely a statement of the factual
position and of the current professed intentions of the two governments.
The Article did not accord recognition to Northern Ireland nor did it
acknowledge the principle of consent and those who claimed that it did,
or that it was in some way an advance, 'were either ignorant of the history
of the question or were misrepresenting the position'. Further, Article 1

was the 'weakest statement yet' of the position of Her Majesty's Government: in its declaration in the Sunningdale Agreement, the British government had declared that it was, and would remain, its policy to support the wishes of the majority of the people of Northern Ireland and it confirmed the status of Northern Ireland as part of the United Kingdom. Unionists now noted that it was no longer the policy of Her Majesty's Government to support the wishes of the people of Northern Ireland, and that Her Majesty's Government were no longer concerned to identify the present status of Northern Ireland. This latter point was significant in view of the textual differences between the British and Irish versions of the text: the British version described the AIA as an agreement between the government of United Kingdom of Great Britain and Northern Ireland and the government of the Republic of Ireland; the Irish version described the AIA as an agreement between the government of Ireland and the government of the United Kingdom. The British text recognised Northern Ireland as part of the UK; the Irish text did not. These differences, taken with the failure to identify the status of Northern Ireland, confirmed for unionists their suspicion that the AIA was in fundamental breach of the principle of consent.

The AIA had the effect of provoking unionist thinking on the application of the principle of consent. Subsequently, unionists demanded that any new agreement replacing the AIA should state and respect the sovereignty of both governments. This had a number of aspects which together represented a major extension of the notion of consent. It involved two major principles and a set of subsidiaries. First, with regard to Northern Ireland, there had to be a clear and unambiguous statement of the status of Northern Ireland as a part of the United Kingdom. Second, and logically consequent, there had to be a firm acknowledgement of the principle of consent for constitutional change. A new agreement had also to apply to the whole of the British Isles; it had to respect the democratic rights of the people who might be affected by it, especially those of Northern Ireland and the people of the Republic of Ireland; and it had to ensure that there was full and proper accountability so that those persons and bodies exercising any function under the same were fully responsible and accountable to those affected by the exercise of those functions. If a function was exercised solely in respect to the people of an area, such as Northern Ireland, then accountability for the exercise of that function had to be to the people of that area. The new agreement and its operation had to be fully transparent, with no possible ground for a suspicion of a hidden agenda which might subvert the consent principle. One way of ensuring this objective was to enable the elected representatives of those concerned to be directly involved in the framing and operation of the agreement and any institutions it might create. The new agreement had to be fully acceptable and a means had to be found to demonstrate that it had the informed and freely given consent of the people; it had to apply equally to both governments and be equally applicable within both states (Northern Ireland Assembly Report 1986).

The UUP, led by David Trimble, achieved all of these aims during the negotiations that led to the Belfast/Good Friday Agreement of 1998. The memory of 1985 was always active in the determination to find an acceptable formulation. In terms of 'Constitutional Issues' the Irish government explicitly conceded the principle of consent at the heart of the Agreement: all parties agreed that there would not be a united Ireland without the consent of a majority of the people in Northern Ireland voting for it.

> (1) It is hereby declared that Northern Ireland in its entirety remains part of the United Kingdom and shall not cease to be so without the consent of a majority of the people of Northern Ireland voting in a poll held for the purposes of this section in accordance with Schedule 1 [see below].

> (2) But if the wish expressed by a majority in such a poll is that Northern Ireland should cease to be part of the United Kingdom and form part of a united Ireland, the Secretary of State shall lay before Parliament such proposals to give effect to that wish as may be agreed between Her Majesty's Government in the United Kingdom and the Government of Ireland.

Articles 2 and 3 of the Irish Constitution were redrawn to separate nation and state in Irish constitutional law. The new Article 2, rather than as before, claiming that all of the territory of the island of Ireland constituted the national territory, stated: 'It is the entitlement and birthright of every person born in the island of Ireland, which includes its islands and seas, to be part of the Irish nation.' The new Article 3 enshrined the consent principle: 'recognising that a united Ireland shall be brought about only by peaceful means with the consent of a majority of the people, democratically expressed, in both jurisdictions in the island.' The phrase 'both jurisdictions in the island' recognised that two states on the island – Ireland and the United Kingdom of Great Britain and Northern Ireland – rather than one as the 1937 Constitution had. The Government of Ireland Act 1920 (Belfast Agreement: Constitutional Issues Paragraph 1; Annex A; Schedule 1; and Annex B) was repealed but was replaced by the Northern Ireland Act 1998 which reasserted, explicitly, the sovereignty of the Westminster Parliament over Northern Ireland (Northern Ireland Constitution Act 1998, Clause 43).

There was to be a North-South Ministerial Council (NSMC) that would be a consultative body with no executive powers – there could be no evolution of an all-Ireland government by-passing consent – as had been inherent in the 1973 Council of Ireland (Belfast Agreement: Strand

2, Paragraphs 1–19; and Annex). Strand 3 saw a British-Irish Council established. It too was a consultative body. It was to be made up of all devolved administrations within the United Kingdom, Crown dependencies within the British Isles and the sovereign governments in London and Dublin (*ibid.*). A British-Irish Inter-Governmental Conference (AIIC) replaced the Anglo-Irish Intergovernmental Conference set up by the AIA. British and Irish ministers and officials would be unable to discuss matters devolved to the Assembly while Northern Irish ministers would be allowed to attend Conference meetings as observers (Belfast Agreement: Strand 3; British-Irish Intergovernmental Conference, Paragraphs 1–10).

Trimble's success did not prevent anti-Agreement unionists, mainly in the DUP, attacking him and the constitutional gains he had secured. On this they were wrong as the DUP's subsequent working within the Agreement framework shows. But critics' opposition to the Belfast Agreement did reveal a deeper, fundamental concern with the principle of consent – in essence the point Harold McCusker had made in opposition to the AIA. And here the memory of 1985 also played its part, as if critics could no longer trust the guarantees given. For example, Peter Robinson complained that the Northern Ireland Constitution Act of 1998, giving legislative effect to the Belfast Agreement, meant the 'people of Northern Ireland' were allowed only to go into a united Ireland or remain in the United Kingdom. They could remain in the United Kingdom not like other citizens, but in a transitional form 'as they move gently out of the United Kingdom and into a united Ireland' as ascribed for them in Clause 1 of the Act concerning a referendum on Northern Ireland's membership of the UK. Only one option – a united Ireland – was offered to them in the clause because the whole purpose of the Act was to lead towards that very option: 'to take the people of Northern Ireland out of the United Kingdom and into a united Ireland.' Robinson asked if anyone really believed that, if the Secretary of State for Northern Ireland was, 'on the basis of a handful of votes of a majority, to put Northern Ireland into a united Ireland, that will provide a peaceful future for the people of Northern Ireland?' It was a 'preposterous' thought. For the DUP it should take more than a simple majority for Northern Ireland to be put out of the United Kingdom, and there was 'clearly' an advantage in having a weighted majority within the new Northern Ireland Assembly suggesting to the Secretary of State when it was time to call a vote on the Border: 'a simple majority would cause chaos and disaster, clearly a minority voting for a united Ireland – perhaps a majority of those who came out to vote, but a minority of the people of Northern Ireland – would clearly cause considerable violence in our community and would not produce a peaceful way forward', concluded Robinson (HC Deb., 26 November 1985).

Robert McCartney, leader of the United Kingdom Unionist Party (UKUP) and whose influence can be traced to opposition to the AIA, argued that democracy meant majority rule, but not unbridled majority rule. Principles for the protection of minorities were encapsulated in all modern constitutions, particularly written constitutions. The essence of the Belfast Agreement, and the Northern Ireland Assembly established by it, was that there could be no majority decision making or majority democracy, even with built-in protections; there must be equality of treatment. There were a First Minister and a Deputy First Minister, elected jointly and who would fall jointly; that was why every important decision required consensus in both communities, even though, numerically and electorally, one of the communities was significantly smaller than the other. An accommodation based on consensus had been accepted as the price that had to be paid for agreement. But, argued McCartney, on the most fundamental issue of all – whether Northern Ireland remained part of the United Kingdom or departed into a united Ireland – the ordinary principles of democracy and majority decision making were imposed: 'In other words, we may not have a majority decision about anything Unionist, but a final and unalterable decision that may be made at any time by a nationalist majority – to abandon for all time the British link and the Union and become part of a united Ireland – may be decided on a single vote. That is a dramatic reversal' (HC Deb., 22 July 1998). This replayed the AIA fear – that the principle of consent was subsidiary to the objective of Irish unity.

Ian Paisley too highlighted the constitutional nuances between the principle of consent in the AIA and, now, in the Belfast Agreement. He pointed out that the governments 'have always told the people of Northern Ireland that there is no change' and that if 'in the future, the majority of the people of Northern Ireland should indicate a wish to become part of a United Ireland, the British Government would support that wish.' But, Paisley noted, 'we turn to the Anglo-Irish agreement, because we are told that the Belfast Agreement is a development of that'. The Anglo-Irish agreement stated: 'the two Governments – Affirm that any change in the status of Northern Ireland with the consent of the majority of the people of Northern Ireland'. But now 'we are not getting the majority of the people of Northern Ireland; we are getting the majority of those who take part in a poll, which is entirely different' (HC Deb., 22 July 1998).

This view was not only the view of anti-Agreement unionists. Trimble believed it was 'quite clear' that – provided that the issue of leaving the United Kingdom was raised – any number of questions could be asked in a poll. An obligation would be placed on the Secretary of State only when the question arose of going into an all-Ireland state. He pointed out that, in the Assembly's operation, under the concept of cross-community support, 'we will use a weighted majority of 60 per cent. It is therefore appropriate also to raise the issue of such a majority in a poll.' In Clause 1(2), of the Northern Ireland Act, the government were taking a further significant step in the development of the United Kingdom constitution, by making the results of a referendum binding on the government (no other referendum results had been binding on a British government before). Trimble, therefore, also considered it appropriate to examine more closely the concept of 'majority', and to operate, by analogy with the Agreement's other provisions, a 60 per cent weighted majority in any Border poll. The meaning of consent for unionists had been modified yet again (HC Deb., 22 July 1998).

Conclusion

For unionists the principle of consent has evolved in response to the changing circumstances of their principal foe: Irish nationalism. From the first Home Rule Bill in 1886 to the Framework Document's north-south body with executive powers, unionists have refused to consent to any institution that might constitute an Irish government for the whole of the island of Ireland. At its simplest the principle of consent remains the right of the people of Northern Ireland to self-determine their constitutional position in a referendum. For unionists this means their continued membership of the United Kingdom. But, for a significant section of unionism this remains their inalienable right, if not to remain within the UK, then to remain outside an Irish Republic. There is no doubt that the AIA alarmed unionists into reflection about the meaning of consent if only because it had revealed its possible limits to protect that status. It provoked a re-assessment of how it was to be meaningfully coded into a subsequent agreement which all unionists, however reluctantly, accepted as the consequence of the AIA. This chapter has argued that the consent clauses of the 1998 Agreement are related to the experience of 1985 and represent a major success for Trimble's tenacity during its negotiation. Moreover, the position on consent continues to change and this can be seen in the adoption of the nationalist concept of parallel consent by some to argue that the unionist community should have a veto over Irish unity. Thus, even when unionists have secured the principle of consent in the GFA, there is an element that, for all its talk about democracy and majority rule, will continue to develop increasingly subtle interpretations of that principle to avoid absorption into a united Ireland.

References

British Government (1995) *The Framework Documents: A Framework For Accountable Government In Northern Ireland*, 22 February (London: Downing Street).

British Government, Irish Government, and the Northern Ireland Executive designate (1973) *The Sunningdale Agreement: Tripartite agreement on the Council of Ireland*, 9 December (Belfast: Northern Ireland Information Service).

British Governments, Irish Government (1995) *The Framework Documents: A New Framework For Agreement*, 22 February (London: Downing Street; Dublin: Department of the Taoiseach).

Bunreacht na hÉireann (Constitution of Ireland) (1937), Dublin.

Dicey, A.V. (1973) *England's Case Against Home Rule* (Surrey: Richmond Publishing).

Great Britain Parliament (1920) *Government of Ireland Act 1920* (10 & 11 Geo. 5 c. 67) (London: HMSO).

—— (1949) *Ireland Act 1949* (London: HMSO).

—— (1985) *Agreement between the Government of the United Kingdom of Great Britain and Northern Ireland and the Government of the Republic of Ireland* [The Anglo-Irish Agreement] (London: HMSO).

—— (1998) *Northern Ireland Bill 1998*, 15 July (London: HMSO).

—— (1998) *Northern Ireland Act 1998*, 19 November (London: HMSO).

Hadfield, B. (1989) *The Constitution of Northern Ireland* (Belfast: SLS Legal Publications).

House of Commons Debate (Hansard) 18 November 1985, vol. 87, cols 19–35.

—— 26 November 1985, vol. 87, cols 767, 774–7.

—— 27 November 1985, vol. 87, cols 918, 951–2.

—— 22 July 1998, vol. 316, cols 1192, 1214, 1217.

Northern Ireland Assembly (1986) *Official Report of the Assembly* (Belfast: HMSO).

Northern Ireland Office (1998), *The Agreement*, 10 April (Belfast: HMSO).

Stewart, A.T.Q. (1967) *The Ulster Crisis* (London: Faber).

Ulster Unionist Party (1984) *Devolution and the Northern Ireland Assembly: The Way Forward* (Belfast: UUP). Available online at http://cain.ulst.ac.uk/events/assembly1982/docs/uup260484.htm (accessed 19 May 2011).

6 Nationalism and the Anglo-Irish Agreement: equality, identity and ideology

Cillian McGrattan

This chapter revisits the contemporary reactions of Irish nationalists to the AIA and attempts to place them in a longer historical context. I concentrate in particular on constitutional nationalism (namely, the belief that reunification and reform of the Northern Irish state must occur gradually and peacefully), rather than the physical force tradition, which advocates immediate change through violent means if necessary (Edwards and McGrattan, 2010: 11). The Agreement sought to address long-standing grievances held by nationalists regarding the apparatus of the state in Northern Ireland. Core nationalist beliefs about the injustice of partition and commonly held feelings of marginality and estrangement from the way Northern Ireland was administered – including, isolation from and mistrust of the police, disaffection with employment legislation, and a distance if not outright hostility to the Conservative government of Margaret Thatcher – were to be given a voice by the government of the Irish Republic through the AIIC. The chapter explores the background to those perceptions and suggests that northern nationalists incorporated and understood the AIA and, in particular, the AIA's equality provisions as a stepping-stone towards attenuating the Union.

That interpretation of the Agreement occurred primarily due to the presence of the SDLP as the principal political voice of northern nationalism, and, in particular, the increasing focus within the party on national grievances over social ones (Campbell, 2010). From the foundation of the Northern state, and, increasingly from the onset of the conflict in 1969, Northern nationalists had understood Dublin involvement to be a means of alleviating discrimination and injustice (Staunton, 2001). While the Agreement facilitated closer inter-governmental relations (O'Kane 2007), its impact on northern nationalism was to inspire not so much a re-think of the political situation or, more specifically, of nationalists' relationship with unionism, as a reinforcement of existing perceptions about how the conflict might be managed or resolved through an increased role for the Irish state.

The legacy of the AIA in the nationalist imaginary reflects that accumulating character of northern nationalism (McGrattan, 2009a). The earliest reactions of northern nationalists to the AIA revealed that mindset and the early framing of the Agreement, by the SDLP's leader, John Hume, coloured later judgments. In this regard it is not unfair to say that the prevailing nationalist interpretation of the AIA remains that it was a catalyst for the peace process and the April 1998 Belfast/GFA. This interpretation is based on the idea that by addressing nationalist perceptions of inequality in the areas of socio-economic opportunity and cultural identification, the AIA ushered in a new era of Catholic self-confidence and openness to political accommodation. Although I do not dispute the basic causal sequence of that narrative, I do question the facile linkage of the 1985 Agreement with later events. Indeed, in providing an instrument for rectifying grievances, the Agreement also opened nationalists' eyes to the opportunities and the limitations of reform. As Sean Farren points out, the failure of the SDLP to achieve radical transformations in, for example, the policing and justice system highlighted the structural powerlessness of constitutional politics while at the same time serving to emphasise the need to maintain pressure on the British government for further concessions (Farren, 2010: 223–7). As such, the nationalist response to the AIA saw equality not only as a civic principle but one that was bound up with ideological imperatives.

Background to the Agreement

Formed in 1970, the SDLP represented a marked contrast from the abstentionist, oppositional and ad hoc style of politics of the old Nationalist Party. The party identified itself as left-of-centre and socialist – as a self-conscious outgrowth of the Northern Irish civil rights movement, the SDLP initially argued for reform of the Northern state, the principle that Catholics and nationalists should enjoy the same rights and opportunities as Protestants and unionists. Reunification was downplayed and the party espoused the idea that constitutional change must be based on the consent of the majority of Northern Ireland's population – importantly, the border question was not written out of the party's philosophy, rather it stressed the need to win over unionism to a leftist and all-island perspective. However, as Sarah Campbell has pointed out, 'apart from the party's first press conference in August 1970, where [the first party leader] Gerry Fitt detailed the party's socialist aims … the SDLP's policies on socioeconomic issues were cursory' (Campbell, 2010: 206). In addition, the long-term crisis of the Northern state and the fragmentation of the once-dominant unionist elite had led to a resurgent nationalist discourse – as evidenced by the belief among sections of the SDLP and the Irish government that real progress towards ending partition was possible (McGrattan, 2010: 102–8).

In addition, the muting of the leftist agenda and the emphasis on nationalist concerns was in part a reflection of John Hume's prominence and increasing pre-eminence within the party. Having failed to convince unionists to share those concerns, Hume and the SDLP looked to external interventions to compensate for the party's electoral and structural marginality. Indeed, the party recognised the new role for the Irish government as a victory for this project:

> By affording the Irish government a formal consultative role on key issues affecting Northern Ireland, it formalized and strengthened its role as guarantor of the rights of the nationalist community, and vindicated the party's claim that the two governments had to share responsibility for dealing with the North's crisis. (Farren, 2010: 210)

For its part, the Irish government had been exercised by the mobilisation of support for Provisional republicanism during the hunger strikes of 1980–81. According to the then Taoiseach, Garret FitzGerald, the decision to convene a body to discuss future options for the constitutional, legal and social frameworks on the island of Ireland was a direct response to the fact that around one out of every three Catholics were voting Sinn Féin. FitzGerald quickly dropped his desired rapprochement with Ulster unionism and instead began to concentrate on buttressing the SDLP (FitzGerald, 1994: 193). The subsequent conclusions of New Ireland Forum largely conformed to John Hume's strategic vision, particularly the ideas that any 'genuine reconciliation' must be based on 'mutual recognition and acceptance of the legitimate rights of unionists and nationalists', and that any settlement that recognises those rights 'must transcend the context of Northern Ireland' (New Ireland Forum, 1984, paragraphs, 4.15 and 4.16). For unionists, however, these ideas appeared to be (a) mutually exclusive, since unionists perceived the Northern state to be a legitimate constitutional entity in and of itself; and (b) democratically problematic, since they were based on the idea that Britain should work to 'persuade' unionists that their best interests lay in a reconstituted Irish state. Because of these misgivings, critics of the report questioned whether it in any way represented a genuine reappraisal or revision of nationalist ideology. Clare O'Halloran, for example, concluded that: 'Far from constituting a reassessment of nationalist ideology, the New Ireland Forum has breathed new life into its fundamental myths. Its rhetoric has given respectability to the tattered remnants of an irredentism which had become anachronistic and devalued in its traditional form' (1987: 210).

Although the AIA reaffirmed the principle that constitutional change could not be imposed on the north in the absence of support from 'a majority of the people' (Article 1), it did represent a substantial political gain by the SDLP – notably in its provision for a consultative role for the Irish government in the day-to-day administration of the north. Thus, Article 2a of the Agreement established the remit of the Inter-Governmental Council, which would cover political, security and legal affairs, together with having responsibility for 'the promotion of cross-border cooperation'. While this fell considerably shorter than the 'executive and harmonising' functions that the projected Council of Ireland would have provided under the Sunningdale Communiqué of December 1973 (paragraph 7), it nevertheless conformed to John Hume's long-standing prioritisation of external 'solutions' – particularly, cross-border cooperation and the 'Irish dimension' of Dublin involvement (McGrattan, 2009a). The 1985 Agreement, however, tempered Dublin's role with the possibility that a Sunningdale-type power-sharing arrangement might be restored: 'The United Kingdom Government accept that the Irish Government will put forward views and proposals on matters relating to Northern Ireland within the activity of the Conference in so far as those matters are not the responsibility of a devolved administration in Northern Ireland' (Article 2b).

Contrary to the assessment by some political scientists (O'Leary and McGarry, 1997: 234) the restoration of devolution would not 'knock-out' the IGC, whose functioning and responsibilities remained subject to a three-year review by the two governments (see, for instance, Article 5c and Article 11). Its main function, as described by FitzGerald was, to provide a means of dealing with 'the alienation of much of the nationalist population from the political and security systems in Northern Ireland' (1994: 198). FitzGerald later admitted that the immediate exigency of counteracting Sinn Féin's electoral mobilisation had in fact passed by 1985 (1994: 202), with the party's vote levelling off at around 11 per cent. However, the emphasis on the need for inter-governmental cooperation had a longer lineage within the SDLP's analysis. For instance, Gerard Murray and Jonathan Tonge explain that by 1979 the SDLP had settled on the conclusion that the main lesson of the Sunningdale power-sharing experiment (1973–74) was that unionist obduracy was all but insurmountable and that 'the two governments had to create the necessary mechanism for political progress to take place' (Murray and Tonge, 2005: 141).

The Inter-Governmental Conference and nationalist grievances

According to Eamon Delaney, who was then centrally involved in the Irish Department of Foreign Affairs' Anglo-Irish Division, 'The full institutional impact of the AIA has never been highlighted or documented. Seeing how mad the unionists were at its symbolism, they would go crazy altogether if they knew its full practical detail (Delaney, 2001: 289).

In lieu of the release of the state files, Delaney's memoir remains the most comprehensive and most revealing account of the day-to-day operation of the IGC and its Secretariat, which was responsible for overseeing the implementation of the Conference's decisions. The IGC and the Secretariat gave Irish ministers and officials unprecedented access to the British government's policy-making apparatus. According to Delaney, Dublin sought to take full advantage of this opportunity: 'There was not a hospital closure, fisheries initiative or cultural programme that the Irish government didn't have a "view" on' (2001: 289–90; original emphasis). These 'views' were formed as a result of close cooperation with the SDLP who advised the Irish government on which individuals would be 'appropriate' for civil service promotions or appointment to public bodies. In addition, Delaney claims that community workers were in constant contact with either the Dublin government or the Secretariat directly to complain about military harassment, which officials followed up with the relevant British authorities. Despite its initial opposition, he points out that Sinn Féin 'cottoned on to its nuisance potential and … filled in [harassment forms] with amazingly similar details' (2001: 291).

In 1989, responding to criticisms that it was adopting a lackadaisical attitude to the IGC, the British government claimed that it had given rise to several legal and social reforms, including the repeal of the Flags and Emblems Act (1954), which had outlawed the flying of the Irish tricolour; the establishment of an Independent Commission for police complaints; the publication of a code of conduct for RUC officers; a new Fair Employment Act that strengthened laws against discrimination and promoted equal opportunity employment practices; and measures to promote the use of the Irish language (O'Leary and McGarry, 1997: 260–1). In addition, Murray and Tonge claim that the Secretariat was responsible for 'the demolition of run-down housing schemes in nationalist areas' in Belfast and Derry (2005: 143). Importantly, the IGC was also instrumental in attracting US aid through the International Fund for Ireland (IFI), which became in the eyes of some nationalists 'a sort of Marshall Plan' (author interview with SDLP member, 5 October 2009). Hume nominated Paddy Duffy (who had represented the party in Mid-Ulster at the 1973–74 Assembly and 1975–76 Convention) to the board, who was later succeeded by the party's former chair, Eamon Hanna. The IFI not only contributed to the amelioration of deprived nationalist areas in the North, but it brought the US into play in Northern Ireland in a significantly new way and offered a justification for Hume's long-term strategy of courting Irish-American congressmen (Murray and Tonge, 2005: 143).

According to Delaney gaining these concessions involved intricate and long-drawn-out negotiations with the British. Their 'foot-dragging', he claims, created an opportunity to add further complaints: 'Everything they gave was done so begrudgingly and slowly that by the time it trickled down it was accepted in the same spirit, and replaced by some new demand' (2001: 290). Delaney's description of the process of nationalist engagement with the AIA captures an essential characteristic of modern northern nationalism – namely, that it proceeds according to an underlying teleological understanding of history in which political developments are understood to conform to the inevitable goal of reunification and political strategies are devised on the premise of moving towards that goal (McGrattan, 2009a). Delaney points out that this was fundamentally rational and quotes the opinion of the then head of the Anglo-Irish Division, Seán Ó hUiginn – nationalism is 'like a shark. It must keep moving or it dies' (Delaney, 2003: 305).

The Agreement in retrospect

During the House of Commons debate on the AIA, John Hume echoed the language of the Agreement by stating that it provided a 'framework for genuine reconciliation' (HC Deb., 26 November 1985). The idea resurfaced in his later reflections on the conflict: 'We [the SDLP] pointed out that the Agreement was not a solution, but a framework within which a solution could be found' (Hume, 1996: 43). Hume's framing was not simply a rhetorical intervention in the political debate; it has in fact resonated beyond electoral politics and, in many ways, has formed the basis of an academic discourse on and about Irish nationalism, which depicts the foregrounding of equality concerns as evidence of a new or 'revised' ideology (McLoughlin, 2005). That discourse has become largely internalised and is often unthinkingly reproduced by many academics working on Northern Ireland and modern Irish nationalism.

The idea that the AIA provided a 'framework' for reconciliation is echoed by Paul Arthur, who, for example, has argued that the Agreement so profoundly changed the political context that it ushered in a 'ripe moment' or an 'optimum' environment for engaging in 'mediation and negotiation' (2000: 223). While warning against 'exaggeration' and the dangers of ignoring the part the Agreement played in alienating Ulster unionists and marginalising Provisional republicans, Mark McGovern has similarly claimed that the AIA initiated 'a long-term strategy of conflict management' that 'helped to create' the peace process (1997: 55). Writing in the post-Good Friday period, McGovern developed these insights and applied them to what he perceived as the historical trajectory of Sinn Féin and Provisional republicanism. While the 1998 Agreement represented the manifestation of the SDLP's vision, McGovern argued that Sinn Féin appealed to northern nationalists by monopolising the equality language associated with the GFA: 'The concept of equality has become the means of expressing Sinn Féin's worldview in every area of its social, political and economic outlook' (2004: 623).

A more subtle exploration of the same argument, Katy Hayward and Claire Mitchell (2003) have highlighted the slipperiness and all-purpose nature of the term 'equality'. It was this vagueness, they claim, that proved so attractive for political strategists: 'Virtually indisputable as a democratic principle, the term's ambiguity meant that it could be seen to address the fundamental political and constitutional grievances of the minority while allowing for a politics of "normality"' (2003: 269). Hayward and Mitchell argue that the emergence of an equality discourse had a self-reproducing effect and increasingly the northern Catholic vote coalesced around which party, Sinn Féin or the SDLP, could best vouchsafe and promote Catholic rights. This represented a potentially profound realignment of political dynamics in the north, for, as Hayward and Mitchell explain, 'Catholics are now politically refocused in the short term in reforming Northern Ireland rather than achieving immediate constitutional change' (2003: 307).

The idea that the AIA radically transformed the environment in the north is, therefore, partially based on the reactions by various political groupings – and, in particular, the angry response by unionist parties. A key feature of Farren's discussion, for example, concerns how unionist discontent played a critical role in shaping northern nationalist support for the SDLP – including the election victories of Séamus Mallon and Joe Hendron (2010: 210–16; 220–21). Similarly, Paul Arthur outlines how the AIA provided for not only inter-governmental cooperation but also a return of devolved administration to Northern Ireland, provided that it occurred within power-sharing institutions. He argues that while unionists may have been dismayed at the idea that Dublin was to be given a consultative role through the IGC in the affairs of the north, by agreeing to share power with nationalists they could initiate a review of the workings of the IGC and thereby reduce the influence of the Irish government. However, as Arthur goes on to explain: 'Unionists made no attempt to take advantage of this offer. They did not realise fully that their resistance to change had been surmounted for the first time this century' (1999: 253). This reductionist treatment of the AIA echoes ideas first articulated by Hume who spoke of how the AIA had 'lanced the unionist boil' and predicted that it would force unionists to negotiate with nationalist Ireland 'by the end of 1986' (quoted in Patterson, 2006: 313).

When continued unionist resistance to the Agreement frustrated Hume's vision, the SDLP leader turned instead to his intra-communal opponents, the Provisional IRA and, in 1988, he entered into a series of talks with Gerry Adams that continued sporadically and behind the scenes until 1993. The AIA coincided with a series of military setbacks that contributed to the ongoing political marginalisation of Provisional republicanism – including the loss of materiel in the capture of the *Eksund* by Irish and French authorities and the killing of eleven people by an IRA bomb in Enniskillen on Remembrance Day in 1987. Insofar as the AIA represented a potent indication of the fact that constitutional nationalism could dramatically alter British government strategy in the north, the Sinn Féin leadership began the process of engagement with the SDLP (McGrattan, 2009b: 157). As Peter McLoughlin points out, this Sinn Féin perception was itself coloured by 'Hume's presentation of the accord' not as a solution in and of itself but as a framework for fostering a solution (2005: 262–9). This series of events allows McLoughlin to draw a line from 1985 to the 'outgrowths' of the Brooke-Mayhew talks in 1991–92 to the Downing Street Declaration of 1993, which reaffirmed the principles of inter-governmental cooperation and the need to gain unionist consent for any constitutional change – and, by way of further extrapolation, to the GFA of 1998, which ratified those principles (see also Murray 2003).

Within this perspective, the 'outworkings' of the AIA ultimately conform to a familiar narrative turn based on the idea that political developments must necessarily move in one direction. In other words, in creating a new political environment, the AIA cultivated a more accommodative approach within Northern Irish nationalism that foregrounded equality as a political priority rather than reunification. However, while an equality discourse may indeed have grown since the 1985 Agreement, the idea that the Agreement acted as a 'catalyst' for that growth is based on a logical distinction between the two. Thus, Christopher McCrudden charts the emergence of an equality discourse to the mid-1980s when, he argues 'inequality of opportunity between Catholics and Protestants became a key political issue' (1999: 98). Although McCrudden points out that this competitive dynamic arose because of the insistence by the US that investment be linked to anti-discrimination principles rather than the AIA *per se*, his analysis depends on a backwards-looking narrative. Thus, what he identifies as the twin goals of the 1998 Agreement, 'equality and the search for a settlement', became increasingly intertwined during the peace process and were established as political goals following the election of New Labour in May 1997 (1999: 103).

That the AIA transformed the face of Northern Irish politics and presented Irish nationalism with a radically changed political environment is indisputable. However, the received wisdom regarding the AIA – that it inaugurated a period of growing nationalist equality and precipitated the peace process – leaves several questions unresolved. The first problem relates to the counter-factual, 'what if' – that is, 'what if' Sinn Féin's adoption of an equality agenda had proven unsuccessful and the peace process had not been successful? Or, in more qualified terms, what if the Gerry Adams-Martin McGuinness leadership had been more resolute in maintaining a commitment to the armed campaign? Perhaps even more crucially given Hume's decision to foster talks with Adams, what if the alternative option – as advocated by key SDLP personnel – of talking to the unionists had been taken up in the late 1980s? The point is not to indulge in speculative historical exercises but the counter-factuals demonstrate that, post-1985, alternative options were open to 'bringing in the extremes' and there was no reason to expect the Agreement to unfold as it did.

The second problem is that despite perceptions of movement towards parity of socio-economic opportunity and recognition of cultural-identity, nationalists' concerns with equality did not disappear in 1998. Rather, as Enda Staunton has pointed out, equality and the perception of 'justice denied' forms a deeply embedded substratum in northern nationalist ideology and continues to play a critical role in influencing nationalist perceptions of political change (2001). In this conceptualisation, equality is not just a distinct part of the nationalist outlook; it is intrinsically related in a formative and causal way to nationalist policy direction.

The third problem relates to the idea that nationalist reaction to the AIA was not uniform but that unionist reactions played a crucial role in convincing many nationalists that it was a positive development. This interpretation is, of course, accurate, but what it fails to appreciate is the fact that there may have been some deeper truth in the unionist reaction, particularly pertaining to northern nationalism. This 'truth' relates to the idea that not only are identities – individual and communal – formed in opposition to others, but they are maintained across time through others' perceptions (Booth, 2006). Unionists reacted to the Agreement because they recognised that it constituted a 'gain' for nationalists and that nationalists also perceived it as such; on the other hand, Northern nationalists had little incentive to repudiate what appeared to be, and what was touted as, a positive step for them. In this regard, the unionist reaction to the Agreement was not simply indicative of entrenched obduracy or a failure to recognise their strategic limitations (Arthur, 1999); it also represented an awareness of the likelihood of nationalism using the Agreement to further its goal of ending partition. John Hume's turn to talks with Sinn

Féin and away from negotiations with unionism merely confirmed these suspicions (Farrington, 2006: 125).

'Stop worrying about the unionists': nationalism and the Anglo-Irish Agreement

Writing in the build-up to the Agreement, the *Irish Times* journalist Mary Holland admonished Garret FitzGerald for alluding to the idea that Irish unity 'must now be regarded as a distant aspiration' (Holland, 1985). Holland noted the increasingly apprehensive tone of the speeches by the SDLP deputy leader, Seamus Mallon, to the effect that the forthcoming Agreement would fail to satisfy nationalist demands that the UDR be reformed and that it could reinforce the constitutional *status quo*. Holland advised FitzGerald to leave unionist concerns to Margaret Thatcher and instead concentrate on the SDLP: 'If Northern nationalists are to have any confidence in this deal they need to be told, quite unequiv-ocally, that this settlement marks an irreversible step forward and that the Irish government is determined to implement the gains which it has made' (Holland, 1985: 10).

In fact, nationalists – both north and south of the border – resolved Holland's dilemma by refusing to settle for the 'gains' instituted by the Agreement. Instead, the AIA was assimilated within the established nationalist project of targeting gradual reunification. Whatever conces-sions the AIA provided in terms of equality were 'banked' and made to service the underlying reunification project. Furthermore, 'banking' or 'pocketing' the AIA effectively meant that unionist retrenchment could be avoided: future negotiations would have to be based on the starting posi-tion of Dublin having a consultative role in the north.

It is understandable therefore that some in the SDLP depict the 1985 Agreement as a more significant historical event than that of 1998:

> ... it gave the Irish government a say in what was happening; it gave them a foot in the door. I suppose that was another outworking of gradualism and reformism ... In some ways it was nearly more important a step than the '98 Agreement, because, as [Seamus] Mallon said, that was basically a reworking of '73 ... I think the Anglo-Irish Agreement was a really vital step. (Author interview with SDLP member, October 2009)

The nationalist press, in particular the Belfast daily the *Irish News*, recog-nised the AIA as a major political intervention. Indeed, the *Irish News* counselled that despite unionist anger the Agreement could not be allowed to be usurped by the 'threat of force' as had happened in 1914 and 1974 (31 October 1985). One of its regular columnists – an ex-SDLP strategist, John Duffy – argued that it had been nationalists, not unionists, who had been forced to adapt to the northern state: 'whatever way one looks at it, "compromise" by nationalists had become the order of the day by the time the Second World War broke out in 1939' (Duffy, 1985). Similarly, at the party's annual conference, Hume described how the 'only political lesson' that unionists had learned from history was that the *status quo* could be defended through threats (*Irish News*, 11 November 1985).

Although the *Irish News* highlighted the fact that the AIA provided for reform of 'human rights', legal justice and equality issues, its support for the Agreement was also based on its constitutional aspects. Thus, while it admitted that the Agreement reiterated the principle of consent, it pointed out that that was qualified by 'an important rider' – namely that London would 'implement Irish unity ON ITS OWN INITIATIVE in the event of a majority emerging in favour of that proposal' (16 November 1985; upper case in original). This proviso, it said, undercut Provisional republicanism's understanding of the British presence because it meant that Britain 'has no ulterior motive, strategic or otherwise for remaining in Ireland' (ibid.). From the outset, therefore, constitutional nationalism associated the Agreement's equality provisions with its constitutional and security implications, all of which it believed must be protected against the threat of unionist violence:

> The British government is totally convinced as to the necessity to accommodate the rights and identities of the two traditions in Northern Ireland. The structures of state from the highest level to the lowest must reflect such accommodation. That is the stumbling block for unionists. Their persistent blind rejection of it will be their undoing. (*Irish News*, 18 November 1985)

Nationalists, therefore, effectively side-stepped Mary Holland's dilemma; in fact, contrary to McCrudden's (1999) depiction, equality did not 'become a political issue' – the initial responses by nationalists to the AIA reveal that its equality provisions were saturated with political and constitutional importance. This was implicit in the commentaries on the Agreement written by the former Irish Labour Party spokesman on Northern Ireland, Conor Cruise O'Brien (O'Brien, 1985a; 1985b). O'Brien criticised FitzGerald for his lack of 'prudence' in ignoring the emerging unionist backlash (1985a) and warned that the Agreement could actually give the 'kiss of life' to the Provisionals' violent campaign, which had been rejected and marginalised by the vast majority of nationalist Ireland (1985b). Although O'Brien was mistaken in his 'malign scenario' prediction where he envisaged Provisional republicans attempting to take advantage of loyalist discontent by escalating their campaign in the north, the subsequent convergence at the level of policy direction, if not quite ideology, between Sinn Féin and the SDLP- Dublin government nexus underlined the inherent amenability of the AIA to traditional nationalist interpretation.

Where O'Brien was mistaken was in his implication that FitzGerald had a choice between recognising unionist concerns and supporting the SDLP. Arguably, a more nuanced appreciation of the politics of the AIA was that offered by the then Bishop of Down and Connor, Dr Cahal Daly, who suggested that what was required from nationalists was a more restrained discourse (Curry, 1985). For Daly, the nationalist interpretation of the AIA as an 'opportunity' was to be expected. However, he urged nationalists 'to refrain from triumphalism' since that would endanger the potential in the Agreement for both communities to 'move together out of the impasse'. Although Daly's words were echoed in the *Irish News*'s subsequent editorial (28 November 1985), by that stage – almost a fortnight after the Agreement – the nationalist discourse on the AIA had effectively been set down and the political dynamic of nationalist gain and unionist loss already established.

Conclusion: reconciliation and equality

Certainly the AIA raised the self-esteem of many northern nationalists. Fionnuala O'Connor, for instance, records the reaction of one 'non-voter': 'The only political development that's involved me for years was the Anglo-Irish Agreement. When that was announced live at Hillsborough I remember it reverberating right through my whole body, that I would never apologise again for where I was coming from' (1994: 55).

However, it is important to remember that nationalists adapted to the Agreement, understood the Agreement in the light of their previous experiences and, according to the ideological framework through which their political leadership had interpreted political events, conflated the Agreement's language of equality with the objective of Irish unity. This is made explicit in the explanation offered by O'Connor's 'non-voter': 'I remember [Northern Ireland Secretary of State] Tom King saying there are *de facto* two traditions in Northern Ireland, and our role is to acknowledge the validity of both. Whether it's because I was thirty that year, I'd come to a stage in my life where I wanted to hear that, but it actually meant a lot to me' (ibid.). In other words, the political and the cultural are, in this particular ethno-centric worldview, intertwined with the constitutional and the ideological.

I have tried to stress that an equality discourse was implicit in the terms of the AIA, but more than that, for nationalists that discourse was saturated with political and constitutional meaning, drawing its language from long-standing nationalist experience of inequality and political marginalisation. The reconciliation envisaged by Hume, and reflected in the earliest nationalist responses to the Agreement, was one that was inflected with the colouring of traditional Irish nationalism. As Mary Holland pointed out, nationalists were in fact initially divided about how to respond to the Agreement, caught between two contradictory views: either that it reinforced partition (as was argued by Gerry Adams and Fianna Fáil leader, Charles Haughey) or that it achieved substantive gains in terms of equality (as was argued by John Hume). However, it appears that this dilemma was solved early on – in fact, within days of the Agreement – as nationalists looked to the Agreement as an opportunity for securing equality in the area of national identity and opening the door to eventual Irish unity.

This reading of events challenges the idea that an equality discourse emerged during the peace process of the 1990s to replace traditional nationalist concerns with reunification. Not only was the equality discourse part and parcel of the terms of the AIA, it was also intrinsic to how nationalists interpreted political events. As I have pointed out, that interpretation fitted within the established direction of nationalist policy-making in terms of capitalising on concessions.

The 'Whiggish' linking of the AIA with later developments profoundly obscures the intimate relationship of equality and identity within modern Irish nationalism. In fact, the direct linking of the Anglo-Irish Agreement with the Good Friday Agreement involves more than simply bad history, but in fact may be seen as amplifying a distinctive nationalist understanding of political events. While equality concerns were a major influence in the framing of the GFA, the implication that it was so because John Hume had always emphasised equality (McLoughlin, 2005), is misleading and reflects a profound misunderstanding of nationalist ideology and politics. Put simply, it misrepresents the way in which Hume and other nationalists conceptualised equality – a point implied in the reflections of contemporary commentators such as Conor Cruise O'Brien, Bishop Cahal Daly and Mary Holland.

Indeed, in many ways, it is only to be expected that nationalists interpreted events according to a pre-existing narrative. That narrative, as Eamon Delaney (2001) notes, was centred on the notion of perpetual and gradual progress towards Irish reunification. Equality was, in this understanding, a concession to be won from the British – even, as Garret FitzGerald later admitted, if it was on the back of the threat of republican violence. As such, it had intrinsic and inescapable political, constitutional and ideological importance. The enduring legacy of the Agreement within nationalist memory and its emblematic role as a stepping-stone towards both equality and the attenuation of the Union is both reflective and constitutive of that narrative.

References

Arthur, P. (1999) 'Anglo-Irish relations and constitutional policy', in P. Mitchell and R. Wilford (eds) *Politics in Northern Ireland* (Oxford: Westview Press and PSAI).

—— (2000) *Special Relationships: Britain, Ireland and the Northern Ireland Problem* (Belfast: Blackstaff Press).

Booth, W.J. (2006) *Communities of Memory: On Witness, Identity and Justice* (London: Cornell University Press).

Campbell, S. (2010) 'New Nationalism? The SDLP and Northern Nationalism, 1969-1975', unpublished PhD thesis, University College Dublin.

Curry, T. (1985) 'Don't ignore Unionist wrath – Bishop attacks "irresponsible" political leaders', *Irish News*, 28 November.

Delaney, E. (2001) *An Accidental Diplomat: My Years in the Irish Foreign Service, 1987–1995* (Dublin: New Island).

Duffy, J. (1985) 'Disturbing strand of thought', *Irish News*, 6 November.

Edwards, A. and C. McGrattan (2010) *The Northern Ireland Conflict: A Beginner's Guide* (Oxford: Oneworld).

Farren, S. (2010) *The SDLP: The Struggle for Agreement in Northern Ireland, 1970–2000* (Dublin: Four Courts Press).

Farrington, C. (2006) *Ulster Unionism and the Peace Process in Northern Ireland* (Basingstoke: Palgrave Macmillan).

FitzGerald, G. (1994) 'The origins and rationale of the Anglo-Irish Agreement of 1985', in D. Keogh and M.H. Haltzel (eds) *Northern Ireland and the Politics of Reconciliation* (Cambridge: Cambridge University Press).

Hayward, K. and C. Mitchell (2003) 'Discourses of equality in post-agreement Northern Ireland', *Contemporary Politics*, 9: 3, 293–312.

Holland, M. (1985) 'Stop worrying about the Unionists, Garret', *Irish Times*, 13 November, p. 10.

House of Commons Debates (Hansard), 26 November 1985, vol. 87, col. 783)

Hume, J. (1996) *Personal Views: Politics, Peace and Reconciliation in Ireland* (Dublin: Town House).

McCrudden, C. (1999) 'Equality and the Good Friday Agreement', in J. Ruane and J. Todd (eds), *After the Good Friday Agreement: Analysing Political Change in Northern Ireland* (Dublin: University College Dublin Press).

McGovern, M. (1997) 'Unity in diversity? The SDLP and the peace process', in C. Gilligan and J. Tonge, *Peace or War? Understanding the Peace Process in Northern Ireland* (Aldershot: Ashgate).

—— (2004) '"The Old Days Are Over": Irish Republicanism, the Peace Process, and the Discourse of Equality', *Terrorism and Political Violence*, 16: 3, 622–45.

McGrattan, C. (2009a) 'Dublin, the SDLP, and the Sunningdale Agreement: maximalist nationalism and path-dependency', *Contemporary British History*, 2009, 23: 1, 61–78.

—— (2009b) 'Northern nationalism and the Belfast Agreement', in B. Barton and P.J. Roche (eds) *The Northern Ireland Question: The Peace Process and the Belfast Agreement* (Basingstoke: Palgrave Macmillan).

—— (2010) *Northern Ireland, 1968–2008: The Politics of Entrenchment* (Basingstoke: Palgrave Macmillan).

McLoughlin, P.J. (2005) 'John Hume and the revision of Irish nationalism', unpublished PhD dissertation, Queen's University, Belfast.

Murray, G. (2003) The Good Friday Agreement: an SDLP analysis of the Northern Ireland Conflict', in J. Neuheiser and S. Wolff (eds) *Peace at Last? The Impact of the Good Friday Agreement on Northern Ireland* (Oxford: Berghahn Books).

Murray, G. and J. Tonge (2005) *Sinn Féin and the SDLP: From Alienation to Participation* (Dublin: O'Brien Press).

New Ireland Forum (1984) 'The New Ireland Forum Report' (Dublin: The Stationery Office).

O'Brien, C. C. (1985a) 'A sleepwalker heads for a fog-bound summit', *Irish Times*, 12 November.

—— (1985b) 'Why war clouds could rend the silver lining', *The Times*, 26 November.

O'Connor, F. (1994) *In Search of a State: Catholics in Northern Ireland* (Belfast: Blackstaff Press).

O'Halloran, C. (1987) *Partition and the Limits of Irish Nationalism: An Ideology Under Stress* (Dublin: Gill & Macmillan).

O'Kane, E. (2007) *Britain, Ireland and Northern Ireland since 1980: The Totality of Relationships* (Abingdon: Routledge).

O'Leary, B. and McGarry, J. (1997) *The Politics of Antagonism: Understanding Northern Ireland* (London: Athlone Press).

Patterson, H. (2006) *Ireland since 1939: The Persistence of Conflict* (Dublin: Penguin).

Staunton, E. (2001) *The Nationalists of Northern Ireland 1918–1973* (Dublin: The Columba Press).

7   Republicanism and the peace process: the temptations of teleology

Henry Patterson

Scholars writing about the AIA a quarter of a century later have the advantage of perspective unavailable to their predecessors trying to make sense of its immediate aftermath. They can also benefit from the reflections of some of those politicians and officials who were involved in the negotiations and which have been published since. Key players have also been prepared to respond to the questions of researchers both academic and journalistic.

However, contemporary analysis of the AIA faces a temptation which those writing earlier were largely immune from: that of reading the events of the mid-1980s through the prism of subsequent developments. This has produced the distorting mirror of what can be termed the teleology of the peace process whereby the AIA is read in terms of a purpose assigned to it by subsequent developments and not in term of its specific causes and purposes at the time. The contingencies and contradictory impulses and forces at work in 1985 are flattened out into what Cillian McGrattan refers to as the 'Whiggish' view of the peace process (McGrattan, 2010). A good example is the account of the negotiations given by Michael Lillis who was responsible for Anglo-Irish affairs at the Irish Department of Foreign Affairs. For Lillis the Belfast Agreement of 1998 was the fulfilment of the core purposes of the AIA. He refers to Mrs Thatcher's defence of the Agreement against fierce unionist denunciations where she argued that the intrusive role allotted to the Irish government could be dispensed with in the event of devolution: 'It is regrettable that almost two decades had to pass before this message was digested fully by the unionist leaders. It was remarkable that Dr Paisley cited precisely Mrs Thatcher's arguments as the grounds for his "reluctantly" acceding to the St Andrews Agreement' (Lillis and Goodall, 2010: 20). In fact the Agreement did not provide for the end of the AIIC in the event of devolution so the link between 1985 and Paisley's eventual embrace of devolution has at most a vestigial relationship to the events of 1985.

It is not surprising that a similar approach has been adopted in narratives of the response of Sinn Féin and the Provisional IRA to the AIA. Republicans' narrative of their movement is profoundly teleological: the Catholics of Northern Ireland were an oppressed and demoralised group who went through the 'Calvary' of August 1969 to be shaken into militancy and struggle by that 'pogrom' and subsequent events from internment to Bloody Sunday. Although that struggle has had its ups and downs – often explained by the mistakes of previous leaders of the movement – the trajectory has been an upward one driven by the impossibility of a partitionist state providing full satisfaction to nationalist aspirations. For all the undoubted revisionism of Sinn Féin leaders since the 1980s this narrative still grounds their discourse.

From within the republican narrative the AIA was both a counter-insurgency move by governments alarmed by Sinn Féin's post-hunger strike political breakthrough and, according to one senior Sinn Féiner, a 'kick in the balls' for unionists (English, 2003: 243), given Thatcher's preparedness to introduce such a radical extension of Irish state influence in Northern Ireland. In his influential history of the IRA, Richard English has noted a tension within Gerry Adams' response to the AIA which denounced its attempt to enrol the Irish government in legitimising partition while noting the 'concessions' to improve the quality of life for northern nationalists (English, 2003: 242). This tension was, he claims, to define the ambiguous nature of republican politics in the subsequent period.

English (2003: 242) treats the AIA as a watershed marking the beginning of the peace process while adding that this established the ironic nature of the process: 'It had begun in 1985 with an AIA intended to strengthen the SDLP at republicans' expense; it had now produced this strikingly different outcome' (i.e. the 1998 Agreement and Sinn Féin's replacement of the SDLP as the dominant force in northern nationalism). However, there is a central flaw in this argument. The future of the SDLP did figure in Irish arguments for an agreement that addressed nationalist 'alienation' from the northern state but there is little evidence that it was a major consideration for the British negotiators. Based on interviews with key players in the negotiations, Eamon O'Kane concluded: 'The alienation thesis is not as acceptable an explanation of the British motivation as it is for the Irish for the simple reason that the British doubted that nationalist alienation would be alleviated by institutionalising a role for Dublin as a spokesperson for the nationalist community' (O'Kane, 2007: 59). On the British side the driving motivations were to improve radically the Republic's contribution to cross-border security cooperation against the Provisional IRA and to fireproof the UK internationally against criticisms of policy in Northern Ireland, particularly in the United States. From this perspective it is difficult to posit 1985 as the beginning of the peace process since at its core this process has come to mean the 'bringing in of the extremes'.

Revising republican history

The ambiguity in post-AIA republican politics noted by English has been given a Machiavellian explanation by the veteran journalist, Ed Moloney, in his controversial history of the evolution of republican strategy since the early 1980s. For Moloney the origins of the peace process were in a developing dialogue between Gerry Adams and the West Belfast priest Alex Reid that started in 1982. Out of this came a tripartite strategy for ending the violence: ending attempts by constitutional nationalists to isolate and marginalise Sinn Féin and instead opening a dialogue leading to a 'pan-nationalist front': a declaration by the UK government of neutrality on the union of Great Britain and Northern Ireland and an inclusive conference of all the parties to the conflict out of which an 'agreed Ireland' would emerge. This would provide a non-violent alternative to armed struggle (Moloney, 2002: 224). As part of the process Sinn Féin mellowed its previous commitment to radical socialism and its critique of the mainstream nationalist parties as bourgeois collaborators with imperialism.

Moloney, who has been writing about and talking to republicans since the start of the Troubles and whose work is characterised by serious research and critical intelligence, is not to be dismissed lightly. There is also evidence that supports some of his claims. Sinn Féin in the late 1970s and early 1980s did emphasise its radical and leftist credentials. The core leadership group around Adams made much of the party's vocation as a vanguard of the oppressed working class in the Republic of Ireland as well as its traditional role of militant defenders of northern Catholics. It couched its critique of its nationalist rival, the SDLP, in class terms as the representative of the Catholic middle class. Emphasis was put on the 'Uncle Tom' nature of the SDLP who were abused as the 'Stoop Down Low Party' and even 'domestic cockroaches' with a former Provisional claiming that senior IRA figures had considered assassinating John Hume (O'Callaghan, 1999: 173 and 284).

These sentiments reflected the early stages of the development of the 'Armalite and Ballot-Box' strategy according to which electoral gains would legitimise rather than, as fundamentalist republicans claimed, undermine armed struggle. Republicans were dizzy with the success of their early electoral interventions and hoped that Sinn Féin would soon displace the SDLP as the dominant nationalist party in the north. Thus Adams, now the MP for West Belfast, predicted that the 1984 European elections would be 'part of the work of supplanting the SDLP as the party representing the Nationalist People in the Six Counties ... the smashing of the SDLP is an ongoing process' (Patterson, 1989: 176). In fact the Sinn Féin candidate, Danny Morrison, was easily defeated by Hume. In the local government elections in 1985 the SDLP vote held up and the Sinn Féin vote declined compared with its high point in 1983. It was therefore unsurprising that Adams broached the idea of a pan-nationalist front at the Sinn Féin *Ard Fheis* in November 1984 and in February 1985 he asked Hume, during a radio interview, to establish a 'united nationalist approach' to dismantling the 'Unionist veto' (Moloney, 2002: 238).

However, such overtures did not mean any let-up in IRA violence. By 1985 the Provisional IRA (PIRA) had conducted the longest armed campaign in the violent history of republicanism. An assessment of the IRA threat produced within the Ministry of Defence in November 1978 had concluded that the Provisionals had the capacity to maintain current levels of violence for the foreseeable future:

> PIRA's organisation is now such that a small number of activists can maintain a disproportionate level of violence. There is a substantial pool of young aspirants nurtured in a climate of violence, eagerly seeking promotion to full gun-toting terrorist status and there is a steady release from the prisons of embittered and dedicated terrorists. (Taylor, 1997: 215)

This predated the hunger strikes with their boost to both IRA recruitment and Sinn Féin electoral advance. In this context it is difficult to accept Moloney's argument that Adams was looking for an alternative to armed struggle from the early 1980s or that change was provoked by the AIA. Such a judgement fails to register the fact that Adams had long been a critic of the militarist mentality within republicanism which looked to armed struggle as the sole lever to force a British withdrawal. The point of violence for Adams was to keep the situation fluid and to prevent what republicans feared most: an internal settlement that would accommodate unionism and the SDLP. Up until the early 1980s, this seemed a distant prospect given the unionist resistance to any form of settlement acceptable to constitutional nationalists. However, the first faltering signs of increased Anglo-Irish cooperation at a political level during Mrs Thatcher's first administration, followed by the deliberations of all the Irish constitutionalist parties at the Forum for a New Ireland in 1983, threatened to change the context in a manner that was harmful to Sinn Féin. As early as the Thatcher/Haughey summit of 1980 with its communiqué acknowledging Britain's 'unique relationship' with Ireland and announcing the creation of joint study groups to consider ways of expressing that uniqueness in 'new institutional structures', an analysis in *Republican News* warned that such talks might presage a British willingness to ignore unionist resistance and work out a deal with Dublin which could extend to either a condominium or even a new confederal Ireland (Dowling, 1981). Although republicans rejected all such possibilities because some form of northern state would continue to exist, they could clearly anticipate that either of these developments would have been popular with the majority of northern Catholics – which the AIA was to be.

The call for a pan-nationalist front did *not* anticipate the dynamics of the peace process in the 1990s. Its aim was to prevent cross-border unity of constitutional nationalists and thus avoid Adams' nightmare scenario of republican political isolation which the AIA was designed to achieve. To argue, as Moloney does, that as '1986 dawned much of the groundwork of the peace process had been done' (2002: 245) is to strain the available evidence considerably. It makes the assumption that the undoubted priority attached by Father Reid to ending violence was one shared equally by his IRA interlocutor. Moloney makes much of a letter sent by Adams to the British Secretary of State for Northern Ireland, Tom King, towards the end of 1986 or early 1987, in which he posed six questions. These included the nature of the British government's interest in Ireland; its attitude to self-determination; whether it would act to persuade unionists of the virtues of self-determination and give public declaration of its intention to withdraw from Ireland along with a date for the completion of the process.

As Moloney admits the questions did not depart from past republican demands (2002: 250). Seeking to talk to the British, while continuing the armed campaign, was something that the previous leadership of the IRA had attempted in 1976 and owed nothing to the AIA. On 21 July the IRA had blown up the car of the British Ambassador to the Irish Republic, killing the Ambassador, Christopher Ewart Biggs and Judith Cooke, private secretary to the Permanent Under-Secretary of the NIO. Despite this, two months later three members of the 'IRA leadership' gave an extensive interview to the journalist Vincent Browne in which they declared 'We want to keep talking with the British' (Provisional IRA Interview, 1976).

Republicans had a history of episodic contacts with representatives of the British state as part of their collective memory. It served to convince them that, for all the anathemas of the British tabloid press, the British would negotiate a satisfactory peace settlement with them. What this settlement would ideally involve, certainly, would have been nothing like either the AIA or the subsequent peace process. The important element of continuity in Provisional calculations has been downplayed. The fact that

Adams opened up a line of communication with King should not therefore be seen as a radical innovation which kick-starts the peace process.

Educating the British

Nevertheless, from this perspective the AIA did have a significant effect
on Provisional calculations. For Thatcher, at Hillsborough, had done
precisely what had been anticipated as a possibility in 1981: she had been
prepared to risk and then to withstand a torrent of unionist opposition.
This aspect of the AIA was noted by one of Sinn Féin's main allies in
British politics, the Labour MP, Clare Short: 'My optimistic scenario is
that this deal, and its ultimate failure, will make it easier to bring about a
shift in British public and parliamentary opinion. You know – "We tried
and that failed and the Unionists are so intransigent and it really is time
that we moved further more rapidly and extricate ourselves"' (Short,
1986: 23–4).

Adams referred to the 'educational effects' of the AIA on loyalists and
welcomed the signs of divisions in loyalist ranks over how to effectively
oppose it. Like Short he also saw loyalist resistance as deepening the division between British and unionist opinion: 'the British public watched
loyalist opposition to what very many people see as a very mediocre
treaty. Their response and behaviour alerted many people to the fascist
nature of loyalism' (Patterson, 1989: 183).

The AIA, precisely because of the evidence it provided of the British
state's willingness to ignore unionist interests, challenged a traditional
element of republican analysis: that the British presence reflected its own
'selfish' interests both economic and strategic rather than the interests of
any section of the Irish population . However, by the 1980s the extent to
which Northern Ireland was a drain on the British Exchequer meant Sinn
Féin leaders were reduced to pleading Britain's supposed strategic interest
in partition. The only remaining shred of plausibility for this claim lay in
the occasional reference by Conservative politicians to the danger of
Ireland becoming a 'Cuban' threat on the western fringe of Europe. This
might have gained traction from the party's earlier leftist phase but by
1986 Adams could tell a journalist that socialism was not on the agenda:
'What's on the agenda now is an end to partition. You won't even get near
socialism until you have national independence' (Patterson, 1989: 185).
The objective of creating a broad nationalist front around the issue of self-
determination inevitably meant republicans junking the language of class
struggle. If such an alliance was constructed then Adams admitted that
republicans would not be the hegemonic force within it and by implication the attainment of Irish unity would take place on terms favourable to
'conservative forces' north and south. This meant *de facto* the creation of

the old pan-nationalist Sinn Féin alliance which had negotiated the Treaty in 1921 and which had subsequently fractured. Such an alliance, while hostile to unionism, had no quarrel with Ireland's existing economic system or its pattern of external relations. The implication of republicans' strategic direction by the mid-1980s was that there was no fundamental British interest in maintaining the link with Northern Ireland and that the main obstacle to unity was in fact the unionist population. Given the time to reflect on these issues in prison, Danny Morrison was prepared to admit that one of the 'realities' of the conflict was that the British did not want to be seen to capitulate to armed struggle (Morrison, 1999: 235). In other words, the obstacle to talks was the continuation of armed struggle but the problem remained that if the IRA stopped 'there would be no longer an overt conflict and therefore a less pressing need for a "solution"' (1999: 177). This was the republican peace dilemma with which the AIA intersected.

The fury of the unionist reaction to the AIA and its apparent lack of influence on Thatcher allowed John Hume to argue that the Agreement was a watershed in Anglo-Irish relations in that it had demonstrated that Britain was now neutral on the Union with Northern Ireland.

However, the Agreement had another important implication for Hume and the SDLP: it strengthened a pre-existing tendency to look to the Irish government to press the British for a radical new initiative on a basis that transcended Northern Ireland. By consolidating the position of the SDLP as the predominant force in Northern nationalism, the AIA had also opened up the possibility that republicanism might have to reconcile itself to becoming part of this initiative if it was not to be condemned to the bleak prospect of fruitless' armed struggle'. Hume was encouraged by an interview that Adams gave to the Dublin magazine *Hot Press* in December 1987 in which he recognised that there could be no military solution to the conflict and that he would be prepared to consider an alternative 'unarmed struggle' to attain Irish independence:

> The difficulty is that no one had outlined a scenario by which unarmed struggle would achieve Irish independence and peace ... most of my discussions, and most of my statements are aimed at opening up a dialogue to seek an end to the causes of violence. (Hennessey, 2000: 39)

Adams' admission that there could be no military solution and his talk of dialogue encouraged Hume to enter into discussions with Sinn Fein implying that they would both be centrally involved in any future negotiations involving Dublin, London and the unionists. This was of course exactly the opposite scenario to the one envisaged by Thatcher who had seen the Agreement as part of a process of the marginalisation and defeat of republicanism. Perhaps this was the most unintended consequence of the Agreement: that something designed to shore up and defend constitutional nationalism from republican challenge would instead see a gradual osmosis between the two dominant currents of northern nationalism.

But whatever Hume's calculations, what lay at the heart of republican strategic debate in the late 1980s was not an emerging peace process provoked by the AIA but a recalibration of the relationship between violence and politics. From this perspective while violence might not force a Vietnam-style withdrawal, it was essential to 'persuade' Britain to include republicans in the all-party talks which lay at the core of the Reid and Adams proposals. These were not seen by republicans as an alternative to violence but the result of the continuation of armed struggle after which a ceasefire would be called on terms favourable to them. From this perspective the relationship between the two poles of the 'armalite and ballot box' strategy needs exploration.

Armed struggle and politics

Rogelio Alonso has pointed out what he sees as the contradictions in standard republican narratives of the origins of the peace process. He counterposes two conflicting statements made in the same interview by Danny Morrison as an example of this. In one Morrison claimed that down to 1984 he had believed that Sinn Féin could overtake the SDLP but 'I began to realise around about 1984 that it could not be done while the armed struggle continued. I believe that others in the leadership were of the same opinion' (Alonso, 2007: 120). Later Morrison says that with the IRA's successful importation of large amounts of weaponry and explosives from Libya he had expected a qualitative leap in the effectiveness of the campaign in the late 1980s but when this did not occur, he began to reconsider the utility of armed struggle (Alonso, 2007:139). Alonso sees the contradiction between these two statements as residing in fact that Morrison was aware of the ineffectiveness of the dual strategy of violence and politics as early as 1984. However, registering that armed struggle put a limit on the electoral ambitions of Sinn Féin was not the same thing as admitting to the ineffectiveness of the dual strategy. Even if Sinn Féin had become the largest nationalist party in Northern Ireland it would remain a minority in electoral terms and its electoral mandate in the Republic remained marginal. Violence seemed the most formidable lever it possessed in influencing British policy.

The debates which developed in the movement in the early and mid-1980s over the policy of abstentionism in elections for the Dáil, have been reread by Moloney and others as a dress rehearsal for later debates during the peace process which eventually led to the formation of the Real IRA in 1997. This is a prime example of reading history backwards. At the time the proponents of the traditional position predicted that taking seats in the Dáil was a precursor to the constitutionalisation of the Provisionals who would follow the paths of Fianna Fáil and the Workers' Party. But if Adams was following the footsteps of Cathal Goulding, Chief of Staff of the IRA in the 1960s, it is important to realise that for Goulding political development was seen as a supplement to, not a replacement of, armed struggle (Hanley and Millar, 2009). If we accept Moloney's analysis it is necessary to view Adams and his closest allies as arch-manipulators of a gullible movement who lied about their true intentions behind a smokescreen of orthodox pieties about the 'cutting edge' of armed struggle. The problem about such an approach is that it cannot be subject to the essential test of any historical hypothesis – it is impervious to contrary evidence. As a 'secret' strategy its existence can only be inferred by what subsequently happened. It cannot be disproved by pointing to the counter-evidence of intensifying violence and very public commitments to the necessity of armed struggle – if only because Moloney argues that these were necessary concessions to prevent a split while Adams was accumulating support for his deeply laid peace strategy.

As Martyn Frampton has pointed out there was little in the way of ideological revisionism within the Adams-McGuinness leadership either before and or after the AIA intimating an incipient peace process. In 1986 Adams claimed he would 'prefer a situation where armed struggle was unnecessary' but that unfortunately 'in the six counties armed struggle is a terrible but necessary form of resistance' (Frampton, 2009: 63). Even more telling is the observation of Tom Hartley, then General Secretary of Sinn Féin, at an internal conference of the party in 1988 where he commented that the continuation of IRA violence was necessary to 'keep the pot boiling' (Frampton, 2009: 64).

That there were disputes over the relationship of armed struggle to politics throughout the 1980s is undeniable. The consolidation of the SDLP's position in the aftermath of the AIA inevitably raised republican fears of marginalisation and a recognition that IRA 'mistakes', particularly those that killed Catholics, would lose Sinn Fein votes. Tensions between those whose central activity was to organise and carry out the campaign and those who straddled the politico-military realms were inevitable. At the core was a debate between those concerned that political development would restrict the IRA's campaign and those concerned that some IRA actions could risk support for Sinn Féin in the broader Catholic community. A leading IRA man, Brendan Hughes, talked revealingly of the tensions as he experienced them on release from prison in 1986:

> I saw myself as a soldier and not a politician ... By and large I saw my strengths [as being] in the Army and I was pretty well accepted throughout the whole of Ireland with IRA volunteers. There were places...I could go and sit down with IRA volunteers where Gerry could not go because some people believed that Gerry was not really a soldier, that he was more of a politician. (Moloney, 2010: 263)

But as Hughes makes clear, although a 'soldier', he was also a close ally of Adams and strongly supported his strategy. Involvement in the military campaign did not inevitably mean a suspicion of politics and those like Adams who promoted it as long as they made it clear that ultimately they did not conceive politics as a replacement of violence. As Adams explained in 1990, while he was 'intellectually and emotionally' for a purely political struggle, 'the hard republican reality' was that this was impossible: 'there is going to be an armed struggle but what sort of armed struggle?' (Hearst, 1990). This question of the type of armed struggle raises two issues which are commonly seen as indicating the contradictions at the heart of the dual strategy: the criticisms by Adams and other members of Sinn Féin of specific IRA actions and the launching of the republican 'peace strategy' in 1987.

The criticism of operations that threatened to alienate the 'softer' sections of Sinn Féin electoral support was not new. In his address to the 1983 *Ard Fheis* Adams had stated that 'revolutionary force must be controlled and disciplined so that it is clearly seen as a symbol of our people's resistance' (Patterson, 1989: 177). The disappointing performance in the 1984 European election was also put down in part to the fact that some voters could not stomach 'some aspects of IRA operations'. There was clearly a contradiction between electioneering and violence but it did not contain within itself the seeds of the peace process. It was in the terms of Mao Tse-Tung's famous essay, a 'non-antagonistic' contradiction which required management to avoid it becoming 'antagonistic' (Mao Tse-Tung, 1968: 70). One way in which it could deepen divisions within the movement was over competing demands for resources. However in 1985 and 1986 Colonel Gaddafi resolved this potential conflict by gifting the IRA with more weaponry and explosives than they had the capacity to use. For Moloney the Libyan weapons complicated significantly Adams' secret strategy:

> Gerry Adams and the small group of advisers around him had, with one hand, approved an ambitious plan to end the IRA's war while, with the other, and in concert with the hardliners on the Army Council, given the go-ahead to import hundreds of tonnes of modern weaponry which they planned to use to launch a Vietnam War Tet-style offensive designed to sicken British public opinion and stimulate withdrawal sentiment. (Moloney, 2010: 262)

That any intensification of the IRA campaign would create problems for widening Sinn Féin's electoral support was inevitable. Apart from the disastrous attack on the Enniskillen Remembrance Day commemoration in 1987, there were other 'mistakes' which gave Adams frequent occasion for hand-wringing and public pleading with the IRA to be 'careful and careful again'. Yet there was little evidence by the beginning of the 1990s – nearly five years after the AIA – that such problems had spurred a re-thinking. Peter Brooke's speech in November 1990 in which he had declared Britain's lack of a 'selfish strategic or economic interest' in Northern Ireland was seen by republicans as symptomatic of a section of the British establishment tiring of its Ulster commitment. At the same time it was believed that this was but one tendency and there were other elements that maintained a traditional position. Only force would shift the balance in the republicans' favour. As David McKittrick, a journalist with good connections to the republican leadership read the situation in 1990, Northern Ireland was far from an end to violence: 'My belief is that we're going out of a political period now. You're now into a military period where it [IRA] goes to the Continent, goes to Britain and tries to create enough havoc there to blow the British out of Ireland' (McKittrick, 1990)

A telling piece of evidence against peace process teleology – and the role of the AIA within it – is the number of deaths from violence. In 1985 it was fifty-nine; by 1986 it had risen to sixty-six and it then shot up to 106 in 1987 and 105 in 1988. Although it dropped after that it did not go below the 1985 level to 1994 – the year of the IRA's first ceasefire. (McKittrick et al., 2004: 1526) The narrative which treats the second half of the 1980s as part of the incipient peace process has to ignore the deci-sion of the army council of the IRA – on which the current leadership of Sinn Féin was well represented – to intensify the armed struggle. The Libyan weapons were to be the basis for a major escalation of Provisional violence. The IRA's attacks were supposed to bring home to the British public and the political class that they would pay a high price if a radical initiative was not taken. The Tet analogy was in some central aspects misleading. The core targets of the Vietnamese Tet attacks were the cities of South Vietnam. The Provisionals 'Tet' was to be an offensive concen-trated in the border counties of Northern Ireland reflecting the increasing difficulties the IRA had in mounting major operations in Belfast and Derry. Still the idea was to administer a shock that would force a funda-mental re-thinking of policy as the twentieth anniversary of the arrival of British troops in Derry and Belfast approached.

One of the central arguments of those trying to persuade Mrs Thatcher to sign the AIA was 'the often overlooked and scandalous fact that the only place in the world where British soldiers' lives were being

lost was in the United Kingdom' (Lillis and Goodall, 2010: 15). The
Provisonals' 'Tet' tested that argument to destruction. In 1985 two
soldiers had died – in 1988 the number was twenty-two and in 1989 it
was twenty-four (McKittrick et al., 2004: 1526). Thatcher expected the
AIA to deliver significant improvement in anti-terrorist cooperation from
the Republic but was bitterly disappointed. But as Sir Kenneth Bloomfield
(a senior member of the Northern Ireland Office at the time) has pointed
out, RUC-Gardai cooperation had been 'close and friendly' before the
Agreement and the issues which had caused most difficulty – British
requests for direct contact between the British Army and the Irish security
forces and a liberalisation on the strict regulations on overflights by
British military aircraft – were not resolved by the AIA (Bloomfield, 2007:
66).

The struggle over 'peace'

Therefore the AIA did not increase the use of the language of 'peace' in
the late 1980s pointing to the end of the IRA's campaign. The republican
peace strategy was initiated with the publication of a 'Scenario for Peace'
document in 1987. Frampton has argued convincingly that the significance of this document lay not in a revision of republican ideology or
strategy but rather in the manner in which that ideology would be
presented. The aim was to prevent the notion of 'peace' being monopo-
lised by republicanism's enemies: in the words of Mitchell McLaughlin the
aim was to 'reclaim' the language of 'peace' (Frampton, 2009: 59). Rather
than pointing towards the peace process of the 1990s, the peace strategy
was designed to manage the predictably damaging effects of the *planned
escalation of violence*. Although launched in May 1987 it had to be
relaunched in 1989 due to the overwhelming focus of the media in 1987
on the results of the Provisionals' 'Tet' offensive. It was overshadowed by
what one commentator referred to as an 'ugly turn' in Provisional strategy (Cusack, 1987). The IRA logic was to destroy the 'veneer of normalisation' by a range of spectacular attacks which had included an economic
bombing blitz of Belfast; the killing of a lecturer in leather-work and two
RUC men in the grounds of the Magee campus of the University of Ulster
and the failed car-bomb attack on crowds of football supporters attend-
ing Windsor Park ground in Belfast (*Irish Times*, 2 February and 25
March 1987). Even the wiping out of the feared East Tyrone unit of the
IRA at Loughgall was put into this context by an IRA spokesman: 'The
Loughgall attack was part of the IRA's plan to hit areas which have
remained untouched. We want to show that there in no normalisation and
the SAS action proves we are in a war situation' (Walsh, 1987).

'Scenario for Peace' was redolent of Adams' arguments in the mid-

1970s that the greatest danger to republicans was isolation around the armed struggle. Commenting on the brief eruption of the Peace People movement with its call for an end to all violence in 1976, he had warned of the dangers of the peace movement being exploited by Britain: 'The Brits intend to isolate us from the people' (Patterson 1989: 172). The AIA represented a more substantial threat than the Peace People but ironically its unintended effects served to dilute this danger for the Provisionals. The hostile unionist reaction meant that any hope of the achievement of devolution was dashed. Neither the Irish government nor the SDLP would agree to the unionist precondition of a scrapping of the main institutional gains for nationalism which the Agreement provided. Therefore political progress would now be measured in new terms which, while not strictly compatible with the fundamentals of republican ideology, were more congenial to mainstream Irish nationalism than anything on offer since the start of the Troubles. The replacement of FitzGerald's government by one led by Charles Haughey in 1987 was a major fillip for the peace strategy. Haughey was seen by Adams as embodying the 'grudging respect for republicanism' – the tolerance and ambivalence in Irish political culture for the IRA's campaign – as long as it was confined to the six counties. Haughey was later to be lambasted for permitting the extradition of IRA men to the UK and his state denounced as 'neo-colony' but Sinn Féin hoped to work on the residual republican component in Fianna Fáil mentalities to inveigle it into talks. Similarly the 'Stoop-Down-Low Party' had, under Hume and Mallon, adopted a distinctly 'greener tone' and was prepared to declare that it had 'no ideological commitment to devolution'. In its 1988 talks with Sinn Féin the SDLP agreed that an 'internal Six County settlement is no solution ... the real question is how do we end the British presence in Northern Ireland' (Patterson, 1997: 209).

Conclusion

If one aim of the AIA was to isolate and marginalise republicanism then it failed almost as much as Mrs Thatcher's hopes for improved cross-border security cooperation which most key British players were later to acknowledge was not delivered on in any significant way (O'Kane, 2007: 85). Apologists for the Agreement may point to the fact of the unanticipated intervention of Libya and the effects of this on the IRA's military capacity. There is something in this argument but the Glover report of 1978 did not envisage any foreseeable end to the IRA's war even without the assistance of Colonel Gadaffi. Glover had also been bitterly critical of the role of the Republic:

The headquarters of the Provisionals is in the Republic. The South also

provides a safe mounting base for cross border operations and secure training areas. PIRA's logistic support flows through the Republic where arms and
ammunition are received from overseas. Terrorists can live there without fear
of extradition for crime committed in the North. In short the Republic
provides many of the facilities of a classic safe haven so essential to any
successful terrorist movement. (Glover Report, 1979)

This was spectacularly confirmed by the Libyan arms shipments, four of
which were landed on the coast of the Republic without problem. The
capture of one of the vessels, the *Eksund*, had nothing whatsoever to do
with intelligence gleaned from the Irish security forces. Increasingly the
IRA campaign focussed on the border counties of Northern Ireland and
cross-border mobility by active service units, essential to it, was largely
unimpeded by the structures agreed at Hillsborough (Patterson, 2010).

Rather than create the basis for a serious cross-border offensive
against the IRA, the AIA altered the structure of political expectations in
a manner that was favourable to republicanism's dual strategy. It removed
any hope of the internal settlement between the unionists and the SDLP
which was Adams' nightmare scenario. There is a direct connection
between the AIA and the seven months of talks between Sinn Féin and the
SDLP in 1988. This might be seen as the start of the process of forging a
settlement based on bringing in the extremes but if so it was contrary to
the desires of all those who had framed the AIA. As far as the evolution
of republican strategy was concerned the Agreement brought not more
than the glimmer of revisionism or of a peace process. That would await
the momentous events of 1989 and the impetus that the collapse of the
Soviet Union gave to the disintegration of the traditional paradigm of
Marxian national liberation struggles.

References

Alonso, R. (2007) *The IRA and Armed Struggle* (Abingdon: Routledge).
Bloomfield, K. (2007) *A Tragedy of Errors: The Government and Misgovernment of
    Northern Ireland* (Liverpool: Liverpool University Press).
Cusack, J. (1987) 'Ugly turn in Provo strategy', *Irish Times*, 25 March.
Dowling, P. (1981) 'Dublin summit opens dangerous option', *An Phoblacht/Republi-
    can News*, 17 January.
English, R. (2003) *Armed Struggle: A History of the IRA* (London: Macmillan).
Frampton, M. (2009) *The Long March: The Political Strategy of Sinn Féin*
    (Basingstoke: Palgrave Macmillan).
Glover Report (1979) 'Future Terrorist Trends', National Archives, FCO 87/976, 15
    May.
Hanley, B. and S. Millar (2009) *The Lost Revolution: The Story of the Official IRA
    and the Workers Party* (Dublin: Penguin Ireland).
Hearst, D. (1990) 'In the shadow of the gun', interview with Gerry Adams, *Guardian*,
    2 February.

Hennessy, T. (2000) *The Northern Ireland Peace Process: Ending the Troubles?* (Dublin: Gill and Macmillan).

Lillis, M and D. Goodall (2010) 'Edging towards peace', *Dublin Review of Books*, 13: Spring, 1–20. Available online at www.drb.ie/more_details/10-02-17/Edging_Towards_Peace.aspx# (accessed 22 March 2011).

McGrattan, C. (2010) *Northern Ireland 1968–2008: The Politics of Entrenchment* (Basingstoke: Palgrave Macmillan).

McKittrick, D. (1990) 'Assessing the current situation', *Fortnight*, September.

McKittrick, D. et al. (2004) *Lost Lives: The Stories of the Men, Women and Children who Died as a Result of the Northern Ireland Troubles* (Edinburgh: Mainstream).

Mao Tse-Tung (1968) 'The correct handling of contradictions among the people' in *Four Essays on Philosophy* (Peking: Foreign Languages Press).

Moloney, E. (2002) *A Secret History of the IRA* (London: Allen Lane, The Penguin Press).

—— (2010) *Voices from the Grave* (London: Faber and Faber).

Morrison, D. (1999) *Then the Walls Came Down: A Prison Journal* (Cork: Mercier Press).

O'Callaghan, S. (1999) *The Informer* (London: Corgi Books).

O'Kane, E. (2007) *Britain, Ireland and Northern Ireland since 1980: The Totality of Relationships* (Abingdon: Routledge).

Patterson, H. (1989) *The Politics of Illusion: Republicanism and Socialism in Modern Ireland* (London: Hutchinson Radius).

—— (1997) *The Politics of Illusion: A Political History of the IRA* (London: Serif).

—— (2010) 'Sectarianism revisited: the Provisional IRA campaign in a border region of Northern Ireland', *Terrorism and Political Violence*, 22: 3, 337–56.

Provisional IRA Interview, Telegram from Dublin Embassy to the Foreign and Commonwealth Office, National Archives, FCO 87/513, 20 September.

Short, C. (1986) 'The beginning of the end? The Anglo-Irish Accord', A Roundtable Discussion, *Marxism Today*, January 1986. Available on line at Amiel and Melburn Trust Archive: www.amielandmelburn.org.uk (accessed 22 March 2011).

Taylor, P. (1997) *Provos: the IRA and Sinn Féin* (London: Bloomsbury).

Walsh, D. (1987) 'History may hold clue to Loughgall', *Irish Times*, 4 April.

8 Loyalists: from killing to common sense

Jonathan Tonge

The AIA provoked the last united unionist and loyalist resistance to the Westminster government. This chapter assesses how, encouraged by successful mobilisation against the Sunningdale Agreement eleven years earlier, loyalists launched a concerted campaign of opposition to a deal they believed drew up the deeds of transfer for the Union. Beyond the immediate post-Agreement unity of opposition, however, lay sharp divisions among unionists and loyalists over the most appropriate means of defiance against a deal which formalised a role for the Irish Republic in the affairs of Northern Ireland. These divisions reflected, first, divergent ideological positions over the extent and nature of conditional loyalty to the Westminster government and the responsibilities of allegiance accruing to UK citizenship; second, political rivalries between the UUP and the DUP and, third, moral issues surrounding the utility of the threat of violence to resist any shift towards Irish 'encroachment' in Northern Ireland. Internal rivalries within unionism and loyalism, allied to the nature of an Agreement impervious to boycott, ensured that the unity of Protestant protest was soon to dissipate.

The chapter analyses the internal tensions within loyalism over the tactics, morals and nature of loyalty and protest, concentrating particularly upon the violent threat to the AIA posed by the paramilitary Ulster Volunteer Force (UVF) and Ulster Defence Association (UDA). Both organisations engaged in armed actions against an Agreement signed by a government whose sovereign claim to Northern Ireland they claimed to defend. Whilst demonstrating the conditionality of their loyalty to Britain's political leaders and engaging in considerable violence, loyalist paramilitaries, via their political associates, were among the first to understand the new realities of political accommodation represented by the AIA. It was within loyalism that the first serious response, in terms of a power-sharing alternative, began to emerge. This new realism, analysed below, eventually paved the way for acceptance of the enshrinement of north-south relationships in the GFA thirteen years later.

Loyalism, pro-British and pro-Ulster 'ultraism'

Although the terms 'loyalism' and 'unionism' are offered interchangeably, loyalism offers a distinctive variant of support for Northern Ireland's position in the United Kingdom. Amid the crisis engulfing Northern Ireland in 1969, loyalism emerged as a working-class form of unionism. The differences are not merely class-related. Loyalism's primary allegiance appears to be to Northern Ireland, rather than the UK state. The repositories of loyalism's fidelity have varied from those held by unionism, which has been defined predominantly by support for the Union of Great Britain and Northern Ireland. Unionism is thus allegiant to a contractual position, the placement of Northern Ireland within the United Kingdom. Whilst usually sharing support for this position, loyalism has flirted with the idea of an independent Northern Ireland, with loyalists criticised for being allegiant only to themselves. Moreover, loyalism emphasises the distinctive characteristics of the 'Ulster people', who tend to be perceived within unionism as 'simply British'. Loyalism's limits of allegiance to UK institutions are more sharply defined than is the case with unionism. Whilst both ideologies share support for the Crown, support for Her Majesty's government at Westminster is more conditional, prompting the labelling of unionists and loyalists as 'Queen's Rebels' (Miller, 1978). Cautious support for the rule of British law and respect (falling far short of veneration) for institutions nonetheless ensures that rebellion against the 'parent state' is unwelcome and exceptional for unionists. For loyalists revolt is also unusual, but the rejection of authority is less ideologically problematic. Rebellion against the law, even possibly violence, can be justified when the always-conditional loyalty of the British state to the Ulster people extends to outright betrayal.

In conceding to the Irish government extensive (if not intensive) consultative rights over future political directions in Northern Ireland, the AIA provided the biggest test yet of the conditional loyalty of the Protestant community and teased out divisions between unionists and loyalists. Ulster Britishness, or traditional unionism, was based upon primary identification of Northern Ireland along a horizontal axis as an essentially ordinary region of the United Kingdom (Todd, 1987) and had already been sorely tested by the 1973 proposals for a Council of Ireland. The Council formed part of the Sunningdale Agreement and contributed heavily to the demise of that deal. The Irish dimension to that agreement constituted a breach of the relationship between the British government and unionists in the view of the majority in Northern Ireland. On an

Ulster-British reading, the position of Northern Ireland as a normal part of a UK State based upon British values was changed. Twelve years later, the role conceded to the Irish government was seemingly even more extensive and subject to no local checks and balances. It was scarcely surprising, therefore, that the AIA was strongly opposed even by that Ulster-British tradition within unionism more closely associated with moderation and respect in terms of its relationship with the governing institutions of the UK than its Ulster loyalist counterpart. As Northern Ireland was placed within an overarching Anglo-Irish axis and subject to the workings of a permanent Inter-Governmental Conference with its own Secretariat, it was difficult to view the region as once outlined by the then British Prime Minister, Margaret Thatcher, now signatory to the Agreement, as 'British as Finchley'.

The Ulster loyalist tradition identified by Todd (1987) was even more enraged by what was described as 'a more crushing end to unionist ascendancy than the suspension of Stormont in 1972' (O'Leary and McGarry, 1996: 227). Such ascendancy had long disappeared for all except the most delusional and working-class loyalists later came to dismiss the notion that they had ever enjoyed ascendancy. At the time of the AIA however, Loyalists were determined to prevent the unwarranted 'interference' of the Irish Republic and the 'betrayal' by the Westminster government in conceding such a widespread role for a 'foreign' government. Given that the AIA promised consultation with the Irish government on political, legal, security and cross-border matters, (i.e. virtually everything) it was clear that the parameters of scope for Irish involvement were hardly constrained.

For Ulster loyalists, the duty to obey laws passed by the Westminster Parliament was dependent upon the proper protection of the sovereign Ulster people (effectively Northern Ireland Protestants in their outlook) by that institution. In the view of Ulster loyalists, an Agreement which afforded a substantial role to a hostile neighbouring state which still lodged an irredentist claim to Northern Ireland was entirely unacceptable. The loyalist interpretation of the deal emphasised that 'Dublin's foot was now in the door', with the binding obligation, produced by an international treaty, upon the British government to produce legislation for Northern Ireland acceptable to another government (Robinson, 1995: 10). Loyalist criticisms were hardly assuaged by the retreat of the British Secretary of State, Tom King, from his position that the Agreement represented the permanent end of the pursuit of Irish reunification by the Dublin government, when the deal clearly said no such thing. The sense of betrayal was not diminished by the profoundly unionist instincts of the then British Prime Minister, nor by awareness that concessions to the Irish government were intended to improve cross-border security and thus help defeat the IRA. Rather, the AIA was seen as a process of gradual West-minster retreat from the Union. In this (erroneous) perspective, loyalists were joined by various journalists and academics (e.g. Fisk, 1975; Kennedy-Pipe 1998).

The Ulster loyalist tradition's guarantees of loyalty to political insti-tutions and laws rested upon both providing adequate defence of North-ern Ireland's position within the UK and protection of the identity of that people. There is a lack of consensus over what constitutes that identity, from the overtly Protestant traditions of fundamentalism or Orangeism, to a much less religious, even secular, urban loyalism. Indeed McAuley (2008) correctly opposes the reductionism of perceptions of Ulster loyal-ism as those of a Protestant people desirous of a Protestant 'homeland'. Nonetheless, what temporarily united Ulster loyalists against the AIA was the perceived threat to their identity from a neighbouring Catholic state which, according to its own unchanged constitution, still perceived Northern Ireland as an 'occupied', illegitimate statelet, whose ultimate future rested in reunification with the rest of the island, within a sover-eign Irish State. That the British government had engaged in bi-national-ism with the Irish Republic meant that it could not be trusted and need not be obeyed. Within the Orange tradition, the sense of Ulster distinc-tiveness was heightened. Amid anger at the bid of the Irish Republic to assert political influence, the executive officer of the Orange Order, George Patton, claimed that he eschewed any Irish identity from the time of the AIA, in favour of Ulster and British associations (Hennessey, 2008).

Moreover, the particularism of the Ulster loyalist identity, in terms of its self-identification as 'The People' (Shirlow and McGovern, 1997) has been translated politically into a desire for local autonomy within the British State. Briefly, this extended beyond that state, with the desire for an independent Northern Ireland supported by the UDA, although many within the organisation did not support this extreme manifestation of Ulster nationalism (Bruce, 1994; Loughlin, 1995). With few takers for independence, an impossible prospect given the desperate state of North-ern Ireland, the UDA rowed back from this policy and the Ulster loyalist tradition is much more commonly associated with support for a devolved, but strongly British, Northern Ireland within the UK. Yet the AIA offered nothing in terms of immediate local autonomy, bypassing the local citi-zenry who saw themselves as the most stalwart defenders of the Union. It was clear that local control of political affairs would only be restored by acceptance of the Irish dimension and seeming dilution of Protestant Britishness, upon which the Ulster loyalist tradition was based.

The Ulster British and Ulster loyalist traditions were thus united in opposing the AIA as a breach of the trust each placed, to differing degrees, in the UK government to uphold the security of Northern

Ireland's position within the UK and to define Northern Ireland as an essentially British country. In the view of these traditions, the AIA represented an eventual threat to the Union and a clear shift in British policy towards joint authority. Moreover, implementation of the deal was perceived not as a rational reward for improved security cooperation from the government of the Irish Republic, but rather as a desire to placate the SDLP's demand for Dublin custodianship of northern nationalist interests (Aughey, 1989; McGrattan, 2010). This aspect particularly antagonised unionists and loyalists across the political spectrum, given that the SDLP had joined Sinn Féin in boycotting the Northern Ireland Assembly established under the 'rolling devolution' experiment begun in 1982. Nationalist abstention now appeared rewarded and the Assembly was wound up within one year of the AIA being implemented.

Given the breach of trust which had occurred, constitutional and extra-constitutional opposition to the Agreement was politically and morally justified in the view of loyalists. Yet, whilst the AIA's Dublin referents were clearly at odds with the desires of the majority of the unionist community, the deal, on any literal interpretation, could not end the Union. Even an academic sympathetic to the unionist cause and critical of aspects of the Agreement, criticised unionists, arguing that they should have 'acknowledged and emphasised the importance of the constitutional guarantee' (of no change in Northern Ireland's position within the UK without majority consent) rather than seeking the impossible of outright destruction of the Agreement (Wilson, 1989: 200). The defeatist discourse and cries of betrayal which characterised unionism and loyalism in the decade following the Agreement offered an unrealistic reading of the deal as a constitutional sell-out. In contrast, the deal was based predominantly upon the need for an element of consultative, not executive, bi-nationalism, which would eventually pave the way towards the parity of esteem for nationalists on which a peace process was based (Finlay, 2001; Gallaher, 2007). Margaret Thatcher's successor, John Major, argued that loyalist reaction was overblown, as the Agreement meant little change (Major, 1999).

Across the political spectrum, republicans were, publicly at least, dismissive of the Agreement's contents, the Sinn Féin President, Gerry Adams, labelling it 'undemocratic in terms of Ireland' and, more curiously, describing it as 'reassurance given to the Protestant ascendancy' (Adams, 1995: 122). Adams argued that the deal was a denial of all-Ireland democracy, 'because now the London government could say not only that the majority of the people in 'the province' as they call it, want the union, they could also say that the Dublin government also supported the loyalist veto' (ibid.). Such republican unhappiness, however, made no impact upon loyalists, as they embarked on their campaign of opposition.

The initial purposefulness of this campaign dissipated, as intra-loyalist differences were soon evident over the appropriate means of opposition, which ranged from demonstration and abstention, through the 'intermediate' threat of armed resistance, to the considerable use of violence. These divisions were to become increasingly manifest as it became clear that the AIA could not be defeated.

The tactics of futility

Protest against the AIA went beyond the constitutional. The responses to the deal highlighted the tensions between the 'constitutional people and the sovereign people', the former supportive of British institutions and laws, the latter seeing the State as residing in the will of the Northern Ireland population (see Aughey, 1997). The sovereign people felt greater justification and less unease in attempting to defy the will of Westminster. Their strategy came closer to a 'by all means necessary' approach to protest than the more modest actions of constitutionalists, yet the division between constitutional and non-constitutional activity was sometimes blurred.

Northern Ireland's loyalists, the sovereign people, took the view that extra-constitutional, even violent, activity paid dividends. The IRA's armed campaign had contributed to the downfall of Stormont in March 1972. Loyalist paramilitaries had been buoyed by their success in bringing down the Sunningdale Agreement in May 1974, via their role in the Ulster Workers Council (UWC). The perception of loyalists was that IRA violence had 'delivered' the AIA to the SDLP, that party and the Irish government enjoying political advancement as a 'trade-off', designed to help dilute a republican armed campaign which had nearly wiped out the British Cabinet one year earlier. The conclusion of loyalists was that if violence introduced the AIA violence might also remove the deal.

Moreover, loyalists were sceptical over whether nationalists or republicans could be adequately challenged within existing arenas. Unionist isolation of Sinn Fein's elected representatives within local council chambers made no impact on the IRA's campaign; in some cases, they found themselves sharing political space with 'politicians' whose 'evening job' was assassination. The 'constitutional people', such as elected UUP representatives, had been entirely outmanoeuvred in the making of the AIA, having failed to foresee, and not been consulted on, the deal. Loyalist suspicion of the DUP leader, Ian Paisley, as offering mainly bluster and rhetoric, was profound. Paisley's attempts to control strikes in 1974 and 1977 had irritated loyalists, whilst there was scepticism over how far he would take extra-constitutional protest.

Yet there was no *guarantee* that loyalist militancy offered by the sovereign people, *or* constitutional protest, could defeat an elite level, intergovernmental deal. A combination of popular support for a protest and paramilitary intimidation led to widespread backing for the strike organised by the UWC. As Bairner (1996: 195) notes in respect of the downfall of Sunningdale, 'this achievement was a coming-of-age for the loyalist paramilitaries', but led them to overplay their hand, calling a preposterous 'constitutional stoppage' in 1977, bereft of tangible, realisable aims and based upon vague demands for a tougher security policy, ironic given that the Secretary of State for Northern Ireland, Roy Mason, was pursuing his avowed policy of crushing the IRA (Tonge, 2002). The loyalist 'coming-of-age' of the early 1970s was followed by 'the fantasies of childhood, particularly the belief that the spirit of the 1974 strike could be invoked at any later moment when the Union was perceived by the UDA and UVF to be in jeopardy' (Bairner, 1996: 195). The 1977 lesson should have provided a guide as to how to avoid futile action in 1985; instead the lesson was not heeded.

Unlike the 1977 stoppage, the protests against the AIA did at least have a defined aim, of defeating the deal. The forces of constitutional unionism, helmed by the UUP leader James Molyneaux and the DUP's Ian Paisley (who was to flirt with quasi-constitutional means) found sufficient unity in opposition to produced a joint unionist election manifesto for the 1987 Westminster election. An immediate offer of some form of devolved power-sharing was rejected by the British government (and would have failed to convince the Irish government). Given the scale of unionist and loyalist opposition to devolved power sharing in 1974, both governments had reason for scepticism concerning the commitment to such an emergency offer. The inter-governmental axis of the AIA, which made boycott virtually impossible given the bypassing of local politicians, insulated its exponents from protests, regardless of opinion poll evidence suggesting that the percentage of unionists and loyalists supporting the Agreement was tiny.

Opponents of the Agreement found themselves politically isolated beyond Northern Ireland. Parliamentary opposition at Westminster beyond unionist MPs was confined to twenty-one Conservative MPs, thus it was evident that another arena of protest would be required. In echoes of the Solemn Covenant of 1912, a petition of protest to the Queen attracted over 500,000 unionist signatures, but made little impact. Within Northern Ireland, a sustained and coherent campaign of opposition from the main Protestant organisation in civil society, the Orange Order, proved impossible, its leadership being still entwined with the unionist political leadership. Indeed the Agreement merely emphasised the 'disorientation of the Orange elite' (Patterson and Kaufmann, 2007: 203). Its leadership rejected all forms of power-sharing as routes out of the AIA and resolved to oppose the deal 'by all lawful means', clinging on to a belief that the withholding of consent would defeat the deal, even after the main unionist parties had realised the impossibility of that ambition (Kaufmann, 2007). The Order's alternatives to the Agreement were an unrealistic federation of the British Isles or the establishment of minor devolved assemblies throughout the UK.

The loyalist campaign of opposition began promisingly enough one week after the Agreement, with over 100,000 protestors assembled outside Belfast City Hall to hear the strident rejections of a united unionist leadership, most graphically articulated in the 'Never, Never, Never' rhetoric of Paisley. The resignation of all fifteen unionist MPs to contest by-elections, supposedly operating as local referenda in which the Irish Foreign Minister, Peter Barry, was listed as a dummy candidate where there was otherwise no opposition, backfired when Newry and Armagh was lost to the SDLP. The total unionist vote, 418,230, fell below the target of half a million votes. A sustained campaign of abstention from local councils and Westminster and the refusal to set or pay rates and rents, whilst well-supported initially, did not shift the British government, nor did a one-day general strike. The actions of local councillors folded under threats of suspension and surcharge.

Pro-state extra-constitutionalism and violence

Between the outright paramilitarism of the UDA and UVF lay a greyer area of semi-constitutionalism accompanied by forms of quasi-paramilitarism, occupied by those whose militancy went beyond advocacy of unequivocally peaceful protest. Within this sector of ambivalence towards physical forms of loyalist resistance to the AIA resided Ulster Clubs, a movement formed just before the AIA primarily to oppose the rerouting of Orange Order parades and whose support was drawn predominantly from an Ulster loyalist tradition which had little regard for Westminster. Outright hostility to 'Lundys', prepared to sell out the Union and whose ranks now startlingly included even Margaret Thatcher, loomed large in this school of thought. Ulster Clubs had a UDA member, John McMichael, on its committee. Given the unpopularity of the AIA, McMichael viewed involvement in Ulster Clubs as a useful means of extending the influence and credibility of the UDA beyond its urban base. The leader of Ulster Clubs, Alan Wright, although stressing his religious credentials and eschewing violence under normal circumstances, indicated that physical force might be justified in the exceptional circumstances which prevailed, whilst the future UUP leader, David Trimble, argued that violence might be 'inescapable' (Dixon, 2001: 7). Other religiously oriented Protestants within Ulster Clubs felt unease with the group's drift towards associations with loyalist paramilitaries. Politically the organisation offered strong Ulster nationalism.

Ulster Resistance's formation in Autumn 1986 heralded a further shift of the anti-Agreement campaign towards quasi-paramilitarism. The sight of Ian Paisley and (the DUP's then Deputy Leader) Peter Robinson, donning military-style red berets was important in giving political cover to a new 'Third Force', an idea first advocated by Paisley in 1981, when he urged the recruitment of an irregular army of Protestants into the security forces. Paisley's advocacy of a 'Third Force', in this case an amalgam of Ulster Resistance and Ulster Clubs (Taylor, 2000) was on the basis of a citizens' army using legally held weapons, prepared to 'defend Ulster' and organise loyalists in a manner reminiscent of James Carson earlier in the twentieth century, but one, which, unlike the UDA and UVF, would not target innocent Catholics. Whilst the large initial gathering of Ulster Resistance suggested that it could become a major force, its collaboration with the UDA and UVF in importing arms meant that it was soon disowned by the DUP 'midwives' present at its birth. Aughey (1989), Cochrane (1997) and Dixon (2004) all indicate that Paisley's influence may have moderated Ulster Resistance, which might otherwise have developed far more of a 'military' role. Its existence, although attracting considerable publicity because of the initial involvement of Paisley, proved little more than a footnote in the antagonism against the AIA.

Many within the DUP preferred to flirt with the idea of armed actions, rather than marry into the cause, to the chagrin of the UDA and UVF leaderships, who were sceptical of the involvement of Paisley and other DUP members from the outset. The arguments of Cochrane and Dixon may thus be correct, less through any DUP control of Ulster Resistance, but rather, that its creation provided a safety valve for those loyalists who wished to demonstrate their militancy in radical form without making a commitment to paramilitarism. Ulster Resistance made clear that it did not seek confrontation with the current forces of the Crown. It offered an outlet for those whose sense of powerlessness was as acute as those who had joined the UVF and UDA, but nonetheless felt some disdain for, and distant from, those who followed that course. The contempt was reciprocated by loyalist paramilitaries when it became clear that Ulster Resistance's DUP connections would not inject new legitimacy into their campaign. The common criticism from the loyalist paramilitaries was that the incendiary language, occasional ambiguity over loyalist violence and description of confrontation as inevitable (common, post-Agreement) of constitutional politicians disappeared when those paramilitaries did indeed take violent action (see Farrington, 2008).

Concurrently, the UDA and UVF stepped up their campaign of violence and sectarian killings of members of the nationalist community, but 'pro-state' terrorism took a new form, with a campaign of intimidation against RUC officers, for their supposed role in implementing the AIA. The paradox of those pledging fidelity to the Crown taking on a section of the 'Crown Forces' (to use republican parlance) appalled the 'constitutional people'. That loyalists were prepared to attack the legitimate force of the state, the RUC, highlighted several viewpoints. First, it indicated that loyalty to the state was highly conditional. Second, loyalists no longer believed Northern Ireland to be 'their' state, having instead become an alien bi-national construct. Third, organisations such as the RUC could only be repositories of community loyalty when they defended the sovereign people. If RUC actions were designed to implement an agreement which harmed that people, the force forfeited the loyalty invested by Protestants.

The activities of loyalist paramilitaries removed the sympathy for the anti-Agreement protestors held by sections of the RUC. These Anti-Agreement police officers were tentatively encouraged by local unionist politicians to make their feelings clear to their Westminster political masters, but the possibility of a rebellion was remote, given robust instruction to obey laws from the RUC command and the lack of prospects of success for any coup (Dixon, 2001). Sympathy for anti-Agreement protests amongst officers was eroded by the actions of the UDA, one of whose leaders boasted of how his organisation was 'taking the police and army on almost hand-to-hand in the streets' (Taylor, 2000: 182).

Violence increased in the aftermath of the Agreement as the pro-state irregulars of paramilitary loyalism terrorised 'their' legal forces, already under extra pressure from a revitalised IRA campaign. Shootings more than doubled from 237 to 674 from 1985 to 1987 and the fifty-one deaths of members of the RUC during this period represented a 30 per cent increase in the preceding two years. RUC injuries, at 622 in 1986, reached their highest peak of the Troubles, forty-seven being sustained during the one day general strike against the Agreement in March that year. During this period, loyalist attacks upon 'their own' police force reached 'epidemic proportions' (Ryder, 1989: 328) in areas previously seen as relatively safe unionist havens, with 120 police families forced to rehouse and an increase in the number applying to leave the force. Ironically, given all this, the AIA failed to deliver many of the improvements in policing or increase the accountability of the security forces in Northern Ireland. As attacks by loyalist paramilitaries upon the RUC subsided, the focus of post-AIA security policy moved towards a phase of collusion between elements of those forces and loyalist paramilitaries, subsequently documented in the enquiries conducted by Sir John Stevens.

Loyalist paramilitaries believed that by increasing the level of violence the deal could be wrecked, but their strategy of ungovernability was one of more obvious benefit to their enemy, the Provisional IRA. Loyalists also had the possible option of bombing the Irish Republic to try to force a retreat from the Agreement. The killing of thirty-three civilians in the Dublin and Monaghan bombings of May 1974, for which responsibility was claimed by the UVF almost two decades later, indicated how loyalists were prepared to use violence to destroy a political agreement. A similar tactic was considered in the aftermath of the AIA, but loyalist paramilitaries preferred a (slightly) more targeted northern strategy of attacking known republican supporters.

By the 1990s, electoral demands and the need to justify the continuing utility of two rival unionist parties were such that post-AIA unity had been displaced. A normal model of intra-unionist electoral competition, evident since the emergence of the DUP in 1971, had been restored. At this point, the Ulster British wing of protest had divided between its integrationist element and those favouring continuing direct rule, without a green tinge, or the return of limited devolution (Loughlin, 2004). The Ulster loyalist tradition was divided (untidily) between constitutionalists and paramilitaries; overt Protestants and secularists and between believers in devolved unionist majority rule and those who accepted the long-term necessity of power-sharing. The DUP's dual approach; brief flirtation with extra-constitutional forces and alliance with the UUP had failed to pay electoral dividends, its vote falling by an average of 6 per cent at the three elections following the AIA.

Beyond the Anglo-Irish Agreement: *Common Sense* and *An End to Drift*

Amid continuing violence, the realisation that the AIA would be difficult to dislodge and that fresh political thinking was required dawned earlier among loyalist paramilitaries than some unionist counterparts. The outworking of this revisionism was the document *Common Sense*, produced by the political advisors to the UDA, the Ulster Political Research Group (UPRG). *Common Sense* was recognition that it was insufficient to oppose the Anglo-Irish Agreement without offering a credible alternative. It moved the UDA's loyalism away from its earlier flirtation with the unworkable idea of an independent Northern Ireland towards its grounding securely within the existing Union, but based upon a revamped political entity which offered power sharing to the nationalist minority. Although the UPRG rejected an 'Irish dimension' the internal proposals in *Common Sense* had much in common with what was to emerge in the GFA thirteen years later. They included devolved legislative government, a set of laws agreed by Protestants and Catholics; a referendum to confirm such agreement; proportional representation to elect political leaders, shared responsibilities within government and assembly committees, based upon proportionality of seats and a bill of rights. *Common Sense* also advocated a fully written constitution.

Common Sense used the language of 'co-determination' (UPRG, 1987: 4) regarding the future of Northern Ireland. Loyalists intended co-determination to mean cross-community determination of internal structures, whereas the 1993 Downing Street Declaration and 1998 GFA went further in facilitating all-Ireland co-determination of constitutional arrangements. Nonetheless, the commitment to inclusive, power-sharing government and the support for the D'Hondt method for the choosing of ministerial portfolios by unionist and nationalist parties was ahead of its time. The document foresaw a Sinn Fein presence in a new Northern Ireland Assembly, but that party's electoral strength was insufficient at the time for ministerial seats to be envisaged, regardless of the political changes required for republican entry into northern state institutional arenas. Moreover, the document insisted that it did not 'deny any section of the community its aspirations. Any group which aspires to a united Ireland, an independent Ulster or any other constitutional change may achieve its objective if it commands a broad consensus of support for change' (UPRG, 1987: 6). Despite this claim, the proposals for a two-thirds majority of those voting in a (Northern Ireland-only) referendum removed any hope of realisation of the long-term constitutional aspirations of the minority for Irish unity. Nonetheless, the document offered internal political advancement for nationalists.

The progressive tone of *Common Sense*, one which advocated internal consociation and political reform, was juxtaposed with a continuing campaign of loyalist violence, one which eclipsed any reception for new loyalist politics. Furthermore, one of the architects of the document, John McMichael, was killed by the IRA in 1987. A combination of revitalised loyalist paramilitarism, diminished racketeering, collusion with the security forces and a 'military' strategy somewhat more targeted at republicans (although the majority of killings remained those of 'civilian' Catholics) characterised activity in the late 1980s and early 1990s. However, by the end of the following decade, *Common Sense*, with an added Irish dimension, was to form the basis of the GFA. The significance of *Common Sense* was apparent. First, it provided a realistic possible route from inter-governmentalism into devolved government, on the basis of local power sharing, for which the AIA provided the carrot (local control) and stick (unregulated Irish input in the absence of local agreement). Second, the proposals indicated that loyalist paramilitaries might contribute more than sectarian killings (and, following the AIA, the targeting of state forces) in the event of movement away from conflict. The tabling of a serious political plan (at that stage still not available from mainstream unionism) boosted the credibility of loyalists and facilitated later input to the drafts of the Downing Street Declaration (O'Kane, 2007) and, post-ceasefire, the GFA.

What *Common Sense* lacked was any acknowledgement of the need for the Dublin government to act as a guarantor of the rights of nationalists. In this respect McGrattan's (2010: 134) heavy criticism of the document (he also criticises its academic backers, such as Bruce (2001)) as a 'stolid internalist settlement' is accurate, although the same can be said for constitutional unionism's alternative. He also correctly highlights that any document released by a group linked to an organisation which has terrorised innocent Catholics for nearly two decades would suffer a major credibility problem. Where McGrattan (2010: 134) is incorrect is to describe *Common Sense* as merely 'majoritarian', given that D'Hondt, coalition government and weighted voting would provide the mutual vetoes associated with consociational forms of government. It was unclear however, how extensive was support within the UDA for the power sharing ideas of *Common Sense*. Although the UDA's 'Inner Council' backed the plan, its applause was deafened by the sound of its own gunfire. As one UDA 'commander' commented, many members 'would have seen that idea [of power-sharing] as surrender and the militarists were dominant' (Spencer, 2008: 57). The proportionality in government ideas of *Common Sense* were a hard sell to some within the UDA, given the IRA's continuing armed campaign (Bruce, 1992; Loughlin, 2004).

Common Sense was a logical document for the UDA to produce. It rowed back from independence to realign the UDA with the broader loyalist community in terms of constitutional preferment: autonomy (i.e. devolved self-government) within the Union was much more popular. Common Sense encouraged loyalist allegiance to a Northern Ireland within the Union, on the basis that it was presided over mainly by a devolved power-sharing government, able to command the loyalty of the majority of people to a far greater degree than the mistrusted Westminster government. The proposals asked a great deal of the minority community, given their lack of support for the northern state, but the UDA calculated (correctly) that a majority of nationalists and even republicans might frontload a stake in the state and equality over the long-term desire for Irish reunification.

Within the UVF, political thinking was less developed relative to the UDA at this stage, although this position would be reversed by the peace process of the 1990s. At the time of the AIA, the Progressive Unionist Party (PUP) was bound by the umbilical cord linking it to its paramilitary parent. Nonetheless, during that year, the party had issued the document, *Sharing Responsibility* (PUP, 1985). This went further than the UDA/UPRG in accepting cross-border activity, provided that it was conducted in a transparent, non-intergovernmental manner. However, the

PUP's proposals were less definitive in terms of political structures in Northern Ireland, offering a tentative suggestion of a system of committees, chaired by unionists, but with nationalist deputies, to assist in the government of the region (Spencer 2008).

Within unionism and mainstream loyalism, the joint UUP-DUP task force set up in 1987 to remove the AIA offered the document, *An End to Drift* (Task Force, 1987). This was more constructive in tone than the protests which preceded the document and arguably laid foundations for subsequent ideological change, by offering to replace abstention and protest with negotiations (McCall, 2006). *An End to Drift* was also tacit recognition that the protests of late 1985 and throughout 1986 had failed. Nonetheless, the document was an amalgamation of contradictions and confusions, failing to chart any coherent way forward for unionism, let alone Northern Ireland society in its entirety. The AIA was equally unforthcoming as to how to move towards inter-communal reconciliation, given its inter-governmental grandstanding. The conclusions of *An End to Drift* nodded, first, in the direction of the full integration of Northern Ireland into the UK, asserting that this option 'continues to attract substantial support in the Unionist community' (Task Force, 1987: 8). The logical derivative of this, that electoral integration should take place, was rejected on the grounds of the need for local representation for local needs and amid the preposterous claim that 'all the principal parties in Britain favour Irish unity' (ibid.), which distorted the true position of the governing Conservative Party.

An End to Drift acknowledged that devolution was a more attainable objective than full integration, but, whilst ruling out a return to straightforward majority rule, gave little indication of the form devolved government should take and failed to provide any specifics over what form of power sharing might be adopted. Finally, in the most frank expression of the conditionality of unionist loyalty to the UK, *An End to Drift* threatened that 'failure to arrive at consensus would leave the unionist leadership no alternative but to seek an entirely new base for Northern Ireland *outside* the present constitutional context' (Task Force, 1987: 9: emphasis in original). The report then insisted that 'membership of the United Kingdom or membership of an Irish Republic are *not* the only options available to the people of Northern Ireland' (ibid.). Thus integration (administrative only), devolution (unspecified in form) and independence were *all* mooted as possibilities, with the supposed cover that it would be unwise to begin negotiations by stating the unionist hand. It was unsurprising that the report was not considered as a serious document by the British government. Its significance lay, first, in highlighting the exhaustion of the protests of unionists and loyalists and, second, in emphasising the lack of clarity of their political alternative.

The Ulster British tradition which dominated the UUP leant towards integrationist solutions under Molyneaux, but the devolutionist wing was far from negligible. A campaign for equal citizenship emerged beyond the UUP as the most staunchly integrationist wing of the constitutional protest, with some associated with the campaign setting up (ironically) Conservative Party branches in Northern Ireland, which eventually gained official recognition from the parent party. The Ulster loyalist tradition favoured strong local devolution, but the only semi-coherent plan came from those close to paramilitaries engaged in a sectarian terror campaign. Ultimately, even Molyneaux and Paisley, having effectively commissioned *An End to Drift*, ignored the document even though it was produced by their party's general secretary and deputy leader respectively. Paisley led the section of loyalism profoundly opposed to full power-sharing, whilst Molyneaux eschewed Ulster nationalism.

The new reality of a permanent inter-governmental axis to political arrangements gradually won curmudgeonly acceptance. Loyalists continued to demand removal of the AIA prior to talks, a pre-condition rejected by the British government, although the temporary suspension of the IGC Secretariat was offered as inducement to negotiation. The 1992 Brooke Talks, examining how devolution might be restored, were facilitated by a hiatus in the secretariat's work. The 1993 Downing Street Declaration contained an important acknowledgement of the unacceptability of aspects of the Irish Republic's constitution and, for loyalists and unionists across the spectrum, the removal of the constitutional claim to the north was a non-negotiable feature of the GFA. Eventually, the Anglo-Irish inter-governmental arrangements were subsumed (not abandoned) within the British-Irish axis which underwrote the 1998 Agreement.

By this point, acceptance of an Irish dimension and full institutional recognition of the minority community extended from the majority of the UUP to loyalist paramilitaries, but with the DUP still resistant. By 2007, even the DUP had abandoned its brand of constitutional uber-loyalism which protested that an Irish dimension hollowed out the Britishness of Northern Ireland, in favour of pragmatic and ring-fenced cooperation with the Dublin government. Loyalist protest against Irish 'interference' appeared confined to the small Traditional Unionist Voice party. Amid a transformed security context, the reworking of Articles 2 and 3 of the Irish Republic's constitution and the lack of an all-Ireland dynamic, as Strand 1 local power-sharing formed the dominant post-GFA political forum, loyalist opposition to an Irish 'dimension' contracted to the point where, twenty-five years after the AIA, it appeared a dated relic of a long-gone era.

Conclusion

At the time of its implementation, the AIA was seen by a majority of unionists and loyalists as the latest addition to the catalogue of attempted betrayals of the Ulster people, following Home Rule and Sunningdale. Resistance to the latest nefarious activity was to be added to a chronicle of Ulster heroism dating back centuries (Graham, 2004). The truth was rather less impressive. The 1985 deal paved the way for a regularisation of Irish influence in the affairs of Northern Ireland, subjected to local accountability amid the devolved power-sharing arrangements established in the 1998 GFA and accepted by most shades of loyalism and unionism following the amendments to the 1998 deal in the 2006 St Andrews Agreement. Given that Irish influence in Northern Ireland was to become routine so quickly, it is tempting to regard the loyalist furore of the mid-1980s as much ado about nothing. The Union was not seriously threatened, but its external relationship with a close neighbour merely renegotiated. This interpretation would be to ignore the backdrop to the AIA, one in which an armed conflict was endemic and seemingly without end, taking place in a polity not recognised by a signatory to the deal and occurring in a part of the UK where unionists had enjoyed unbroken rule for the five previous decades. Given this, it is scarcely surprising that loyalists felt inclined to protest.

More surprising is that it was among the most militant and brutal section of loyalism, its paramilitary component, that the resistance to the AIA was accompanied by the development of an embryonic form of civic unionism, a development undetected amid the stepping up of the armed activities of the UVF and UDA. Devolved power-sharing, proportionality in government, the use of the D'Hondt mechanism for cross-community allocation of ministerial portfolios and functional cooperation with the Irish Republic are all now accepted as routine, yet seemed far off when advocated by a section of loyalism in 1987. The political institutions in which mandatory coalition and proportionality reside are now repositories of local allegiance for most loyalists. A devolved, power-sharing Northern Ireland Executive and Assembly was advocated soon after the AIA, evidence of embryonic new realism amongst loyalists. As such, loyalists could not credibly oppose the proposed introduction of such arrangements when the GFA was offered as a replacement for the offending 1985 deal. Accordingly, the successor to the UPRG, the Ulster Democratic Party, along with the PUP, campaigned strongly for acceptance. Although some loyalist ultras objected, these wild elements, comprising the Loyalist Volunteer Force (LVF) and a rejectionist section of the UDA, were marginalised.

Ultimately, the significance of the AIA lies less in the deal *per se*, but in what it later achieved: (grudging) acceptance of the bi-nationalism of

Northern Ireland and recognition that the Agreement would only ever be replaced by a set of local political institutions fundamentally different than those which had governed the province in the past. As these local institutions grow in strength, so constitutional Ulster loyalism is thriving, but on a reconstituted basis, adopting the civic and inclusive forms tentatively mooted from the late 1980s onwards. Loyalism has not entirely desectarianised and residual symbols of paramilitarism and of a distinctive, exclusivist Protestant-Britishness, in the form of slogans, murals, marches and territorial disputes still exist, but these have diminished and become less threatening. Where loyalism has failed, however, is to turn credible political thinking into major political organisation. The absence of a major working-class political party for loyalists, arising from the conflict, contrasts sharply with developments within republicanism. Devolved power-sharing with republicans became part of the political mainstream and the loyalist idea was absorbed and implemented by those parties which once scorned. However, as the SDLP also discovered on the nationalist side, political architects are not always vote beneficiaries.

References

Adams, G. (1995) *Free Ireland: Towards a Lasting Peace* (Brandon: Dingle).

Aughey, A. (1989) *Under Siege: Ulster Unionism and the Anglo-Irish Agreement* (London: Hurst).

—— (1997) 'The character of Ulster unionism', in P. Shirlow, P and M. McGovern (eds) *Who are 'The People'? Unionism, Protestantism and Loyalism in Northern Ireland* (London: Pluto).

Bairner, A. (1996) 'Paramilitarism', in A. Aughey and D. Morrow (eds), *Northern Ireland Politics* (London: Longman).

Bruce, S. (1992) *The Red Hand: Protestant Paramilitaries in Northern Ireland* (Oxford: Oxford University Press).

—— (1994) *At the Edge of the Union* (Oxford: Oxford University Press).

—— (2001) 'Terrorism and politics: the case of Northern Ireland's loyalist paramilitaries', *Terrorism and Political Violence*, 13: 2, 27–48.

Cochrane, F. (1997) *Unionist Politics and the Politics of Unionism since the Anglo-Irish Agreement* (Cork: Cork University Press).

Dixon, P. (2001) *Northern Ireland: The Politics of War and Peace* (Basingstoke: Palgrave).

Farrington, C. (2008) 'Loyalists and unionists: explaining the internal dynamics of an ethnic group', in A. Edwards and S. Bloomer (eds) *Transforming the Peace Process in Northern Ireland* (Dublin: Irish Academic Press).

Finlay, R. (2001) 'Defeatism and northern Protestant "identity"', *Global Review of Ethnopolitics*, 1: 2, 3–20.

Fisk, R. (1975) *Point of No Return: The Strike Which Broke the British in Ulster* (London: Deutsch).

Gallaher, C. (2007) *After the Peace: Loyalist Paramilitaries in Post-Accord Northern Ireland* (Ithaca: Cornell University Press).

Graham, B. (2004) 'The past in the present: the shaping of identity in loyalist Ulster', *Terrorism and Political Violence*, 16: 3, 483–500.

Hennessey, T. (2008) 'The evolution of Ulster Protestant Identity in the twentieth century', in M. Busteed, F. Neal, and J. Tonge (eds) *Irish Protestant Identities* (Manchester: Manchester University Press).

Kaufmann, E. (2007) *The Orange Order: A Contemporary Northern Irish History* (Oxford: Oxford University Press).

Kennedy-Pipe, C. (1998) *The Origins of the Present Troubles in Northern Ireland* (Harlow: Longman).

Loughlin, J. (1995) *Ulster Unionism and British National Identity since 1885* (London: Pinter).

—— (2004) *The Ulster Question Since 1945* (Basingstoke: Palgrave).

Major, J. (1999) *John Major: The Autobiography* (New York: Harpercollins).

McAuley, J. (2008) 'Commentary on Todd's two traditions in unionist political culture', in C. McGrath and E. O'Malley (eds) *Irish Political Studies Reader* (London: Routledge).

McCall, C. (2006) 'From "long war' to "war of the lilies": "post-conflict" territorial compromise and the return of cultural politics', in M. Cox, A. Guelke and F. Stephen (eds) *A Farewell to Arms? Beyond the Good Friday Agreement* (Manchester: Manchester University Press).

McGrattan, C. (2010) *Northern Ireland 1968–2008: The Politics of Entrenchment* (Basingstoke: Palgrave).

Miller, D. (1978) *Queen's Rebels: Ulster Loyalism in Historical Perspective* (Dublin: Gill and Macmillan).

O'Kane, E. (2007) *Britain, Ireland and Northern Ireland Since 2007: The Totality of Relationships* (London: Routledge).

O'Leary, B. and J. McGarry (1996) *The Politics of Antagonism* (London: Athlone).

Patterson, H. and E. Kaufmann (2007) *Unionism and Orangeism in Northern Ireland since 1945: The Decline of the Loyal Family* (Manchester: Manchester University Press).

Progressive Unionist Party (1985) *Sharing Responsibility* (Belfast: PUP).

Robinson, P. (1995) *The Union Under Fire: United Ireland Framework Revealed* (Belfast: np).

Ryder, C. (1989) *The RUC: A Force Under Fire* (London: Mandarin).

Shirlow, P. and M. McGovern (eds) (1997) *'Who Are "The People"'? Unionism, Protestantism and Loyalism in Northern Ireland* (London: Pluto).

Spencer, G. (2008) *The State of Loyalism in Northern Ireland* (Basingstoke: Palgrave).

Task Force (1987) *An End to Drift* (Belfast: Task Force), available in P. Taylor (2000) *Loyalists* (London: Bloomsbury).

Taylor, P. (2000) *Loyalists* (London: Bloomsbury).

Todd, J. (1987) 'Two traditions in unionist political culture', *Irish Political Studies*, 2: 11, 1–26.

Ulster Political Research Group (1987) *Common Sense* (Belfast: UPRG).

Tonge, J. (2002) *Northern Ireland: Conflict and Change* (London: Pearson).

Wilson, T. (1989) *Ulster: Conflict and Consent* (Oxford: Blackwell).

9 Europe and the Agreement: beyond influence at the margins?

Elizabeth Meehan

What role did Europe, or the EU, play in the 'moment' of the AIA of 1985 and what has been its subsequent influence? (Except when quoting others, the term 'EU' is to cover the whole period of European integration.) Recent treatment of the influence of the EU on British-Irish relations and the ending of conflict in Northern Ireland focuses primarily on the 1998 GFA rather than its predecessor. Alternatively, there is another view that neither European nor international developments are particularly relevant to the reaching of agreement on and within Northern Ireland. Yet, looking back to the 1980s and even earlier, one can find evidence of some connection between Irish and British EU membership, their relations with one another and the development of a joint approach to Northern Ireland.

The ardour of the view that the external world has little to do with developments on the island of Ireland makes it necessary to state my case carefully. In this respect, Oakshott's scepticism of historical transformations is particularly relevant to the points at which the EU enters the picture. That is, it is necessary to 'avoid the false emphasis which springs from being over-impressed by the moment of unmistakable emergence' (Oakeshott, 1962: 13). For this reason, Oakshott's dry-wall metaphor is appropriate to my endeavour here – and, incidentally, pertinent to the island of Ireland where dry-wall enthusiasts note their abundance in the west of Ireland and the twenty-two miles long Mourne Mountain wall in the east of Northern Ireland. However, Oakshott's imagery refers only to the field or quarried stones that make up the face of the two external sides of a dry stone wall and this is not enough. For such a wall to endure, 'hearting stones' and 'through-stones' are also necessary. These stones provide much of a dry stone wall's strength but they are not visible from the outside. 'Hearting stones', packed within the wall, prevent its total collapse as it settles. They also stop the crowning wedges from falling into voids. 'Through-stones' traverse the width of a wall, helping to bind the two faces together.

As part of the invisible 'hearting-stones' or 'through-stones' the EU provided opportunities that stopped the disappearance of wedges from into voids during the talks leading up to the AIA; it helped to shape the foundational context within which the builders could put into place the face stones of the AIA and GFA; and it had a part in bringing into line with the 'visible hand of self-conscious elites' at least some popular consent for a shift from 'the received wisdom of the past' (see Chapter 1, this volume on Ackerman).

The chapter begins with a brief discussion of the case that European and international factors are but tangential to change in Northern Ireland under the development of British Irish relations. Here is shown an explicit connection, at least on the Irish side, between its EU and British/northern policies. The chapter then outlines the significance of EU meetings for 'self-conscious elites' on both sides – political and administrative – in overcoming obstacles to bringing about change at the level of 'high politics' in the form of the AIA. Thereafter, the chapter moves to EU influence in the development of popular consent through the 'low politics' of policy co-operation across borders and communities. The penultimate section goes beyond the two 'moments' of the AIA and GFA by noting the wider context within which they came about; the interdependence of states as exemplified by the EU and recognition of the implications of this for identity, territory and sovereignty. In conclusion, the chapter considers Oakshott's (1962) 'ripe time' theory and reverts to his dry-wall metaphor, together with the 'test of endurance' for 'constitutional moments', discussed in Chapter 1.

The relevance of the EU and connections in Irish European, British and Northern Irish policies

Dixon (2006: 409–26) argues that analyses of international and European influences on Northern Ireland are overstated; moreover, that they serve the propaganda interests of 'pan nationalists'. It is, of course, true that factors making Ireland, Northern Ireland and Great Britain a little like 'a common market within a common market' – free movement of persons and cross-border cooperation – pre-date and are independent of the two states' EU membership (Kennedy, 2000; Meehan, 2000; Hayes, 2005). And, Dixon could, perhaps, find vindication for the historical part of his case from Maurice Hayes' (2005: 139–41) observation that in 1975 'the real potential of EEC membership had not begun to be realised'. On the other hand, Cox's (2006: 436–8) reply to Dixon points to the importance of the development, throughout EU membership, of strategic analyses by the two governments: '[T]he experience of partnership in Europe ... forced Dublin and London together, led them to conclude that their 'previously poisoned relations' had 'contributed to the conflict in Northern Ireland' and that they 'had to work in tandem to ensure that instability in Northern Ireland did not spill over and render Ireland itself ungovernable.' Neither the AIA nor the 1993 Downing Street Joint Declaration could have happened 'without the longer term revolution that had transformed Anglo-Irish relations after Ireland and the UK joined the EEC back in 1972' (ibid.).

Asserting the importance of the EU is not to claim that common EU membership 'caused' – in the positivist sense – the AIA, the Joint Declaration, the 1995 Framework Documents or the 1998 GFA. Indeed, Lillis (in Lillis and Goodall, 2010) links EU importance with circumstance in the securing of the AIA; the AIA is an 'important example, even if *fundamentally circumstantial*, of the *importance of Europe*'. And, in an analysis that takes matters up to the GFA, Gillespie (2006: 323) refers to 'the *pervasive if usually indirect influence* of the European Community' (emphasis added in both cases).

But arguments such as those of Cox are borne out by accounts of the EU's instrumentality to the negotiation of the AIA in saving wedges from falling inwards. Its foundational significance is evident in studies of how EU membership was used to change Ireland's strategy towards the UK government and Northern Ireland and the explicit connections in Irish policy can be identified.

It was in the 1960s that both Ireland and the UK first sought to join the EU. In an extensive and in-depth analysis of 'Irish official discourse' (speeches, documents, etc.) on nationalism and European integration, Hayward (2009) demonstrates a consistent connection in Ireland amongst its EU, British and northern policies from that first attempt at accession. She shows how common accession to the EU brought about a new understanding in Ireland of its relationship with the UK. The previous assumption had been that 'the path to reunification lay in clearer distinction between Britain and Ireland', whereas in 1972 it lay, according to Taoiseach, Mr Lynch, in 'an Ireland in a friendly relationship with Britain; an Ireland a member with Britain of the enlarged European Communities' (quoted in Hayward, 2009: 182).

The new approach was about Ireland's relationship with the UK in the context of its own need for real autonomy and economic independence. This is summed up by the Irish diplomat who delivered the first application from his subsequent vantage point as a Commission official. Looking back in 1985 to the 1960s, Eamonn Gallagher (1985: 35, quoted by Arthur, 2000: 129) reflected that 'the effects of common United Kingdom and Irish membership of the Community ... are so great that Anglo-Irish relations can hardly usefully be discussed except in that context. This, in my view, is healthy for both partners as it substitutes an agreeably wider embrace for what has been an excessive intimacy'. Dr FitzGerald (2005: 19–31) also notes his longstanding view

> that a normal relationship between Britain and Ireland required the elimina-
> tion of economic inequalities between the two peoples and that this ... could
> not be achieved without two things; Ireland's economic (as well as political
> and cultural) independence and the participation of both Ireland and the
> United Kingdom in the European single market.

As also indicated in Hayward's quote from Lynch, it was thought that moving from distance to friendliness 'could help to overcome differences between north and south'. This, she says, 'was at the heart of negations' that led to the AIA, the 1995 Framework Documents and the GFA (Hayward, 2009: 182). With respect to the EU context of the Northern Ireland dimension of British-Irish relations, Hayward (2009: 56, 60) sets out parallel time lines of key events involving Ireland, Northern Ireland and the EU. The AIA was signed just after the 1984 Irish EU presidency and just as the Single European Act was coming about (see also Fitz-Gerald, 1991: 56–7, 544). The Brooke/Mayhew talks and the Joint Declaration overlapped with the 1992 Maastricht Treaty of Union. The Framework Documents and talks leading to the GFA occurred on either side of the 1996 Irish EU presidency and the Amsterdam Treaty. This reflects something deeper than coincidence. As Hayward (2009: 55) points out, of the five taoisigh involved with these events, three of them – Mr Haughey, Dr FitzGerald and Mr Reynolds – took 'a particular interest in developments in Northern Ireland *and* in the European Union, with significant progress being made in Ireland's policy towards both under their administrations' (emphasis in original). Mr Haughey is often remembered because of the strains he caused in British Irish rela-tions, which had to be salvaged by Dr FitzGerald (1991: 351–2, 408, 412, 428, and 462). But it should not be forgotten that he and Mrs Thatcher had started an 'Anglo-Irish process' and it was he who introduced the subsequently talismanic phrase, 'the totality of relation-ships in these islands'. He and she had agreed to cross-border cooperation and joint studies (Tannam, 1999: 75–7; Arthur, 2000: 177, 183, 209; Gillespie, 2006: 320). Of these, it was, of course, Dr FitzGerald who, with Mrs Thatcher, negotiated and signed the AIA. Gillespie (2006: 329) also notes that 'systematic uses of meetings on the margins of European Councils ... [had been] inaugurated in the mid 70s'. So important were they that they 'deserve a separate study of their own'. It is clear from both sides that they did contribute to the reaching of agreement in 1985.

The EU and 'high politics' among 'self-conscious elites' in the AIA process

The AIA was negotiated by a small team of the two prime ministers, other ministers and senior officials (FitzGerald, 1991: 474; Arthur, 2000: 213; Lillis and Goodall, 2010). At a number of meetings, Dr FitzGerald and Mrs Thatcher discussed issues with only one or two officials present. Officials met frequently in between summits over two years. A former US Ambassador to Ireland, William Shannon (1986: 864, quoted by Arthur, 2000: 214) estimated that, of six meetings between Mrs Thatcher and Dr FitzGerald, four were held on the margins of the European Council. Goodall (in Lillis and Goodall, 2010: 12) suggests that the meetings between the Taoiseach and Prime Minister at EU summits, as well as the two summits at Chequers, 'were key moments in the process'. An explanation for this is given by his counterpart, Michael Lillis.

Lillis argues that, because of tensions arising from the hunger strikes, Mr Haughey's lack of support, when Taoiseach, for sanctions against Argentina during the Falklands crisis, and Mrs Thatcher's own attitudes on Anglo-Irish relations, it was only because of meetings on the margins of European summits that any negotiations at all could take place. These were 'without fanfare of any kind' and, as such, eased Mrs Thatcher's nervousness about 'any publicity which might be interpreted as suggesting she was selling out the Unionists' (in Lillis and Goodall, 2010: 2). 'The negotiation by Dr Garret FitzGerald and Mrs Margaret Thatcher of the Anglo-Irish Agreement of 1985 provided an important example, even if fundamentally circumstantial, of the importance of Europe at a moment of despair in Anglo-Irish relations (ibid.: 1). Moreover, he also suggests that the EU as a meeting place for the two heads of government, in the presence of only one or two senior officials from either side, provided crucial opportunities for settling what came to be known as 'neuralgic' points.

Some of the 'neuralgic' points are discussed by Dr FitzGerald himself (1991: 461, 470, 472, 477, 496, 508, 526, 538, 542, 543, 544, 551, 562, 569, and 601–2; see also, Arthur, 2000: 217, Chapter 9). At meetings around EU summits, numerous matters of misunderstanding or disagreement were discussed, for example: the need to strengthen the SDLP *vis à vis* the republicans; discrimination against and alienation amongst nationalists; the need to think about unionists; the New Ireland Forum (its rationale, report and Mrs Thatcher's reaction to it); the security implications in Ireland of the Dowra case; intimidation and personation in elections in Northern Ireland; Articles 2 and 3 of the Irish Constitution (off the agenda after Mrs Thatcher's response to the report of the New Ireland Forum); Irish involvement in the security processes in Northern Ireland and matters relating to policing, prisons and justice; the proposed International Fund for Ireland (and Mrs Thatcher's reluctance to seek EU funding); and, after it was signed and sealed, unionist reaction to the Agreement.

In addition to the discretion allowed by meetings taking place in the EU context, personal chemistry also played an important part in tackling difficult issues. Both participants and commentators (participants: FitzGerald, 1991: 474; Lillis and Goodall, 2010; commentators: Arthur, 2000; Gillespie, 2006) note that strong personal ties were formed between opposite numbers amongst officials and between Dr FitzGerald and the British Ambassador to Ireland. Dr FitzGerald and his team were touched and impressed by Mrs Thatcher's willingness to continue inter-governmental talks even in the wake of the IRA bombing of the Conservative Party Conference in Brighton on 12 October 1984 (FitzGerald, 1991: 509). Such were these ties that, according to the Secretary to the Office of Taoiseach, Mr Dermot Nally, 'negotiations were unique in the way understandings developed … [E]ventual agreement was not simply a record of hard-won compromises between two opposing sides but a composite accord aimed at achieving an end to which both sides could fundamentally subscribe' (Ivory, 1999, quoted by Arthur, 2000: 213, 293).

As events unfolded after the AIA, the EU continued to serve as a meeting place for Irish and British ministers. As Gillespie (2006: 322, drawing on others) notes: 'in recent years no European Council has been complete without a meeting of *taoisigh* and prime ministers about Northern Ireland on the margins'. And, in this period, some EU influence percolated from the 'high politics' of international diplomacy to the 'low politics' of domestic policy.

The EU and cooperation in the 'low politics' of public policy

The 'visible hand of self-conscious elites' (Ackerman, see Chapter 1) is evident in some cross-border policy cooperation that has both EU and inter-governmental features. A report (Progress Report, 1997; see also Gillespie, 2006: 329) by the two governments emerged from the margins of the December 1997 European Council covering some sixteen policy areas of direct potential impact on people's lives, both east-west and north-south. In the meantime – from the late 1980s, as Tannam (1999: 81) points out – an EU influence 'increasingly encroached on the work' of the Anglo-Irish Intergovernmental Conference on cooperation and EU programmes were used to develop the functional agenda of the AIA. This impact arose from structural funding programmes and other initiatives such as the cross-border INTERREG scheme. By 1994, 'the respective development plans in Northern Ireland [then under Direct Rule] and the Republic of Ireland for EU structural funds [had to include] a common chapter or agreed text' (Magennis, 2007: 245). Inter-governmental cooperation – EU-influenced or not – is often criticised for lacking strategy, for being characterised by 'back-to-back' development, rather than joint planning involving relevant citizens (ibid.). The absence of strategic frameworks for north-south cooperation has been identified as a hindrance to grassroots collaboration where, in the case of education for example, 'an extraordinary growth' in educational projects has been 'driven largely by individual idealism and funded by the EU and other overseas sources' (Pollak, 2007: 156; see also Clarke, 2007, on the health sector).

There are also disputes about how deeply rooted grassroots cross-border and cross-community cooperation really is. As Pollak (2007: 165) points out, it is difficult to assess 'the impact of any programme designed to overcome deeply held suspicions ... in the short term: such programmes typically need to be in place for many years before their effects are felt'. It is also difficult to identify the relative weights of the EU's influence compared with the pre- and post-AIA inter- governmental ambitions (Tannam, 1999, 2007). Hence, the importance of Chapter 1's injunction: 'not to put words into the mouth of history by understanding the meaning of events after 1985 as the intended unfolding of the AIA' – or, indeed, of EU programmes.

But with these caveats in mind, it is worth considering 'Track Two diplomacy' which can complement government-to-government contact. Arthur (2000: 239, drawing on Montville, 1986, and others) describes it as 'seek[ing] to promote an environment in a political community, through the education of public opinion, that would make it safer for public opinion to take risks for peace'. But, as he goes on to point out, it was difficult for people to take risks in the midst of the continuing violence between the mid-1980s and mid-1990s. All the literature on grassroots cooperation, be it of the socio-economic or cultural type, points to the seeming logic of cooperation under the auspices of the EU. For example, economic incentives would encourage it and the EU could provide a neutral (neither Irish nor British) framework for it (e.g., Tannam, 1999: 97, 98, 104, 108-9, 123; Tannam, 2007: 111; Cochrane, 2006: 258). Whether or not these logics are obvious in practice is an open question.

Women's groups in Northern Ireland were quick self-consciously to 'catch on' to the EU's principle of partnership in policy-making, even under structural funding programmes, before new sources of support emerged (*Women and Citizenship*, 1995; Hodgett and Meehan, 2003).

And they drew upon European and international developments and networks in making responses to constitutional developments in the 1990s (Hinds 1999). Cochrane (2006: 257–9) suggests that the growth of a 'large array of NGOs ... that focus on peace and conflict resolution and/or community development' was facilitated by the EU Special Support Programme for Peace and Reconciliation (SSPPR), as well as by the US and the British government. Jacques Delors, Commission President when the AIA was signed, was determined to secure the SSPPR as the EU's contribution to the peace process and it engendered unusual cooperation amongst Northern Ireland's MEPs. Acknowledging the indirect, rather than direct, importance of civil society to the peace process, Cochrane argues 'that its role in contributing to progressive social and political change has nevertheless been an important one over the last thirty years' (ibid.: 261). Others corroborate his view. Even at tense times, 'the extent of cooperation between members of opposing parties and members of different communities [was] quite remarkable' (Williamson, Scott and Halfpenny, 2000: 57; see also McCall and Williamson, 2000; McCall, 2006; Adshead and Tonge, 2009: 219). The SSPPR also had an institutional consequence – albeit a short lived one. The socially inclusive nature of its first funding bodies, the District Partnership Boards, was one inspiration behind the Women's Coalition proposal for a Civic Forum which was included in the GFA (Hinds, 1999: 114).

Similarly qualified observations arise from research on cross-border initiatives, also often EU funded. Tannam (1999, 2007) finds sectorally varied patterns as to the relative importance of the AIA, GFA or EU, the latter often of less importance than the other two, and in people's commitment to cross-border cooperation. On the other hand, research also 'shows that the voluntary sector's promotion of cross-border cooperation can make a distinctive contribution to building peace and reconciliation (O'Dowd and McCall, 2007: 145–6; see also Pollak, 2007 and Clarke, 2007). According to O'Dowd and McCall, for some unionist groups 'cross-border links may be a useful detour on the road to improving links with nationalists and republicans in the North'. In general, they suggest: 'such activities ... creat[e] a space in which difference can be explored and mutual interests advanced' – so long as support is forthcoming, in the right form, from the EU and/or the two governments. (Both they and Cochrane, 2006, outline the difficulties that exist for civil society in the funding bureaucracy.)

To conclude this section, it is necessary to say something about parties, now in government, which define themselves as thoroughly rooted in communities; the DUP and Sinn Féin. It is a commonplace that, to their resentment, unionists were excluded from the AIA negotiations, while the SDLP were in contact with the Irish government. Another

commonplace is that the AIA was intended to marginalise Sinn Féin's electoral threat to the SDLP. Something of a gloss on the former emerges from
Dr FitzGerald's (1991: 381, 499, 529, 533, and 563–4) account of the
negotiations where he refers several times to anxiety about the exclusion
of unionists, especially the UUP, and to enquiries to the British team about
this. The experience of cross-border cooperation modified attitudes
amongst members of the parties outside the AIA negotiations. The transcendence of UUP fears (fuelled by SDLP hopes) of an analogy between
'ever closer union' in the EU and 'rolling reunification' on the island of
Ireland has been discussed elsewhere (Meehan, 2009). Tannam (2007:
341–2) argues that, for both the DUP and Sinn Féin, 'the issue of cross-
border cooperation *per se* has become less politicised' – a trend, she says,
that emerged in the 1990s, stimulated by the GFA and EU initiatives from
1999.

The wider context of EU influence – identity, territory and sovereignty

Common EU accession brought about a new approach in Ireland to the
UK and relations between two formally sovereign states. Other adapta-
tions took place in ideas about identity and territory which, along with
reflections on what sovereignty actually means in an interdependent
world, also contributed to the foundations of the AIA and subsequent
'constitutional moments'.

Regarding identity and territory, Hayward (2009) reveals a story that
exemplifies Oakshott's (1983: 94) observation, discussed in Chapter 1,
that: 'The idea of change is a holding together of two apparently opposed
but in fact complementary ideas: that of alteration and that of sameness;
that of difference and that of identity'. She shows that official discourse
in Ireland about the EU is characterised by traditional notions of national
identity, the nation state and the pursuit of national interests. At the same
time, however, the EU has brought into official discourse new elements of
what it means to be Irish and to be republican; it has occasioned notions
such as 'unity in diversity' and 'diversity in unity'; and has introduced
common phrases and images in discourse about European integration and
conflict resolution. And, she argues, 'the framework, narrative and model
of the European Union has been applied in this redefinition of Irish identity regarding Northern Ireland' (Hayward, 2009: 139, 217). A central
element of this has been 'the drawing of a clearer boundary between Irish
identity (culture, traditions, experience) and Irish nationhood (as a territorial, political entity)' (ibid.: 139). Thus, at the time of the AIA, Dr
FitzGerald called for the setting aside of 'historical suspicions', on the one
hand, and 'unrealistic expectations' on the other. The 'North and South
[were] interdependent partners in the vital search for peace and stability'

(Hayward, 2009: 144). By the 1990s, the shift was possibly even more marked – as indicated in Gillespie's (2006: 326) quote from the 1998 memoirs of Fergus Finlay (1998: 182–3), special advisor in 1992–96 to Tanaiste, Mr Dick Spring. The process, 'so far as I was concerned, was never about unity. The process of twenty-five years, and the new process I was being invited into, was about stability and peace' and that for this purpose, 'both governments had to work together'. Moreover, by the time of the GFA which, unlike the AIA, had an east-west dimension, there was also taking place a territorial 'deconstruction' of 'Britishness' reflected in the UK's devolution programme and the crafting by the then Irish Taoiseach, Mr Ahern, of a diplomatic policy that enabled him to welcome the British Irish Council and to increase contact with the Scotland and Wales (Hayward, 2009: 141; Meehan, 2009).

On sovereignty, Arthur (2000: 126, 128-30) and Gillespie (2006: 321) draw attention to the fact that the Irish recognised much earlier than the British the difficulty in the traditional notion of sovereignty in the context of new forms of international linkages in an interdependent world. Arthur notes the discussion in the 1972 White Paper, *The Accession of Ireland to the European Communities*, of a distinction between independence and sovereignty. This distinction (and others) was echoed in the search for words in negotiations leading to the AIA. By the 1980s, some in the UK were beginning to acknowledge the new 'uncertain world' outside the 'comfortable existence of exclusive territorial sovereignty' (Arthur, 2000: 128). As Arthur (2000: 130-1) notes, the then Secretary of State for Northern Ireland, Sir Humphrey Atkins, observed in 1980 that 'we do improve our chances of success by recognizing that the Republic is deeply interested in what happens in Northern Ireland'. British Conservative MEPs welcomed the European Parliament's 1984 Haagerup Report at committee stage (though they abstained at the plenary vote). This Report 'placed the potential solution [to Northern Ireland] within an identity paradigm ... and argued for power sharing and intergovernmental cooperation as the institutional mechanisms that could provide a way forward' (Adshead and Tonge, 2009: 219; see also Arthur, 2000: 198).

Unionist politicians in Northern Ireland were less able or willing in the 1980s to acknowledge interdependence. The two unionist MEPs (and the traditional Irish nationalist, Neil Blaney, Independent Fianna Fáil) voted against the adoption of the Haagerup Report. It, and subsequent SDLP ideas for an EU role in the governance of Northern Ireland, 'fuelled unionist euro-scepticism because of the threat they saw in integration to the sovereignty of the UK' (McCall, 2006: 306). This was 'bolstered by the fact that the 1985 AIA, which brought an infringement of sovereignty directly to the Irish border, had [according to the DUP] traceable Euro-roots' (ibid.: 306, 315 note 20). But the joint UUP/DUP response in 1987 to the AIA, *An End to Drift*, marked 'an important evolution in unionist thinking' and 'signalled a level of strategic and policy flexibility that was a prerequisite for' the negotiation of the GFA (Coakley, 2002: 144; see also Adshead and Tonge, 2009: 219). And, as Lillis (in Lillis and Goodall, 2010: 9) notes of the AIA: 'In the perspective of twenty-five years, it is beyond question that this perceived "betrayal" of the unionists by Mrs Thatcher ... created over time a gradual but profound reappraisal in the first place by the UUP and finally by Dr Paisley's DUP'. (See also McCall (1999) on the interaction of the EU and politics of identity in Northern Ireland – comparable with Hayward's (2009) treatment of the south.)

Unlike those who draw distinctions between sovereignty, independence and autonomy, etc., Mrs Thatcher did not. And, in this respect, her approaches to the EU and Northern Ireland paralleled one another but in the opposite direction to the association in Ireland. Necessity – the depth of the Northern Ireland problem – became the mother of her accepting a role for the Irish government (Shannon, 1986: 861–2). Knowing that joint sovereignty, explicitly stated, was 'not on' for her, Dr FitzGerald (1991: 475, 476–7, 478, 501), considered alternatives such as 'joint responsibility', though there was Irish confidence that 'experienced British officials would appreciate the underlying [joint] dimension' (Lillis in Lillis and Goodall, 2010: 5). Then, at Mr Haughey's suggestion (made in connection with the New Ireland Forum), he used the phrase, 'joint authority'. Dr FitzGerald explained to Mrs Thatcher that he saw joint authority 'as simply a method that the British government might choose to adopt in exercising its sovereignty in order to regulate affairs in one part of the kingdom'. But to her, joint authority and joint sovereignty was a 'distinction without a difference' (Goodall in Lillis and Goodall, 2010: 16; see also Arthur, 2000: 216–7). Goodall also notes the taxing task that fell upon Sir Robert Armstrong and Mr Dermot Nally to find a form of words simultaneously to satisfy Irish (the government and northern nationalists') aspirations and to assuage the concerns of Mrs Thatcher and unionists about the 'derogation of sovereignty'. In the end, Article 2c of the AIA states explicitly that the Agreement is not a 'derogation of sovereignty'. Nor does it refer to 'joint authority' but it authorised 'in practice a significant degree of joint responsibility over 'a significant range of subjects' (Goodall in Lillis and Goodall, 2010: 17–18) and 'in its mechanisms and formulations came as close as one could imagine in practical political terms to achieving a form of Joint Authority' – though, for reasons of diplomacy, no such large claim was made for it (Lillis in Lillis and Goodall, 2010: 7). Tannam (1999: 77) also argues that the AIA was a 'compromise between Irish demands for joint authority and British reluctance to cede sovereignty'.

In the words of former Ambassador William Shannon (1986: 870, quoted by Arthur 2000: 179), 'the two governments ... set in motion a process of change [for which] the way ahead is uncharted. We may have to wait until the end of the century before it finally becomes clear how far Northern Ireland has drifted from its old habits of conflict.' This brings me to my concluding section on time – Oakshott's 'ripe time' and the test of time for 'constitutional moments' discussed in Chapter 1.

Conclusion: ripe time and constitutional moments

Before discussing the AIA and time, it is worth noting how profoundly innovative many contemporary observers saw it – with implications, not only for Britain and Ireland, but also for other disputes over sovereignty and territory (Arthur, 2000: 116, 220, 223). This is exemplified in remarks, quoted in Arthur (2000: 220), by a later British Ambassador to Ireland, Sir Nicholas Fenn, that the AIA 'was one of those rare diplomatic moments which changes the game thereafter'. In Lillis's (in Lillis and Goodall, 2010: 9) view, without the AIA 'the remarkable and historic achievement of Messrs Ahern and Blair on Good Friday, April 10 1998 would have been unthinkable'. His counterpart agrees. From significant joint responsibility over a wide range of subjects 'developed the mutual confidence between the two governments and successive prime ministers of both countries without which it is doubtful whether the subsequent agreements leading to the GFA could ever have come about' (Goodall in Lillis and Goodall, 2010: 18).

Critics of the idea that Europe and the international community contribute to or influence the resolution of conflict in and about Northern Ireland might also find Ambassador Fenn's comment overstated. He, too, might fall foul of a case that elements of the building blocks of current arrangements pre-date the AIA, including the longstanding link in Irish official discourse between EU membership and northern policy. This link was restated – just as talks leading to the AIA were beginning – by Dr FitzGerald who hoped for a 'new and dynamic relationship with both communities in Northern Ireland, with the British government and with our European friends' and in his determination to use his 1984 Irish EU presidency 'to smooth the path of Anglo-Irish rapprochement' (quoted by Hainsworth, 1985: 128, 130). To follow this line might be to contemplate the AIA in the context of the theory of 'ripe-time' (touched upon by Arthur, 2000: 224).

As outlined by Oakshott (1962: 124–33), society is composed of arrangements that are at once 'coherent and incoherent', forming a pattern that 'at the same time intimates a sympathy for what does not fully appear'. Political activity is the exploration of these sympathies or intimations. The process of change cannot be abridged. It can take place only when anomalies in social arrangements press 'convincingly for remedy' and there is a convincing demonstration that the moment is appropriate. It was clear to both Mrs Thatcher and Dr FitzGerald that there was a convincing need for remedy, albeit that their 'takes' on peace, stability and security differed. It also seems plausible that the adaptation of Ireland's notions of identity, territory and sovereignty and the experience of both states of interdependence and integration were part of the intimations of sympathy for what had not fully appeared.

Finally, I turn to the test of future time for the AIA which, according to Ackerman (Chapter 1), should be a ten-year one and, to Shannon (1986: 870), is one of twenty-five years. Kenny (1986: v) set no limit on the time by which we might know the import of the AIA, remarking that '[w]e must wait a long time before we can make a judgement on the merits and demerits of Hillsborough' – as also indicated by Pollak's (2007: 165) comment, noted above, on the length of time needed to heal suspicion and mistrust.

Within four years, Mr Haughey who, with Mrs Thatcher, had begun the Anglo-Irish approach to tackling Northern Ireland but who, in opposition, had rejected the AIA because he did not accept its acknowledgement of British sovereignty over the north, readily reaffirmed in 1989 his government's commitment to all its provisions and agreed to further functional cooperation (Arthur, 2000: 235). Otherwise, Shannon's time scale seems to have been more prescient. Since neither government, as Goodall (in Lillis and Goodall, 2010: 18) puts it, 'walked away from the AIA', the AIA 'remained in force long enough to change the political chemistry in the north and oblige all the political parties – even in the end Sinn Féin – reluctantly and privately to realise that it would not go away unless and until they could jointly agree on a mutually acceptable alternative' – the 'carrots' 'and sticks' as described by Lillis (in Lillis and Goodall, 2010: 10–11) that 'it took two decades for unionists to digest'.

The coming about of a new register of politics in Northern Ireland has been paralleled by a new EU register on the part of the British government and parties in Northern Ireland. All significant post-AIA developments – the Joint Declaration, Framework Documents and the GFA – acknowledge interdependence, not only between the two states and on the island, but also in their common interdependence in the EU. In the words of the Joint Declaration, 'the development of Europe will, of itself, require new approaches to serve interests common to both parts of the island of Ireland and to Ireland and the United Kingdom as partners in the European Union'. Taking the Declaration and the Frameworks together with the 'Delors package' (SSPPR, see above), Arthur (2000: 245) argues that, in combination, they show 'how managing change in the international system had moved from old-fashioned notions about the role of the nation-state and power politics and from spheres of responsibility and spheres of abstention to that of "functional regimes"'. The culmination of this can been seen in what is now Northern Ireland's close engagement with the EU, exemplified in the devolved government's cooperation with Commission President Barroso's equivalent of the 'Delors package' – the task force, on socio-economic sustainability, he initiated in the wake of the St Andrews Agreement (European Commission, 2008).

Finally, the Kenny test of time may be more in keeping with the dry stone wall metaphor – which implies analysis by the historian rather than the contemporary political analyst: a well-constructed dry stone wall ought to last 100–150 years. Should it collapse within five years, this usually stems from poorly inserted hearting and through-stones – in the interests of cheapness and speed. There was no cheap tendering in the AIA. Both governments committed themselves to it and remained so even in difficult circumstances of claims of 'betrayal' of their respective traditions. And the EU and other states, via the International Fund for Ireland, paid substantial sums to help to make conflict resolution work. Thus, the AIA did not fail within five years and, indeed, for twenty-five years served its function in holding up the new face stones of subsequent 'constitutional moments'.

References

Adshead, M. and J. Tonge (2009) *Politics in Ireland: Convergence and Divergence in a Two-Polity Island* (Basingstoke: Palgrave).

Arthur, P. (2000) *Special Relationships: Britain, Ireland and the Northern Ireland Problem* (Belfast: Blackstaff Press).

Clarke, P. (2007) 'Institutional cooperation: the health sector', in J. Coakley and L. O'Dowd (eds) *Crossing the Border: New Relationships Between Northern Ireland and the Republic of Ireland* (Dublin: Irish Academic Press).

Coakley, J. (2002) 'Conclusion: new strains of unionism and nationalism', in J. Coakley (ed.) *Changing Shades of Orange and Green: Refining the Union and the Nation in Contemporary Ireland* (Dublin: University College Dublin Press).

Cochrane, F. (2006) 'Two cheers for the NGOs: building peace from below, in Northern Ireland' in M. Cox, A. Guelke and F. Stephen (eds) *A Farewell to Arms? Beyond the Good Friday Agreement* (Manchester: Manchester University Press).

Cox, M. (2006) 'Rethinking the international and Northern Ireland: a defence', in M. Cox, A. Guelke and F. Stephen (eds) *A Farewell to Arms? Beyond the Good Friday Agreement* (Manchester: Manchester University Press).

Dixon, P. (2006)'Rethinking the international and Northern Ireland: a critique', in M. Cox, A.Guelke and F. Stephen (eds) *A Farewell to Arms? Beyond the Good Friday Agreement* (Manchester: Manchester University Press).

European Commission (2008) *Northern Ireland: Report of the Task Force*. Communication from the Commission. Brussels COM (2008) 186, 7 April.

Finlay, F. (1998) *Snakes and Ladders* (Dublin: New Island Books).

FitzGerald, G. (1991) *All in a Life: An Autobiography* (Dublin: Gill and Macmillan).

—— (2005) 'The normalisation of the British-Irish relationship', in T. Reilly (ed.) *Britain and Ireland: Lives Entwined* (Dublin: British Council Ireland).

Gallagher, E. (1985) 'Anglo-Irish relations in the European Community', *Irish Studies in International Affairs*, 2: 1, 21–35.

Gillespie, P. (2006) 'From Anglo-Irish to British- Irish relations', in M. Cox, A. Guelke and F. Stephen (eds) *A Farewell to Arms? Beyond the Good Friday Agreement* (Manchester: Manchester University Press).

Hainsworth, P. (1985) 'Northern Ireland in the European Community', in M. Keating and B. Jones (eds), *Regions in the European Community* (Oxford: Clarendon Press).

Hayes, M. (2005) 'The crazy knot', in T. Reilly (ed.) *Britain and Ireland: Lives Entwined* (Dublin: British Council Ireland).

Hayward, K. (2009) *Irish Nationalism and European Integration: The Official Redefinition of the Island of Ireland* (Manchester: Manchester University Press).

Hinds, B. (1999) 'Women working for peace in Northern Ireland', in Y. Galligan, E. Ward and R. Wilford (eds) *Contesting Politics: Women in Ireland, North and South* (Boulder, Colorado: Westview Press).

Hodgett, S. and E. Meehan (2003) 'Multilevel Governance in the European Union', in J. Magone (ed.) *Regional Institutions and Governance in the European Union* (Westport: Praeger).

Ivory, G. (1999) 'The Political Parties of the Republic of Ireland and the Northern Ireland Question, 1980–1995, unpublished PhD thesis, University of Wolverhampton.

Kennedy, M. (2000) *Division and Consensus: The Politics of Cross-Border Relations in Ireland, 1925–1969* (Dublin: Institute of Public Administrations).

Kenny, A. (1986) *The Road to Hillsborough: the Shaping of the Anglo-Irish Agreement* (Oxford: Pergamon Press).

Lillis, M. and D. Goodall (2010) 'Edging towards peace', *Dublin Review of Books*, 13: Spring, 1–20. Available online at www.drb.ie/more_details/10-02-17/Edging_Towards_Peace.aspx# (accessed 22 March 2011).

Magennis, E. (2007) 'Public policy cooperation: the 'common chapter – shadow or substance?', in J. Coakley and L. O'Dowd (eds.) *Crossing the Border: New Relationships Between Northern Ireland and the Republic of Ireland* (Dublin: Irish Academic Press).

McCall, C. (1999) *Identity in Northern Ireland: Communities, Politics and Change* (Basingstoke: Macmillan).

—— (2006) 'From "long war" to the "war of the lilies": "post-conflict" territorial compromise and the return of cultural politics', in M. Cox, A. Guelke and F. Stephen (eds) *A Farewell to Arms? Beyond the Good Friday Agreement* (Manchester: Manchester University Press).

McCall, C. and A. Williamson (2000) 'Fledgling European Union social partnership and the Irish border region', *Policy and Politics*, 28: 3, 397–410.

Meehan, E. (2000) *Free Movement between Ireland and the UK* (Dublin: The Policy Institute (Trinity College), Studies in Public Policy 4).

—— (2009) 'From conflict to consensus: the legacy of the Good Friday Agreement. The British-Irish and European contexts', Institute for British Irish Studies Working Paper 83, Dublin: University College Dublin, available at www.ucd.ie/ibis/filestore/wp2009/83_meehan%20rev%201.pdf (accessed 22 March 2011).

Montville, J. (1986) '"Track two diplomacy": the development of non-governmental peace promoting relationships', Draft paper presented at international conference, Irish Peace Institute, Limerick, 28 April–3 May 1986.

Oakshott, M. (1962) *Rationalism in Politics and Other Essays*, London: Methuen.

—— (1983) *On History and Other Essays* (Oxford: Blackwell).

O'Dowd, L. and C. McCall (2007) 'The voluntary sector: promoting peace and cooperation', in J. Coakley and L. O'Dowd (eds) *Crossing the Border: New Relationships Between Northern Ireland and the Republic of Ireland* (Dublin: Irish Academic Press).

Pollak, A. (2007) 'Cooperative projects: the education sector', in J. Coakley and L. O'Dowd (eds) *Crossing the Border: New Relationships Between Northern Ireland and the Republic of Ireland* (Dublin: Irish Academic Press).

Progress Report on Cross-Border Co-operation between Ireland and the United Kingdom: Developing East/West Relations (1997). Issued by the two Governments in the Margins of the European Council meeting, Luxembourg, 12–13 December 1997.

Shannon, W. (1986) 'The Anglo-Irish Agreement', *Foreign Affairs*, 64: 4, 849–70.

Tannam, E. (1999) *Cross-Border Cooperation in the Republic of Ireland and Northern Ireland* (Basingstoke: Macmillan).

—— (2007) 'Public policy: the EU and the Good Friday Agreement', in J. Coakley and L. O'Dowd (eds) *Crossing the Border: New Relationships Between Northern Ireland and the Republic of Ireland* (Dublin: Irish Academic Press).

Williamson, A., D. Scott and P. Halfpenny (2000) 'Rebuilding civil society in Northern Ireland: the community and voluntary sector's contribution to the European Union's Peace and Reconciliation District Partnership Programme', *Policy and Politics*, 28: 1, 49–66.

Women and Citizenship: Power, Participation and Choice (1995), authored by a collective (Belfast: Women's Resource and Development Agency).

10 Locating the Agreement in evolving conflict theory

Gráinne Kelly

When viewed through the rear-view mirror, many conflict theorists would now conceptualise the AIA as one of several failed attempts to resolve a protracted ethnic conflict through an inter-governmental approach, framing it as a 'ripe moment' (Zartman, 2000), misjudged and an exercise in exclusion – an anathema in an era which promotes inclusiveness above all else. In a post-Cold War context, conflict resolution theory and its application has burgeoned, with models of success and failure dissected to identify the combination of ingredients which can be imported and exported to other regions in need. And yet, the 1985 AIA appears to have been largely overlooked by the conflict analysts whose focus tends to fall on stories of success that can be replicated elsewhere, or tales of failure that have other lessons to impart. Perhaps it is the ambiguity of which stool the AIA falls upon – feat or failure – that has led to the general indifference shown to it by the new breed of conflict specialists and the international community at large. In the spirit of this volume's overall objective, this chapter sets out to consider where the AIA is located – or not – within contemporary theories of conflict resolution internationally, and revisits its relevance and significance within the development of the new industry of peace-making and peace-building, created in the past two decades. It seeks to consider how the AIA might be viewed retrospectively by conflict analysts from a range of disciplines, using the lens of the subsequently developed and evolved theories of conflict resolution. In doing so, it aims to shed some light on the question as to whether the 1985 Agreement was a product of its time, a stepping stone on the long road to the 1998 Belfast/GFA or merely an aberrant footnote in the complex history of Northern Ireland.

The study of, and literature on, conflicts and their resolution has proliferated, particularly over the past two decades, to become a self-conscious, self-contained, albeit interdisciplinary field of both theory and practice. This development is hardly surprising given the upsurge in conflicts in the post-colonial context and the mixture of successes, half-hearted attempts and dire failures to resolve them. However, conflict reso-lution – and its cousins, conflict management and transformation – is a remarkably recent concept only gaining significant momentum since the late-1980s. This advancement and expansion of the field in the past two decades reflects the profound global change taking place, with the conclu-sion of the Cold War in 1989 and the dissolution of the Soviet Union two years later. These global shifts in power resulted, by the early 1990s, in a decline in the number of inter-state conflicts and a surge of 'new wars' (Kaldor, 1999). According to Kaldor, these 'new wars' were marked by three key characteristics, namely that the principal issue of conflict is identity not interests, that the protagonists are mainly paramilitaries not armies, and that the victims are mainly civilians and the impact on their lives is brutal. Traditionally, distinctions between international and inter-nal conflicts were clearly drawn and were treated within the literature as dichotomies of inter-state and intra-state with varying characteristics and modes of resolution. This was useful as it served to define the parameters of intervention available to the international institutions, such as the United Nations or the International Court of Justice. But the validity of such a distinction has been eroded since the Cold War, both normatively and in practice, often centering on the moral debates around intervention on internal conflicts on humanitarian grounds (Wallensteen, 2007: 66) and the blurring of boundaries and spheres of influence in an increasingly globalised context.

This proliferation of sub-regional conflicts in the early 1990s was followed by an upsurge in the delivery of negotiated agreements from East Timor to Kosovo to Sierra Leone by the end of the decade. One study put the number of conflicts which resulted in peace agreement between 1989–2000 at twenty-two, including settlements in South Africa, Cambo-dia, Mozambique, El Salvador and, of course, the Belfast Agreement of 1998 (Sollenberg and Wallensteen, 2001). Many of these accords were successful in curtailing the excesses of violence, building relationships between former enemies and providing the opportunity to create a more comprehensive 'peace', through effective implementation. Some failed miserably in the 'outworkings' of their accords, resulting in little change in the status quo or in a further deterioration and escalation of the conflict.

Locating the 1985 Agreement

The 1985 Anglo-Irish Agreement was born into this period of Cold War antagonism; an era of dirty wars in Latin and Central America, of repression in the Soviet spheres, of apartheid South Africa and dictatorships across Asian states. The global division between East and West made any region a potential object of strategic interest, and therefore vulnerable. The Falklands War of 1982 between Thatcher's Britain and Argentina, Israel's invasion and occupation of a large swathe of Lebanon between 1982–88 and the Iran-Iraq War of 1980–88 captured the attention of strategic and international relations specialists. It was essentially a Westphalian world in which deals were made – and expected to be made – between states in grand halls and the recognition or inclusion of civil society in any significant way was yet to take place. The AIA was a product of this time – an internationally recognised treaty between two sovereign states and took the shape and form of a formally negotiated-behind-closed-doors document. It was presented, not as something to be sold to the populace, but as a fait accompli for acceptance by the people, albeit one which set terms by which it could be modified through negotiation. In this sense, it conformed to all the mechanisms of international diplomacy in form and substance and was not out of kilter with the tradition of the day. What sets the Agreement apart, however, was that it emerged from a series of exhausted attempts to engage and include the key protagonists in efforts to reach resolution from Sunningdale onwards, rather than an assumption that the inter-state approach was the only appropriate option available.

This upsurge in focus on 'ethnic' conflicts – however defined – following the Cold War and their reframing as 'new wars' within the growing conflict literature in the early 1990s, appeared to have resulted in an invisible boundary line beyond which the new generation of conflict analysts tend not to stray. Although one might argue that there was much to learn from the sporadic attempts by the British and Irish governments to manage the conflict since the early 1970s, the international conflict literature tends to focus its gaze on the initiatives from the 1988 Hume-Adams talks onwards and frames them as part of a new 'process' of peace-making, as if divorced from what preceded it. Darby and Mac Ginty define peace processes as 'persistent peace initiatives involving the main antagonists in a protracted conflict' (2003: 2). Timothy D. Sisk is more verbose, describing it as

> step-by-step reciprocal moves to build confidence, resolve gnarly issues such as disarmament, and carefully define the future through the design of new political institutions. In other terms, a peace process is an intricate dance of steps – choreographed by third-party mediators – among parties in conflict that help to gradually exchange war for peace (2001: 787).

No such peace process could be said to have existed prior to the AIA. Indeed, one could argue that the Agreement actually pre-dates the modern peace process formula with which we have become habituated and that it came too early to be seen as a new type of 'peace-making' model. It does not appear, therefore, to find a comfortable or accessible place to sit within the developing conflict resolution literature, with its emphasis on defined phases and characteristics, such as ripeness and inclusiveness, both of which concepts I will return to later. This is borne out by the scant attention paid to the Agreement in subsequent commentary, as they leap-frog in their analysis of, and comparisons between, the Sunningdale Agreement of 1973 to the Belfast Agreement twenty-five years later, comparing and contrasting their content and their passage towards accord (Wolff, 2001; Horowitz, 2002). Interestingly, both in core issues addressed and negotiation format, the Sunningdale Agreement conforms much more closely to the 'ideal' peace process described in contemporary literature than attempts twelve years later, and although it failed at endorsement and implementation phase it is perhaps unsurprising that it garners more attention in contemporary literature than the events of 1985.

Applying a retrospective lens

Although it appears that the AIA came a decade too early to be consid-ered by the theorists as a key moment in the development of new conflict resolution mechanisms at the time, it is no less worthy of retrospective consideration using the new insights subsequently gained. The convention developed in recent conflict analysis literature is to view peace processes through a chronological lens – tracking the process through which an agreement is reached, endorsed and finally implemented. In fact, Guelke (2003) identifies at least seven phases of the process, namely: the pre-talks phase; era of secret talks; the opening of multi-lateral talks; negotiating to a settlement; gaining endorsement; implementing its provisions and the institititionalisation of the new dispensation. Darby and Mac Ginty (2003) concur, noting that the achievement of a peace accord should be viewed as but one in a series of incremental steps within a much more prolonged and complex process of conflict termination. While perhaps unnecessarily schematic and risking simplifying a complex choreography into discrete chucks, this sequencing structure nonetheless has provided the opportunity for further analysis of the key moments which open up during the course of a peace process and its conclusion.

The signing of the 1985 Agreement did not have a neat trajectory through Guelke's seven-phase outlined process and it finally faltered at the phase of endorsement, albeit not as dramatically or comprehensively as Sunningdale. The AIA certainly did not bring an end to political violence in Northern Ireland, nor did it mark the end of antagonism and mutual mistrust between the two main communities. That being said, if it is viewed as part of a staged process in developing new ways of working together and of having a productive, cumulative effect (at least with the benefit of hindsight), the negotiations which led to the Agreement succeeded in addressing one key cog in the machinery – namely the relationship between the British and Irish governments and the institutionalisation of the role of the Irish government in the affairs of Northern Ireland on mutually significant issues. Never again would the relationship between the British and Irish governments become a significant stumbling block in the pursuit of an agreement, and the strengthening and institutionalisation of the working relationships between the two governments would prove significant by the 1990s with the development of the subsequent formal peace process and its outworkings.

Perceptions of 'ripeness'

Concurrently although unconnected with the signing of the Agreement in 1985, an American political scientist I. William Zartman, was proposing an interesting theoretical perspective on conflict dynamics – with an early focus on African experiences – which was to take strong root within conflict resolution literature subsequently (Zartman, 1985). Now known as the 'ripeness theory', Zartman was seeking to understand how conflicts move towards resolution and to provide potential mediators with some indicators that might assist with their timing of intervention. He argued that a conflict is ripe for resolution when it is seen to offer nothing but 'a flat unpleasant terrain stretching into the future' (Zartman, 1985: 268). It is based on the simple proposition that parties only resolve their conflict when they are ready to do so, and it is with the arrival of this elusive 'ripe moment' that 'they grab on to proposals that usually have been in the air for a long time and that only now appear attractive' (Zartman, 2003: 19). The concept of a ripe moment centres on the parties' perception of a mutually hurting stalemate, optimally associated with an impending, past or recently avoided catastrophe. He argues that it is only when the parties find themselves locked into a conflict from which they cannot escalate to victory, and this deadlock is painful to both of them – although not necessarily in equal degree or for the same reasons – that they seek an alternative policy or exit strategy. However, he inserts a caveat: 'Ripeness is only a condition, necessary but not sufficient for the initiation of negotiations. It is not self-fulfilling or self-implementing. It must be seized, either directly by the parties, or, if not, through the persuasion of the mediator' (Zartman, 2003: 20).

The case for viewing the AIA as a 'constitutional moment' has been previously discussed (see Aughey and Gormley-Heenan in this volume).

Considering Zartman's proposition that with a 'ripe moment' comes the opportunity for strategic re-think, how useful is this concept in understanding the motivations of the two governments as they edged, and then dived towards agreement? Were they acting in the face of an identified ripe moment for intervention, or were their actions taken in order to induce some form of future ripeness into the process? Did ripeness exist in 1985, or was it the lack of time for maturation that ultimately weakened the success of the Agreement? Brendan O'Leary's observation quoted in the introduction to this volume takes a pragmatic perspective. He posits that the governments felt: something needs to be done. Here is an option, so let's do something. (1987)

Zartman's use of the terminology of 'ripeness' conjures up images of fruition and an identified opportunity to act. In retrospect, the Agreement reached in 1985 feels more like the product of an exhaustion of ideas, frustration that no acceptable proposals for devolved structures were emerging from the Assembly (Knox and Quirk, 2000: 33) and begrudging recognition that the security-led strategy previously adopted by the British government was patently not working. What was clear was that the heads of both the British and Irish governments were motivated to progress the situation, even if that meant bypassing the positions held by the local power bases – both political and paramilitary. However, if, as Zartman proposes, the mutually hurting stalemate is especially motivated by 'a recent or impending catastrophe' one might argue that the rise of republicanism, both militarily and electorally, in the post-hunger strike period drew both governments towards the negotiating table, first through the Thatcher/Haughey overtures in the early 1980s and the formal negotiations of Thatcher/FitzGerald mid-decade. However, while events may have helped to bring it about, one should not under-estimate the importance of personality and leadership in changing positions on failed policies of the past. It would be difficult to imagine anything similar to the AIA during Charles Haughey's tenure as Taoiseach. FitzGerald's arrival heralded a new strategic and analytical approach and, indeed, a new impatience to seize the opportunity for movement presented. Arthur (2000) presents an alternate perspective on Zartman's concept, viewing the Agreement as the creator of subsequent 'ripeness' through the profound reframing of the political context. This, he argues, provided the framework for the peace process which followed. There are, therefore, at least three positions one might take in relation to the concept of 'ripeness' and the AIA. First, that ripeness did not exist in 1985 – certainly not in the eyes of republicans or unionists – and therefore the Agreement was unsuccessful as neither party was feeling the 'hurt' profoundly enough – or that it was not mutually experienced. Second, that ripeness did exist and it manifested itself in the words and deeds of the two leaders,

Thatcher and FitzGerald, and their insistence that an opportunity for change had arisen and could usefully be seized, before the moment passed. Third, that there were some signs that a maturation of the conflict was occurring and that with some changes in the environment and temperature, future ripeness could be induced and that was the real *modus operandi* of the signatories to the Agreement. As John-Paul Lederach has argued, ripeness is not only 'in the eye of the beholder' but also 'more like a rearview mirror than a windscreen' (2003: 32) making the concept useful only when used in retrospect and weak in its predictive capacity. So, while it is interesting to examine the AIA to assess its ripeness in retrospect, it is unclear how cognisant the negotiating – and non-negotiating – parties were to the ripeness of the moment which was unfolding by the mid-1980s.

Inclusive negotiations

Adrian Guelke (2003) attempts to draw a distinction between international negotiated treaties between states and negotiations taking place within so-called internal conflicts. He suggests that there may be two models of negotiation that can be applied in these contexts, although he recognises the limitations in this argument. '[T]he *realpolitik* model of negotiations is most appropriate to the realm of international relations, the conflict resolution model to that of domestic politics' (2003: 55). In support of this proposition, he argues that the settlement of international disputes through negotiation does not require the parties to abandon their antagonistic relationship whereas, in the domestic context, a negotiated political accord is unlikely to survive if the power dynamics between the parties is not significantly altered. This analysis reflects the shift in thinking within conflict resolution theory, from one which focused on the imperative to settle through legal frameworks and elite negotiations, to a significant emphasis on sustainable working relationships between parties at multi-levels, particularly those bound by history to share the same territory, for better or ill.

It is the recognition of this cheek-by-jowl nature of the 'new wars' which has led to the development of multi-track approaches to negotiation to satisfy the needs of the diverse political and civil society actors. The Belfast Agreement conformed obediently to this formula. Multilateral talks, shuttle negotiations, back-channel discussions, private facilitated dialogues, trainings to improve the parties' capacities to negotiate, all featured in the lead up to the Agreement and assisted in the building of relationships between the key negotiators. As Mac Ginty and Darby put it: 'It was deliberately designed and organised to include those previously on the political margins' (2002: 73). This trend for inclusiveness in conflict resolution appears to blur the distinction between 'high' and 'low' politics, favouring the latter which engages 'diverse groups and individuals to secure their respective interests' as a way of ensuring successful endorsement and implementation (see introductory chapter by Aughey and Gormley-Heenan). Timothy Sisk is more circumspect about the value of inclusion in negotiation processes, recognising that 'it is clear sometimes the table needs to be enlarged to incorporate more negotiators, while other times chairs need to be taken away' (2004: 262). The trick to successful implementation of a peace agreement lies in the tension between these two acts, one which George Mitchell learned only too well in the lead up to the 1998 Agreement.

In 2000, Darby and Mac Ginty proposed five criteria deemed essential for the successful conclusion of a peace accord. Among them was the assertion that 'the key actors are included in the process' (2000: 8). In 2007, Wallensteen confirmed that the general contemporary preference in designing negotiations is for 'a broad agenda and liberal rules of invitation' (2007: 45). While clearly influenced by the language of the New Ireland Forum, the negotiations that led to the AIA were made behind closed doors with a small team of officials. As Lillis recalls, 'The Agreement that eventually emerged was essentially Mrs Thatcher's and Dr. FitzGerald's creation' (Lillis and Goodall, 2010: 3). While conflict analysts might bristle at the idea of such elite decision-making taking place in what has been typically (although not uncontroversially) framed as a domestic conflict, this approach did leave one long-term legacy of note, namely the Unionist conviction that never again could they afford to be left outside of the process. The Mitchell Principles of 1996, which admitted or excluded parties on the basis of compliance, demonstrated that this evolution in thinking was mirrored in Northern Ireland, designed as they were to ensure the most inclusive representation at the tables, albeit with preconditions.

One motivating factor behind this bias towards inclusivity is the gnawing threat of what those outside – in indeed within – the process might do in reaction to an agreement reached and subsequently deemed unacceptable. The concept of 'spoilers', which was introduced in the latter half of the 1990s, is worthy of retrospective consideration and testing against the backdrop of the AIA. In the influential article 'Spoiler problems in peace processes', Stephen J. Stedman (1997) argues that the greatest risk to a peace process comes from both armed and unarmed groups or parties who believe that the outcome of the negotiations do not serve their interests and are intent on 'spoiling' the advances made. He provides a typology of spoilers, with three key points of note. First, under his definition, spoilers exist only when there is a peace process to undermine. As such, they sit in relation to the context of the conflict itself and the actions of others in efforts to resolve the conflict. Second, spoilers can emerge from both inside and outside the peace process. 'Inside' spoilers are those who seek to undermine the process or block the implementation of the agreement reached. 'Outsider' spoilers are those who are excluded – by their own choice or by the decision of others – and their behaviour is relationally determined by their experience. Third, spoilers differ in relation to the type of interests or goals they seek to influence, which he further categorises as limited, greedy and total. While the first two are relatively self-explanatory, greedy spoilers, according to Stedman, are those whose goals expand and contract depending on what they think they can get, based on risk and cost calculations (1997: 11). While this initial formulation of a 'spoiler' has been expanded and critiqued in subsequent literature, both by Stedman and others, the fundamentals remain intact.

When implementing some form of conflict resolution process, it is certainly prudent to be mindful of the potential threats of disruption, obstruction and violence by such spoilers. However, it is equally important that the focus of negotiations does not stray into second guessing who has the potential to spoil before an agreement is even reached, as it will likely result in process paralysis. The signatories of the 1985 Agreement were hardly under any illusion as to the relative positions of the various political parties and any military wings, given all that had preceded it. However, they took a calculated risk as to the possible strength of the reactions and make a judgment on the efficacy of moving the negotiations to completion. In the end, the spoilers were much less ferocious in their reactions than in the aftermath of Sunningdale, at least in the short term. Failure in acceptance of the terms of an agreement and any resurgence of violence cannot be explained through the 'spoiler' lens exclusively. Spoilers arise as a consequence of agreements reached and it is perhaps more helpful to reflect on, and analyse the content and quality of the agreement itself as a means of assessing levels of acceptance from the various protagonists' perspectives.

Third-party intervention

Concurrent with the increasing weight given to the adoption of multi-track approaches to resolving conflicts had come an intensified focus on the role of external intermediaries in the mediation and negotiation of settlement between protagonists. This development has undoubtedly been influenced by the freeing up of foreign policy decision-makers – including the United Nations – in their deliberations on whether, when and how to intervene in intra-state conflicts following the collapse of the Cold War (Regan, 1996: 336). The shift from bi-lateralism to multi-lateralism (where the external mediator is viewed as a key actor in the process) in the resolution of conflict appears complete in the eyes of the international community. Christopher Mitchell reflects that given the complexity of negotiations which are 'subject to many vicissitudes and liable, because of its fragility, to break down frequently and disastrously' that 'a directly negotiated bilateral settlement is [now] something of a rarity' (2003: 77). The standard argument in favour of a third party's intervention is that they offer a less biased perspective than the main protagonists and are unburdened by the hand of history and the expectations of their follow- ers. They come with the promise of offering 'attention, resources and guarantees' (Stedman, 2003: 105). The role of third parties in the lead up to the 1998 Agreement has been well documented (Mallie and McKit- trick, 1996; Mitchell, 1999; Arthur, 2000). In the years preceding and following it, the international dimension weighed heavily on the process and was surprisingly tolerated – nay welcomed – by most of the political leadership, most of the time. This was a marked departure from the 1980s when external referents, in the form of international actors, were much less significant. However, as outlined in Meehan's chapter, it is not valid to argue that the 1980s was a period of disinterest by external parties in comparison to the 1990s which was awash with the influence of the United States and the European Union in particular (Tonge, 2005: 237). While it was the general perception that the US involvement was as supporters of republicanism in the 1980s (and was uninvolved in the lead up to the 1985 Agreement) and cheerleaders for the peace process in the 1990s under Clinton's presidency (and was heavily involved in providing a negotiator to the process), this dichotomy is not so distinct. It was under the Reagan administration that the AIA was to be shored up to the tune of 50 million dollars in its first year of implementation, on the basis that it 'had the potential to address the strong sense of minority alienation in Northern Ireland' (Tonge, 2005: 241).

The intervention of external parties – either invited or imposed – into modern 'peace processes' now appears as an accepted inevitability and a key component in the complex edifice which is constructed (often itself by external parties) to resolve conflicts. It is worth noting, however, that despite alternate perspectives on the success or failure of the AIA, the two governments did manage to reach agreement without the reliance on external parties acting in a mediative role. One might argue that it was the intimacy of the negotiations in 1985 between the British and Irish govern- ments, conducted without intermediaries, which cemented the relation- ships – diplomatic and personal – which proved so valuable in subsequent years. One might further argue that it was the artificial 'distancing' of the parties through the use of mediators moderating the peace process of the 1998 that has resulted in the challenging set of relationships that currently exist among the local political elites, even within the context of a comprehensively devolved Assembly.

The complexity of implementation

As outlined previously (Introduction: Aughey and Gormley-Heenan), one of Ackerman's three criteria by which to assess a constitutional moment is its speed of implementation. Interestingly, despite its rapid growth, the field of conflict resolution has afforded relatively little reflection to this complex post-accord phase of implementation, being 'more practiced than studied' in recent years (Stedman, 2001: 1). Stedman argues that at its most basic level, what has been missing is a clear understanding of the factors that make the difference between successful peace implementation and failure, making the perhaps obvious point that '[T]he greater the difficulty of the environment, the greater the likelihood that peace implementation will fail' (2001: 14). In recognition to the need to understand the crucial implementation phase more clearly, Fen Osler Hampson (1996) offers a number of contemporary factors, based on his analysis of a range of conflicts, which appear pertinent when assessing the prospects of durability of a peace agreement. Granted, the examples of Angola, Cambodia, Cyprus, Namibia and El Salvador from which he draws his analysis are significantly removed from the Northern Ireland context, however, as he was aiming to generalise from these examples, one should assume they have applicability to other contexts. The first is the role of third party interveners in facilitating a resolution to the conflict. He argues that external parties have both a technical and monitoring role in the implementation phase in keeping the parties on track by proffering carrots and wielding sticks and ensuring that the whole process does not derail (1996: 12). As outlined previously, the 1985 Agreement did not have any significant external assistance prior to, or during the negotiation period, although some might argue that the US administration attempted to provide some 'carrots' in the form of financial support to address socio-economic priorities, perhaps in an effort to encourage popular support for an unpopular accord. The second hypothesis that Hampson addresses is the impact of the structural characteristics intrinsic to the conflict processes itself on the success or failure of its implementation, marked by its degree of 'ripeness' at the negotiation phase. This has been previously discussed. The changing dynamics of regional and/or systemic power relations since the late 1980s is the third key factor influencing the degree to which accords are implemented, he proposes. The marked changes to the global political and military balances, which the end of the Cold War heralded, offered the opportunity for new approaches to conflict resolution and have, he argues, been demonstrated in the new role of the international community in resolving conflicts subsequently. The final point relates to the range of issues covered by the peace settlement itself. The dominant literature and practice in conflict resolution since the mid-1990s tends to presuppose a peace agreement which is both comprehensive in actors involved and issues resolved. In 1992, the United Nations Secretary-General, Boutros Ghali, outlined the range of issues which an agreement might address, including

> disarming the previously warring parties and the restoration of order, the custody and possible destruction of weapons, repatriating refugees, advisory and training support for security personnel, monitoring elections, advancing efforts to protect human rights, reforming or strengthening governmental institutions and promoting formal and informal processes of political participation. (1992: 5)

By these standards, it is perhaps unsurprising that the AIA is given little retrospective analysis, limited as it was by the actors involved, the focus of its negotiations and the issues it addressed.

The post-Agreement environment of 1985 certainly did not lend itself to its successful implementation, given the lack of endorsement by both unionist and republicans alike. However, despite this, one cannot dismiss the Agreement as a failure at implementation phase. From the point of view of the British and Irish governments, their ability to hold the line was at least a partial implementation success. It also, as Cillian McGrattan has argued elsewhere, gave northern nationalists a new voice – via the Irish government – in the consideration of public appointments and consultation on public policy, resulting in the SDLP pronouncement after 1985 that it had no ideological commitment to devolution. Unfortunately, the British government was not in a position to play that role for unionism. As far as present conflict-resolution theory goes, with its emphasis on balance and equity both in negotiations and in implementation, the 1985 Agreement seems aberrant, at least in that regard.

Conclusion: the bias of hindsight

In 2001, conflict statisticians Sollenberg and Wallensteen attempted to analyse the reason for the decline in the number of active conflicts recorded at the turn of the twenty-first century and struggled to define a clear trend at work. They made one observation, however: that some of the most significant armed conflicts have a long and violent history and are less susceptible to effective peace-making. They note that 'The degree of complexity [within the conflict dynamics] is a function of not only the age of a conflict but also negative experiences in peacemaking' (2000: 633), noting the Israeli-Palestinian 'Oslo process' of 1993 as a case in point. Over the years, Northern Ireland experienced its fair share of peacemaking efforts, climaxing, although not concluding, with the 1998 Belfast Agreement. How significant were Northern Ireland's prior 'negative experiences' of peace-making in prolonged the duration of the violent conflict?

One might argue that what the AIA lacked in 1985 – and what set it apart from the Agreement reached twelve years later – was inspiration. 'Contemporary peace processes', Mac Ginty and Darby writes 'can be viewed as a cascade of new approaches, borrowing from earlier lessons and mistakes, and lending new experiences to the corpus of knowledge (2002: 167). The 1985 Agreement was reached before this new era, when 'El Salvador was Angola was Northern Ireland was Rwanda' (Stedman, 2003: 105) and the models of peace-making had grown in number and, arguably, complexity. Louis Kriesberg notes: 'Every conflict is unique in some ways, but like some other conflicts in certain ways; determining how a conflict is like and unlike other conflicts helps decide what would be appropriate actions' (2009: 3).

One might ask how different the AIA of 1985 would have looked if the parties involved had had the privilege of the new thinking which would subsequently develop within conflict-resolution theory and the range of international examples from which to draw new frameworks and techniques had been available to the negotiators. Perhaps we already have the answer: it would look like the GFA of 1998. But that would be too simplistic a leap, and the Northern Ireland of the mid-1980s looked significantly changed over a decade later. As John McGarry cautioned: 'One should be careful about exaggerating the effect of parallels. Developments in divided societies, whether of a violent or peaceful kind, are usually influenced by a myriad of exogenous and endogenous factors' (2001: 12).

In the introductory chapter to his book *Nurturing Peace: Why Peace Settlements Succeed or Fail*, Fen Osler Hampson writes, 'Peace agreements sometimes contain the seeds of their own destruction' (1996: 3). When evaluated against the norms of conflict resolution which have subsequently developed, the design of the AIA approach showed glimmers of new thinking: its inter-governmentalism was novel, it set out the conditions for a power-sharing devolved government, it took cognisance of identity issues and the equality agenda, it acknowledged the role of socio-economic development as a contribution to building peace and it sought to win public endorsement through its televised signing and the subsequent rhetoric by the two governments. However, the Agreement was not the game changer that Thatcher and FitzGerald had hoped it would be, and the metaphorical seeds of destruction began to scatter before the ink was dry on this new international treaty. It antagonised a generation of unionists. It, arguably, did little to prevent the continuation of republican or loyalist violence. It failed to stop the electoral rise of Sinn Féin.

What it did succeed in achieving, however, was recognition on the part of the British and Irish governments that failure to act was no longer an option. While the evidence of recent years may highlight the dangers of flawed peace-making attempts, the actions of the two governments sent out a clear message to both unionists and republicans alike: whether this conflict is ripe for resolution or not, we choose to act. In hindsight, the AIA has typically been framed as a key moment in the long-term trajectory towards peace, and the cumulative effect of these efforts is significant, albeit not necessarily all constructive. Reflecting on the Northern Ireland experience, Mac Ginty and Darby wrote: 'A peace process is not like a race, with a guaranteed result at the end. It is more like a sheepdog trial without time limits, when the sheep must be steered through obstacles by whatever means are available. The essential skills are perseverance and ingenuity rather than speed' (2002: 175). While the slow process of implementation of the 1998 Belfast Agreement demonstrates that Northern Ireland may now have perfected its languorous nature, the efforts by the Irish and British governments in the 1980s did demonstrate the existence of at least modest ingenuity, and most definitively exceptional perseverance.

References

Arthur, P. (2000) *Special Relationships: Britain, Ireland and the Northern Ireland Problem* (Belfast: Blackstaff Press).

Boutros-Ghali, B. (1992) An Agenda for Peace. S/24111, Report of the Secretary General, 17 June 1992. Available at www.un.org/Docs/SG/agpeace.html (accessed 22 March 2011).

Darby, J. and R. Mac Ginty (2000) *The Management of Peace Processes* (London: Macmillan).

—— (2003) (eds) *Contemporary Peacemaking* (London: Palgrave Macmillan).

Guelke, A. (2003) 'Negotiations and peace processes' in J. Darby and R. Mac Ginty (eds) *Contemporary Peacemaking* (London: Palgrave Macmillan).

Hampson, Fen Osler (1996) *Nurturing Peace: Why Peace Settlements Succeed or Fail* (Washington DC: USIP Press).

Horowitz, D.L. (2002) 'Explaining the Northern Ireland Agreement: the sources of an unlikely constitutional consensus', *British Journal of Political Science*, 32: 193–220.

Kaldor, M. (1999) *New and Old Wars: Organised Violence in a Global Era* (Cambridge: Polity).

Knox, C. and Quirk, P. (2000) *Peace Building in Northern Ireland, Israel and South Africa* (London: Macmillan).

Kriesberg, L. (2009) 'The evolution of conflict resolution' in J. Bercovitch, V. Kremenyuk, and I.W. Zartman (eds) *The Sage Handbook of Conflict Resolution*, (Thousand Oaks, CA: Sage.).

Lillis, M. and D. Goodall (2010) 'Edging towards peace', *Dublin Review of Books*, 13:

Spring, 1–20. Available online at www.drb.ie/more_details/10-02-17/Edging_Towards_Peace.aspx# (accessed 22 March 2011).

Mallie, E. and D. McKittrick (1996) *The Fight for Peace: The Secret Story Behind the Peace Process* (London: Heinemann).

Mitchell, C. (2003) 'Mediation and the ending of conflicts' in J. Darby and R. Mac Ginty (eds) *Contemporary Peacemaking* (London: Palgrave Macmillan).

Mitchell, G.J. (1999) *Making Peace: The Inside Story of the Making of the Good Friday Agreement* (London: Heinemann).

Mac Ginty, R. and J. Darby (2002) *Guns and Government: The Management of the Northern Ireland Peace Process* (London: Palgrave).

McGarry, J. (2001) *Northern Ireland and the Divided World* (Oxford: Oxford University Press).

O'Leary, B. (1987) 'The Anglo-Irish Agreement: meanings, explanations, results and a defence' in P. Teague (ed.) *Beyond the Rhetoric: Politics, the Economy, and Social Policy in Northern Ireland* (London: Lawrence and Wishart).

O'Leary, B. and J. McGarry (1997) *The Politics of Antagonism: Understanding Northern Ireland* (London: Athlone Press).

Regan, P.M. (1996) 'Conditions of successful third-party intervention in inter-state conflicts', *Journal of Conflict Resolution*, 40, 336–59.

Sisk, T.D. (2001) 'Democratization and peacebuilding' in Chester A. Crocker, Fen Osler Hampson and Pamela Aall (eds) *Turbulent Peace* (Washington, DC: United States Institute of Peace).

Sisk. T.D. (2004) 'Peacemaking in civil wars: obstacles, options and opportunities' in U. Schneckener and S. Wolff (eds) *Managing and Settling Ethnic Conflicts: Perspectives on Successes and Failures in Europe, Africa, and Asia* (London: Hurst & Company).

Stedman, S.J. (1997) 'Spoiler problems in peace processes', *International Security*, 22: 2, 5–53.

—— (2001) *Implementing Peace Agreements in Civil Wars: Lessons and Recommendations for Policymakers* (New York: International Peace Academy).

—— (2003) 'Peace processes and the challenges of violence' in J. Darby and R. Mac Ginty (eds) *Contemporary Peacemaking* (London: Palgrave Macmillan).

Sollenberg, M. and P. Wallensteen (2001) 'Armed conflict 1989–1998', *Journal of Peace Research*, 36: 5, 593–606.

—— (2001) 'Armed conflict 1989–2000', *Journal of Peace Research*, 38: 5, 629–44.

Tonge, J. (2005) *The New Northern Irish Politics?* (London: Palgrave Macmillan).

Touval, S. and I.W. Zartman (eds) (2005), *International Mediation in Theory and Practice* (Boulder, CO: Westview).

Wallensteen, P. (2007). *Understanding Conflict Resolution*, 2nd edn (London: Sage).

Wolff, S. (2001) 'Context and content: Sunningdale and Belfast compared' in R. Wilford, (ed.) *Aspects of the Belfast Agreement* (Oxford: Oxford University Press).

Zartman, I.W. (1985). *Ripe for Resolution: Conflict and Intervention in Africa* (New York and Oxford: Oxford University Press).

—— (2000). 'Ripeness: the hurting stalemate and beyond' in P.C. Stern and D. Drukman (eds) *Conflict Resolution After The Cold War* (Washington, DC: Nation Academy Press).

—— (2003). 'The timing of peace initiatives: hurting stalemates and ripe moments' in J. Darby and R. Mac Ginty (eds) *Contemporary Peacemaking* (London: Palgrave Macmillan).

Appendix 1

ANGLO-IRISH AGREEMENT 1985
between
THE GOVERNMENT OF IRELAND
and
THE GOVERNMENT OF
THE UNITED KINGDOM

The Government of Ireland and the Government of the United Kingdom:
Wishing further to develop the unique relationship between their peoples and the close co-operation between their countries as friendly neighbours and as partners in the European Community;

Recognising the major interest of both their countries and, above all, of' the people of Northern Ireland in diminishing the divisions there and achieving lasting peace and stability;

Recognising the need for continuing efforts to reconcile and to acknowledge the rights of the two major traditions that exist in Ireland, represented on the one hand by those who wish for no change in the present status of Northern Ireland and on the other hand by those who aspire to a sovereign united Ireland achieved by peaceful means and through agreement;

Reaffirming their total rejection of any attempt to promote political objectives by violence or the threat of violence and their determination to work together to ensure that those who adopt or support such methods do not succeed;

Recognising that a condition of genuine reconciliation and dialogue between unionists and nationalists is mutual recognition and acceptance of each other's rights;

Recognising and respecting the identities of the two communities in Northern Ireland, and the right of each to pursue its aspirations by peaceful and constitutional means;

Reaffirming their commitment to a society in Northern Ireland in which all may live in peace, free from discrimination and intolerance, and with the opportunity for both communities to participate fully in the structures and processes of government;

Have accordingly agreed as follows:

A. STATUS OF NORTHERN IRELAND

ARTICLE 1

The two Governments
(a) affirm that any change in the status of Northern Ireland would only come about with the consent of a majority of' the people of' Northern Ireland;

(b) recognise that the present wish of a majority of' the people of' Northern Ireland is for no change in the status of Northern Ireland;

(c) declare that, if in the future a majority of the people of' Northern Ireland clearly wish for and formally consent to the establishment of a united Ireland, they will introduce and support in the respective Parliaments legislation to give effect to that wish.

B. THE INTERGOVERNMENTAL CONFERENCE

ARTICLE 2

(a) There is hereby established, within the framework of the Anglo-Irish Inter-governmental Council set up after the meeting between the two Heads of Government on 6 November 1981, an Intergovernmental Conference (hereinafter referred to as "the Conference"), concerned with Northern Ireland and with relations between the two parts of' the island of Ireland, to deal, as set out in this Agreement, on a regular basis with
(i) political matters;
(ii) security and related matters;
(iii) legal matters, including the administration of justice;
(iv) the promotion of cross-border co-operation.

(b) The United Kingdom Government accept that the Irish Government will put forward views and proposals on matters relating to Northern Ireland within the field of activity of the Conference in so far as those matters are not the responsibility of a devolved administration in Northern Ireland. In the interest of promoting peace and stability, determined efforts shall be made through the Conference to resolve any differences. The Conference will be mainly concerned with Northern Ireland; but some of' the matters under consideration will involve cooperative action in both parts of the island of' Ireland, and possibly also in Great Britain. Some of the proposals considered in respect of' Northern Ireland may also be found to have application by the Irish Government. There is no derogation from the sovereignty of either the Irish Government or the United Kingdom Government, and each retains responsibility for the decisions and adminis-tration of government within its own jurisdiction.

ARTICLE 3

The Conference shall meet at Ministerial or official level, as required. The business of the Conference will thus receive attention at the highest level. Regular and frequent Ministerial meetings shall be held; and in particular special meetings shall be convened at the request of' either side. Officials may meet in subordinate groups. Membership of the Conference and of sub-groups shall be small and flexible. When the Conference meets at Ministerial level an Irish Minister designated as the Permanent Irish Ministerial Representative and the Secretary of State for Northern Ireland shall be joint Chairmen. Within the framework of the Conference other Irish and British Ministers may hold or attend meetings as appropriate: when legal matters are under consideration the Attorneys General may attend. Ministers may be accompanied by their officials and their professional advisers: for -example, when questions of' security policy or security co-operation are being discussed, they may be accompanied by the Commissioner of the Garda Siochána and the Chief Constable of' the Royal Ulster Constabulary; or when questions of economic or social policy, or co- operation are being discussed, they may be accompanied by officials of' the relevant Departments. A Secretariat shall be established by the two Governments to service the Conference on a continuing basis in the discharge of its functions as set out in this Agreement.

ARTICLE 4

(a) In relation to matters coming within its field of activity, the Conference shall be a framework within which the Irish Government and the United Kingdom Government work together
(i) for the accommodation of the rights and identities of the two traditions which exist in Northern Ireland; and
(ii) for peace, stability and prosperity throughout the island of Ireland by promoting reconciliation, respect for human rights, co-operation against terrorism and the development of economic, social and cultural co-operation.

(b) It is the declared policy of the United Kingdom Government that responsibility in respect of certain matters within the powers of the Secretary of State for Northern Ireland should be devolved within Northern Ireland on a basis which would secure widespread acceptance throughout the community. The Irish Government support that policy.

(c) Both Governments recognise that devolution can be achieved only with the co-operation of constitutional representatives within Northern Ireland of both tradi-

tions there. The Conference shall be a framework within which the Irish Government may put forward views and proposals on the modalities of bringing about
devolution in Northern Ireland, in so far as they relate to the interests of the
minority community.

C. POLITICAL MATTERS

ARTICLE 5

(a) The Conference shall concern itself' with measures to recognise and accommodate the rights and identities of' the two traditions in Northern Ireland, to
protect human rights and to prevent discrimination. Matters to be considered in
this area include measures to foster the cultural heritage of both traditions,
changes in electoral arrangements, the use of flags and emblems, the avoidance of
economic and social discrimination and the advantages and disadvantages of a
Bill of Rights in some form in Northern Ireland.

(b) The discussion of these matters shall be mainly concerned with Northern
Ireland, but the possible application of any measures pursuant to this Article by
the Irish Government in their jurisdiction shall not be excluded.

(c) If it should prove impossible to achieve and sustain devolution on a basis
which secures widespread acceptance in Northern Ireland, the Conference shall be
a framework within which the Irish Government may, where the interests of' the
minority community are significantly or especially affected, put forward views on
proposals for major legislation and on major policy issues, which are within the
purview of' the Northern Ireland Departments and which remain the responsibility of the Secretary of' State for Northern Ireland.

ARTICLE 6

The Conference shall be a framework within which the Irish Government may put
forward views and proposals on the role and composition of bodies appointed by
the Secretary of' State for Northern Ireland or by Departments subject to his direction and control including

the Standing Advisory Commission on Human Rights;
the Fair Employment Agency;
the Equal Opportunities Commission;
the Police Authority for Northern Ireland;
the Police Complaints Board.

D. SECURITY AND RELATED MATTERS

ARTICLE 7

(a) The Conference shall consider
(i) security policy;
(ii) relations between the security forces and the community;
(iii) prisons policy.

(b) The Conference shall consider the security situation at its regular meetings and thus provide an opportunity to address policy issues, serious incidents and forthcoming events.

(c) The two Governments agree that there is a need for a programme of special measures in Northern Ireland to improve relations between the security forces and the community, with the object in particular of making the security forces more readily accepted by the nationalist community. Such a programme shall be developed, for the Conference's consideration, and may include the establishment of local consultative machinery, training in community relations, crime prevention schemes involving the community, improvements in arrangements for handling complaints, and action to increase the proportion of members of the minority in the Royal Ulster Constabulary. Elements of' the programme may be considered by the Irish Government suitable for application within their jurisdiction.
(d) The Conference may consider policy issues relating to prisons. Individual cases may be raised as appropriate, so that information can be provided or inquiries instituted.

E. LEGAL MATTERS, INCLUDING THE ADMINISTRATION OF JUSTICE

ARTICLE 8

The Conference shall deal with issues of concern to both countries relating to the enforcement of the criminal law. In particular it shall consider whether there are areas of the criminal law applying in the North and in the South respectively which might with benefit be harmonised. The two Governments agree on the importance of public confidence in the administration of justice. The Conference shall seek, with the help of advice from experts as appropriate, measures which would give substantial expression to this aim, considering inter alia the possibility of mixed courts in both jurisdictions for the trial of certain offences. The Conference shall also be concerned with policy aspects of extradition and extraterritorial jurisdiction as between North and South.

F. CROSS-BORDER CO-OPERATION ON SECURITY, ECONOMIC, SOCIAL AND CULTURAL MATTERS

ARTICLE 9

(a) With a view to enhancing cross-border co-operation on security matters, the Conference shall set in hand a programme of work to be undertaken by the Commissioner of the Garda Siochána and the Chief Constable of the Royal Ulster Constabulary and, where appropriate, groups of officials, in such areas as threat assessments, exchange of information, liaison structures, technical co-operation, training of personnel, and operational resources.

(b) The Conference shall have no operational responsibilities; responsibility for police operations shall remain with the heads of the respective police forces, the Commissioner of the Garda Siochána maintaining his links with the Minister for Justice and the Chief Constable of the Royal Ulster Constabulary his links with the Secretary of State for Northern Ireland.

ARTICLE 10

(a) The two Governments shall co-operate to promote the economic and social development of those areas of both parts of Ireland which have suffered most severely from the consequences of the instability of recent years, and shall consider the possibility of securing international support for this work.

(b) If it should prove impossible to achieve and sustain devolution on a basis which secures widespread acceptance in Northern Ireland, the Conference shall be a framework for the promotion of co-operation between the two parts of Ireland concerning cross border aspects of economic, social and cultural matters in rela-tion to which the Secretary of State for Northern Ireland continues to exercise authority.

(c) If responsibility is devolved in respect of certain matters in the economic, social or cultural areas currently within the responsibility of the Secretary of State for Northern Ireland, machinery will need to be established by the responsible authorities in the North and South for practical co-operation in respect of cross-border aspects of these issues.

G. ARRANGEMENTS FOR REVIEW

ARTICLE 11

At the end of three years from signature of this Agreement, or earlier if requested by either Government, the working of the Conference shall be reviewed by the two Governments to see whether any changes in the scope and nature of its activ-ities are desirable.

H. INTERPARLIAMENTARY RELATIONS

ARTICLE 12

It will be for Parliamentary decision in Dublin and in Westminster whether to establish an Anglo-Irish Parliamentary body of the kind adumbrated in the Anglo-Irish Studies Report of November 1981. The two Governments agree that they would give support as appropriate to such a body, if it were to be established.

I. FINAL CLAUSES

ARTICLE 13

This Agreement shall enter into force on the date on which the two Governments exchange notifications of their acceptance of this Agreement.

In witness whereof the undersigned, being duly authorised thereto by their respective Governments, have signed this Agreement.

Done in two originals at Hillsborough on the 15th day of November 1985

For the Government of Ireland .... *Gearoid Mac Gearailt*
For the Government of the United Kingdom .... *Margaret Thatcher*

Index

Lightning Source UK Ltd.
Milton Keynes UK
UKOW06f1818180616

276556UK00005B/38/P

9 781784 993856